Exploring
the Best Ethnic Restaurants
of the Bay Area

SAN FRANCISCO FOCUS

EXPLORING THE BEST
ETHNIC
RESTAURANTS
OF THE BAY AREA

BY SHARON SILVA AND FRANK VIVIANO

Requests for permission should be
addressed in writing to
San Francisco Focus,
680 Eighth Street, San Francisco, CA 94103.

San Francisco Focus Books are published by
San Francisco Focus magazine, a division of KQED, Inc.

Library of Congress Catalog Card Number: 90-62527
Silva, Sharon and Viviano, Frank.
    Exploring the Best Ethnic Restaurants of the Bay Area.

    First edition
    Includes index.
    ISBN: 0-912333-05-7

Printed in the United States of America

Table of Contents

Preface

I t's no mystery why the Bay Area is the most interesting place in the world to eat. Nowhere else on earth
is there a population that matches its sheer diversity.
Stop any two people on the street in
San Francisco, according to a recent
study, and there is an 83 percent
probability that their ancestors are
from different countries. In Daly
City, the chances are 84 percent. El
Cerrito, Hayward, Newark, Union
City, South San Francisco, and Milpitas all register in
the 80s. Eight of the 15 most ethnically diverse cities
in America—and five of the 10 most diverse counties—
are located on the shores of San Francisco Bay.

At the dinner table, that translates into an ethnic
restaurant scene second to none. In many cities elsewhere, "Asian food" equals Chinese, and Chinese
equals all-purpose Cantonese. In the Bay Area, the Asian
choices alone run to more than two dozen distinct cuisines, with at least seven separate
entries from China.

This grand mosaic, in all its fascinating complexity, is the subject of our
book. In effect, it is a San Francisco
diner's Baedeker—a comprehensive
guide to the culinary possibilities
of the Bay Area. Drawing on more than a decade of
journalism here and abroad, for *San Francisco Focus,*
the *San Francisco Chronicle,* and many other publications,
we have aimed at a volume that also animates the people

and cultures behind the restaurants.

Not surprisingly, given an immigration wave that has increased the Bay Area's Asian-American population to an estimated 1.3 million, the Orient is our strongest culinary suit. But more than a million Latin Americans consider this "their town," too, as does one of the nation's largest communities of single-ancestry European-Americans—Italians and Portuguese, Basques and Russians, Germans and Spaniards, to name just a few.

The Bay Area is not a place that compromises at the table. It's not afraid of spices and delicacies that won't play in Peoria. The people seated next to you in the establishments we describe here don't need an introduction to the gastronomic delights of Luzon or Vientiane, Torino or Jalisco, Bayonne or Managua. Chances are, that's where they were born.

We can't promise that our book will make you as familiar as they are with their native cuisines; but we'd like to think you'll be farther down the road—equipped with the tools necessary to begin deciphering the secret menus of Chinatown and the complexities of a Persian *khoresht*. Along these lines, we've done our best to describe key national dishes, to assemble brief glossaries listing items that may not be translated on English-language menus.

Our premise is that the chief responsibility of a good guidebook is to open the door to independent discovery, not to close it to all but the authors' personal choices. There's a lot more culinary anthropology in these pages than conventional restaurant criticism. But we've got that, too. You'll find reviews of our favorites in each cuisine's "Top Choices."

In those instances where a community resides (and dines) in a distinct ethnic neighborhood, we've also drawn brief demographic portraits, complete with the most dependable population statistics we could find. In most cases, these statistics were secured from community agencies rather than the Census, which has only limited data on all but a few ethnic groups.

Prices are the bane of food writers, given the uncertainties of inflation and the variables of personal taste that contribute to the final dinner check. We've placed the restaurants in this book in three broad categories, reflecting the cost of a meal for one person, including tax and tip but not beverage: Inexpensive (less than $12);  Moderate ($12 to $25); and Expensive (more than $25). Very few of our selections fall into the latter category; generally speaking, the Bay Area has lower restaurant prices than such culinary rivals as New York and Paris. Broad as it is, our system still has its shortcomings. Many European restaurants, for instance, fall into the upper range of the moderate category, with a bill for two running close to $50. By contrast, most of the Chinese and other Asian establishments classified as moderate can probably deliver a dinner for two for less than $30.

Population numbers explain, in part, why Asian restaurants are so heavily represented in this book. More than half of all eating places in the Bay Area serve one of the Far East's cuisines, adding up to the finest, most genuine Asian restaurant scene in the Western Hemisphere. But numbers don't tell the whole story, of course; some ethnic groups with large populations have  shied away from the fickle dinner trade, while others do not have strong restaurant traditions in their ancestral homelands and have yet to generate them here. The Irish are a case in point: their population is booming in the Bay Area, but its evening evidence is largely confined to a fast-growing selection of excellent, friendly pubs. Finally, there is the matter of fashion. French restaurants, for instance, have been on the wane in this area since the rise of California cuisine in the 1980s.

There would be no book at all without the assistance of many friends and associates. Our editors at *San Francisco Focus* magazine, Amy Rennert and Mark Powelson, nourished what once seemed little more than a crazy scheme—a revisionist restaurant guide!—into an actual book. Much of what we know about food is directly the result of warm friendships (and years of congenial dining) with such superb gastronomes as Maggie Gin, Wigbert Figueras, Bruce Cost, Hideo Iwata, Chine Wong, Kimun Lee, Tilda Young, Vu-Duc Vuong, Cecilia Brunazzi, Chan Fook-Chueng, George Csicsery, and Catharine DiGiuseppe.

The Top Twenty

Basque Cultural Center • *Basque*

Buca Giovanni • *Italian*

Cambodiana's • *Cambodian*

Fortune Restaurant • *Chao Zhou Chinese*

Helmand • *Afghani*

Heung Heung • *Cantonese*

Hong Kong Flower Lounge • *Cantonese*

Indian Oven • *Indian*

Maykadeh • *Iranian*

Monsoon • *Nan Yang Asian*

Okina • *Japanese*

Paolo's • *Italian*

Patio • *Spanish*

Quoc Te • *Vietnamese*

Sorabol • *Korean*

Square One • *Mediterranean*

Taqueria San Jose • *Mexican*

Thep Phanom • *Thai*

Tito Rey of the Islands • *Filipino*

Yaya • *Iraqi / Mediterranean*

EAST ASIA

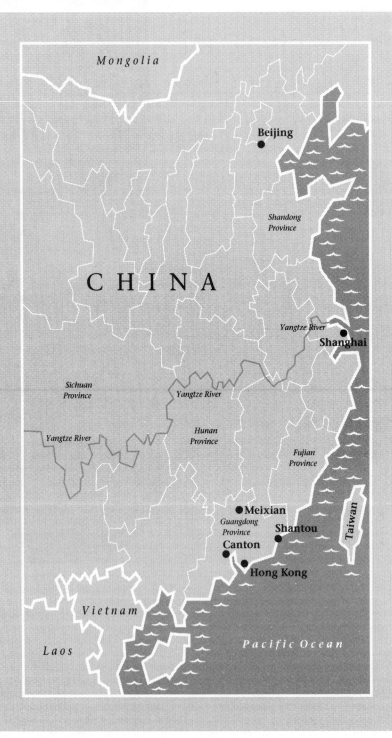

China: An Exotic Banquet of Regional Cuisines

The view from the corner of Clay Street and Grant Avenue in San Francisco is admired by 50,000 tourists per day and probably appears in as many photographs. This is the heart of snapshot Chinatown, the center of a five-block stretch of curio shops and dinner houses. A few yards up Clay, under a red restaurant awning, a Cantonese-American menu offers the usual choice between sweet-and-sour pork and cashew chicken. A few yards down Grant, the skyline is dominated by a four-story beige building with ersatz pagoda trim.

On the surface, these blocks appear to be little more than an Oriental theme park: a tourist trap high on the contrived picturesque, low on the meaningful. The appearances couldn't be further from the truth. Behind the snapshot facade is a neighborhood so laden with historical significance—and matchless culinary quality—that it ought to have been declared a national treasure long ago. Yet its true riches, in the annals of history and dining alike, remain unknown to all but a few of the San Franciscans who live beyond its boundaries.

That beige pagoda is the headquarters of the Sam Yup Association, a gold-rush institution linking

People and Their Neighborhoods

Where they live: Hardly a district in the Bay Area's five southern counties has not seen an enormous increase in its Chinese-American population over the past decade. The largest residential concentration remains San Francisco's fast-expanding Chinatown, which now includes large parts of Telegraph and Russian hills. Ethnic Chinese from Southeast Asia have created secondary Chinatowns in San Francisco's Tenderloin and along San Jose's East Santa Clara Street, and have vastly expanded central Oakland's Chinese-ancestry population. Solidly middle-class Chinese-American communities have settled into San Francisco's Richmond and Sunset districts.

Where they gather: Every residential concentration has its bustling commercial corridors, the most dynamic of which are Oakland's Eighth Street area; the Stockton Street, Clement Street, Irving Street, Noriega Street, and Mission Street market districts of San Francisco; Castro Street in Mountain View; and El Camino Real in northern San Mateo County. Along any of these corridors, you can now find stores selling foodstuffs—including Sacramento Delta–grown Asian vegetables—that until quite recently were unavailable outside of the Far East.

Estimated Bay Area population: 350,000.

Asian San Francisco directly to the Pearl River villages that gave birth to Chinese America in the mid-19th century. The unremarkable restaurant building at 839 Clay? There's no memorial plaque on its door, but in the rooms of the old Yutton Hotel, above the red awning, one of the 20th century's earthshaking events took shape. Sun Yat-sen resided here, and it is here that he plotted the overthrow of the Manchu dynasty. As for the dinner houses, which march far beyond these five blocks—there were an estimated 1500 Chinese restaurants in San Francisco at last count—for those who know how and what to order, they add up to the most authentic Chinese dining experiences to be had outside of Asia.

"Chinatown leads three lives," says Alton Chinn, a longtime community organizer who was himself raised above a storefront on Grant Avenue. "It is a tourist mecca, to be sure. But it is also a living residential metropolis for thousands of people—the Cantonese name for it is *Dai Fao*, the 'big city.' And finally, it is a genuine global capital for more than a billion Chinese, a landmark in their modern history."

The crowded streets and narrow alleyways of Chinatown define a universe that is at once a fundamental source of greater San Francisco's energy and a separate realm of cultural memory and nuance. The real Chinatown is as young as the immigrant kids who dream in its tenements and as old as the customs that tie it to 4000 years of Chinese civilization. To wander the days and nights of *Dai Fao* is to know a world more mutable—and yet more timeless—than any other on the North American continent.

The mutability is both geographic and cultural. Chinatown itself has become a kind of "downtown" for Bay Area Chinese-

Americans, as their population—less than 50,000 in 1960—has soared to more than 350,000. Today, there are bustling Chinese commercial districts along Clement Street and Geary Boulevard in San Francisco's Richmond District (known as *Sun Wah Fao*, "New Chinatown," to Cantonese speakers), and also in the city's Sunset District, central Oakland, Mountain View, and San Jose.

In cultural terms, the changes are equally profound. In 1965, when a new immigration law ended decades of discriminatory restrictions on Asian newcomers, San Francisco was still *Gum Shan*, the predominantly Cantonese "Golden Mountain" that

dated back to the era of the forty-niners. Three decades later, it has become a living textbook on the complex nuances of Chinese subcultures. In the 1990s, Chinatown—or for that matter, its many Bay Area satellites—isn't simply Chinese. It is Cantonese and Hakka, Chao Zhou, Fukienese, Shandong, and Shanghainese. It speaks Putonghua, Hokkien, Teochew, Kechua, and at least four distinct dialects of Guangdonghua, Cantonese.

Along the way, "Chinese food" has become "regional Chinese cuisines," as different from each other as German *Kartoffeln* are from Italian pasta. These cuisines reflect the arrival on our shores of ethnic Chinese immigrants from every part of China, Hong Kong, and Taiwan, as well as from Vietnam, Laos, Cambodia, Thailand, Burma, and Malaysia. Together, they have contributed inordinantly to the Bay Area's reputation as a world-class dining capital.

Cantonese Cuisine

You can lead a horse to water, but you can't make him drink. That sums up a monumental contradiction in the local dining scene. The Bay Area has the world's second greatest collection of Cantonese restaurants, surpassed in sheer numbers and quality only by Hong Kong. And even in Hong Kong, the average diner can't afford some of the delicacies that regularly turn up in modest dining rooms here—tanks full of live lobsters, crabs, and fish, breast of squab and stuffed web of duck. Not to mention fresh vegetables so exotic that no English translation exists for them.

Why, then, do so many Occidental Bay Area diners slog on through the nightmarish swamp of deep-fried egg rolls and sweet-and-sour pork? Why do they regard Cantonese food as little more than a cheap alternative to going hungry?

One answer is that the very term "Cantonese" has a bad name in America, a fact that would be greeted with astonishment in China, where the cuisine of Canton is regarded as the most elegant and subtle in the entire Middle Kingdom. Another is that restaurateurs and diners alike seem strangely determined to keep it that way, even in the city that (supposedly) knows how.

If the non-Cantonese Bay Area really knew how, sweet-and-sour nightmares would disappear forever in the wake of the kind of dinner we regularly sit down to in the far reaches of the Richmond District. Eighteen hefty shrimp, poached to the exact point of rosy perfection. Enormous Tomales oysters, steamed on the half shell in a light sauce of soy and garlic. Clams stir-fried with black beans and fresh chili. A whole New England lobster sautéed with ginger and scallions. A Sacramento Delta black bass, plucked live from a tank and steamed. Black-forest mushrooms braised with sea cucumber. A soup of fresh greens and pork. Chilled tapioca and melon.

The place is **Heung Heung**, an utterly unpretentious little gem on Balboa Street. It's a long, long way from Heung Heung to the restaurants, all over the United States, that gave Cantonese food its lowly reputation in the first place. Isolated in towns where there were no other Asians in sight, generations of Cantonese cooks devised a formula that they *thought* met American expectations.

The reasoning, based on what Orientals saw Occidentals eating elsewhere, went like this: Westerners *don't* like unusual ingredients, steamed dishes, light sauces, unboned meats and fish, plain boiled rice, or anything that hasn't been cooked limp or fried to a crisp. They *do* like thick sauces, sweet flavors, deep-fried dishes, and everything filleted. Plus chop suey, of course,

Gold Cup: The New Upscale Chinese Restaurants

Let's pretend that a brilliant chef, a renowned master on the order of Paul Bocuse, has decided to bid *au revoir* to France and move to San Francisco. Let's further imagine that he is in his 40s, with decades of creativity still ahead of him. Shift the fantasy from the Atlantic to the Pacific, give our genius a Cantonese vocabulary, and stop pretending.

Hui Pui Wing, one of Hong Kong's most celebrated chefs, is alive and well and already living in San Francisco. In a city where Chinese grand cuisine has far more followers than *la gastronomie française*, his arrival in the late '80s was among the Bay Area's most important culinary landings in recent history.

The landing of chef Hui also marks the coming of age here of a type of Chinese restaurant that his native Hong Kong calls "gold cup" and that the Bay Area is more likely to describe as "upscale." Although San Francisco has always had a few posh Chinese dinner houses— notably the Mandarin and the Empress of China—the upscaling process that Hui reflects has been underway in earnest only a few years. It is bringing silver chopstick rests, damask tablecloths, Qing wall scrolls, and elegantly attired waiters to a realm that was once noted for an utter indifference to ambience.

The redefinition of the Chinese restaurant is strikingly evident at the elegant **Harbor Village** in the Embarcadero Center, where chef Hui presides over the kitchen. But it's far from the sole example. Harbor Village stands at the crest of a wave that has deposited upscale Chinese and the ubiquitous fried rice.

The irony is that the *don't* list is precisely what defines genuine Cantonese cooking, the subtle cuisine that China raves about. It places an extraordinary emphasis on the freshest and rarest of ingredients, light-handed cooking styles, and preservation of natural flavors.

San Franciscans are savvy enough to have discovered a few authentic Cantonese treats, such as *shu app, dow see chow heen,* and *chow fun,* aka roast duck, clams in black bean sauce, and fried rice noodles. But that's barely scratching the surface of a cuisine whose variations on the single theme of seafood can run into the hundreds. In a few blessedly helpful establishments the problem is solved by the proprietors. Our fondness for Heung Heung is directly related to the fact that Jane Yang, its owners' daughter, is willing to translate the ever-changing list of the chef's best dishes. Jane, alas, is a rare find.

If you are on your own, seafood is a good place to begin further explorations because it is the focus of preoccupation for the fussiest Cantonese diners. A rule of thumb, applicable to every denizen of the deep, is to avoid anything that tampers with basic character. A catfish or a prawn should taste like what it is, and not like the syrupy sauce it is sometimes swimming in. This is another way of restaurants all over the region, from Sausalito's **North Sea Village** to **Ming's Villa** of Palo Alto. In between lie an ever-growing number of others, many of them branches of Hong Kong gold-cup establishments: **Wu Kong** and **Hong Kong Flower Lounge** in San Francisco, two more **Hong Kong Flower Lounges** and **Fook Yuen** in Millbrae, **Sun Tung Lok** in Burlingame, and **East Ocean** in Emeryville.

To the Bay Area's relentlessly demanding Chinese diners—each one a restaurant critic manqué—"upscale" in these restaurants means a lot more than silver chopstick rests. They also insist on a kitchen that produces verifiably gold-cup food, and nobody has more gold cups in his cabinet than Harbor Village's Hui Pui Wing.

Every year since 1984, he has placed among the top 10 grand masters in Hong Kong's prestigious Courvoisier Chef's Invitational. In 1986, he became the first chef ever to win two platinum medals in the Hong Kong Food Festival and was named one of the 20th century's top 10 Asian chefs in a Japanese-sponsored culinary arts exposition.

To understand why, you might begin with a special order of his prize-winning *sah cheung ying yang,* which translates poetically as "lights and shadows viewed through a window screen." The "screen" is bamboo pith, which is stuffed with the highest quality shark's fin and crowned with rich red crab roe. Or perhaps your taste runs more to the "peacock blossom platter," a combination of walnuts, honeydew, jellyfish, roast duck, ginger, and slices of *you tiao,* a cylindrical cruller, under a delicate sesame and peanut sauce. In the old days, creations of this sort were designed for the likes of the dowager empress; today they're what you order if you're the Hong Kong–born v.p. of a Palo Alto engineering firm trying to impress a venture capitalist.

saying that steamed dishes in general are preferable; they tend not to be oversauced. The same holds true for poultry: steamed or poached chicken—sometimes described on a menu as "white-cut chicken"—is among the chief glories of the Cantonese table.

One way to beat the odds is to patronize the Bay Area's growing number of what the Cantonese call "roast houses," relatively modest establishments that do much more than roasting and literally display their specialties in the front windows. Consider, for instance, **Jan Mae Guey** (1222 Stockton St), set right in the center of the wonderful chaos of San Francisco's Stockton Street market district just south of Broadway. There, for all the world to see, are those roast ducks and poached chickens, alongside whole roast pigs, squabs, and long trays full of the day's braised and stir-fried preparations, ranging from stuffed bean curd to steamed pork trotters. Just go inside, point to what interests you, and take a seat at one of the five tables.

The roast houses, incidentally, also tend to be the top noodle (wheat or rice, fried or in soup) and *juk* (rice porridge) joints. In both categories, two standouts are the late-night **Hing Lung** (674 Broadway), just around the corner from Jan Mae Guey on Broadway, and **Yuen's Garden** (1131 Grant Ave), only a block away. In Oakland's Chinatown, **Sun Tai Wong Restaurant** (729, 733 Webster St) offers a full menu of barbecue dishes, but it is just one roast house among many in that fast-growing neighborhood. And don't forget San Francisco's Clement Street, which is well supplied with its own fine roast houses.

At more elaborate full-fledged dinner houses, the best possible advice is to think not in terms of dishes but ingredients. The Cantonese view menus as nothing more than mild suggestions; what those Chinese-language signs on the restaurant walls often advertise are available components: the freshest fish, the seasonal vegetables. The idea is to determine what you would like—and how you would like it cooked. The patron is in the driver's seat, and the kitchen awaits instruction.

Cantonese Restaurants: The Top Choices

• **East Ocean** At the west end of the Emeryville Peninsula, East Ocean gazes over the waters at the gentle swoop of the Bay Bridge. If the view weren't enough, this branch of a famous Hong Kong restaurant (with other branches in Singapore and Taipei) also offers the East Bay's finest Cantonese cuisine. One way to decide on the meal's centerpiece is to window shop at fresh- and sea-water tanks that line the restaurant's entrance. Another is to order, unseen, such Cantonese classics as panfried fresh conch with tender greens or steamed prawns; the latter come with an outstanding dipping sauce of soy, hot oil, fresh chilies, and scallions. The noon hour brings a very respectable Hong Kong dim sum spread. A favorite with the discriminating dons of Berkeley's East Asia Institute. 3199 Powell St, Emeryville

(415) 655-3389. Lunch and dinner daily. Major credit cards. Moderate.

• **Fook Yuen** This is the branch of another of the big Hong Kong restaurant groups now operating in the Bay Area's lucrative market. It's upscale—a gold-cup establishment with fancy (if a bit overblown) decor and silver plates on white tablecloths. But what really sets it apart is a list of daily specials that deliver gold-cup cuisine at a common man's budget level. Consider, for instance, the possibility of a whole Peking duck, carved right at the table, for one sawbuck; that was the Thursday special one season. Other options, depending on the day, include whole crab, whole lobster, and shark's fin soup. Arrive early: the sales technique draws hordes of diners. 195 El Camino Real, Millbrae (415) 692-8600. Lunch and dinner daily. Major credit cards. Moderate.

• **Gold Kirin** This is a restaurant that takes seriously the Cantonese claim to be the world's most avid seafood lovers. It's one of only a few dining rooms anywhere that feature more than a dozen varieties of live fish and shellfish in its tanks, ranging from sturgeon to geoduck. But the possibilities don't end at the shore. Poussin, poached in salt water and served with a ginger dip, is a house specialty. Alas, this is also one of those Chinese restaurants where the best dishes are not listed on the English menu brought to your table. The aggressive, questioning diner fares far better here than the reticent. 2520 Noriega St, SF (415) 731-6303. Lunch and dinner daily. MC, V. Moderate.

• **Harbor Village** As the essay on upscale Chinese restaurants in this chapter notes, Harbor Village was among the first of Hong Kong's big-name dinner houses to open a branch in California (a second branch has now opened in South-

Chop Suey

For years, chop suey has been synonymous in America with Cantonese food. Both New York and California claim its introduction. According to the Manhattan theory, the dish was born there during the visit of Chinese foreign minister Li Hung Chang in 1896. Li, the story goes, would only eat what his own cooks prepared. When they couldn't find the things he was used to, they stir-fried a hodgepodge of available ingredients. The boss called it chop suey, roughly meaning "pot luck."

California's account starts 40 years earlier, when half a dozen hungry miners fresh out of the Sierra gold fields showed up after closing time at a San Francisco Chinese café. You can't just say "sorry boys" to six tough customers who've been eating stale biscuits and rancid bacon for months. So the chef frantically combined various kitchen scraps. The result was chop suey.

The moral, of course, is that chop suey and a whole range of dishes it is associated with—tomato beef, steak kew, the familiar versions of cashew chicken, egg foo young, and sweet-and-sour pork—aren't Cantonese. They were invented outright in the United States or dramatically altered here to suit the local taste. They are Cantonese-American, a cuisine in its own right, packaged in white cartons down at the corner for takeout in every town in the United States.

ern California and a third is planned for Contra Costa's exclusive Blackhawk community). It's also the base of Hui Pui Wing, one of the most acclaimed chefs in Hong Kong history. The dim sum is as respected as the dinner menu. A gallery of private banquet rooms makes this an ideal place to celebrate. Harbor Village's personable manager, Clifford Chow, will help you set the menu. Four Embarcadero Center, SF (415) 781-883. Lunch and dinner daily. Major credit cards. Moderate.

• **Heung Heung** The Yang family, owners of Heung Heung, preside over one of the most cherished secrets in San Francisco. Their small restaurant in the outer reaches of the Avenues has a clientele that knows extraordinary food and isn't anxious to share it. But it's time the secret was out: for sheer culinary skill, faithfulness to Cantonese tradition,

Taiwanese Cuisine

Although full-fledged dim sum is, by definition, Cantonese, people in the rest of China also eat mid-morning meals. The so-called mandarin dim sum, or *zhao dian*, was pioneered locally in the 1970s by Shui-ho and Florence Lin at their Taiwan Restaurant in Berkeley, where it is a weekends-only attraction. In 1986, they opened a second Taiwan in San Francisco's Richmond district; demand there for the special brunch has put it on the daily menu. Since their pioneering efforts, the northern dim sum trade has grown to include many restaurants in the Bay Area.

But what still sets the Taiwan restaurants apart is Florence Lin's background. Born and raised on the island of Taiwan, she is of Hokkien Chinese ancestry. Little known in the United States, the Hokkiens are the dominant ethnic group of Taiwan, China's Fujian Province, and Singapore. Although Shui-ho is himself a Hakka, he, too, was raised in Taiwan on the local Hokkien fare and has mastered its preparation. Their restaurants are among the few places in the United States where you can eat Hokkien *zhao dian*. "Some of these dishes," says Mr.

Lin, "are pretty hard to find in Taiwan."

Two cases in point are worth mentioning. The first is an exotic concoction called "fried yam cakes stuffed with meat and mushrooms," comprised of taro, bean thread noodles, pork, black forest mushrooms, and three distinct sauces. The second is a kind of pancake made of taro flour, egg, and small oysters. Come dinner, the menu offers plenty more of this fare, in a category denoted as Taiwan Specialties. Notable entrées include "petals of pork soup," thin slices of meat sandwiched with ground fish and served in a thick broth; pickled greens with shredded pork tripe; and a wonderful preparation of glutinous sweet rice cooked in a crock with slivers of vegetables and meat.

Incidentally, walking down Clement, you'll know you're at the Taiwan when you reach a window where three people are hard at work on the morning's dumplings and crullers. There is no such thing as mass-produced food here.

Taiwan Restaurant 445 Clement St, SF (415) 387-1789; 2701 University Ave, Berkeley (415) 845-1456. Lunch and dinner daily. MC, V. Moderate.

and concern for the highest quality ingredients, you can't improve on Heung Heung. Jane, the Yangs' charming daughter, thoughtfully translates special dishes into English, including such wonders as salt-and-pepper sole fillets, eggplant stuffed with shrimp and cooked on an iron teppan platter, and squab with mango. Heung Heung is also known for its homemade noodles and wonton skins. 3608 Balboa St, SF (415) 221-9188. Lunch and dinner daily. MC, V. Moderate.

• **Hing Lung** Come here to sample Hong Kong hip: the walls are pink, the waiters in black tie, the tables set for middle-class Asian immigrant kids with healthy wallets and a taste for the kung fu films screened next door at the World Theatre. At Hing Lung, they can eat after midnight, indulging another Hong Kong taste—the appreciation for a good Cantonese roast house featuring duck, chicken, noodle dishes, and the rice porridge known as *juk*. If you haven't tried the latter, start with Hing Lung's house special, a generous portion of fish and shellfish cooked to tender perfection in the porridge. 674 Broadway, SF (415) 398-8838. Lunch and dinner daily. MC, V. Inexpensive.

• **Hong Kong Flower Lounge Restaurants** When Alice Wong, scion of Hong Kong's Flower Lounge empire—that's no overstatement for a family with four restaurants of the same name in Asia and three in America—announced she was opening a branch in Millbrae in the late '80s, sophisticates guffawed. But today those same sophisticates are waiting in line along with everyone else at the three elegant Bay Area Flower Lounges, and Millbrae has emerged as a Chinese gourmet ghetto. We like the San Francisco Geary Boulevard branch best; it delivers perfection: perfectly fresh ingredients, cooked perfectly. An added attraction is the chef's willing-

ness to experiment with unusual dishes, such as deep-fried catfish showered with scented oil and scallions, spinach tossed with Chinese sausage and black mushrooms, and prawns braised in a clay pot with bean thread noodles and fermented

red bean curd. The dim sum at all three branches draws huge crowds. 5322 Geary Blvd, SF (415) 668-8998; 51 Millbrae Ave, Millbrae (415) 692-6666; 1671 El Camino Real, Millbrae (415) 588-9972. Lunch and dinner daily. Major credit cards. Moderate.

• **In Inn** The name of this busy Sunset District establishment is a pun on both the chef's name and the literal translation, which more or less amounts to "nice guy." The menu is heavily weighted toward seafood, and every table groans under huge platters of perfectly steamed fish, stir-fried crab, and poached shrimp. The daily-specials board lists such highly prized delicacies as fresh Pacific Northwest scallops in the shell stir-fried with black-bean sauce. The kitchen also turns out beautiful chestnut-brown ducks with featherlight buns for stuffing with the crisp skin and moist meat. 1935 Taraval St, SF (415) 753-0828. Lunch and dinner daily. MC, V. Moderate.

• **Lichee Garden** Tucked away on an uncharacteristically leafy block of Chinatown, Lichee Garden also offers a somewhat uncharacteristic combination of superlative Cantonese food and a quiet, almost intimate atmosphere. The helpings here are large, the prices reasonable, and the staff attentive. There are plenty of

ambitious dishes to be had: a rich "salad" of sesame-scented shredded duck and jellyfish (Hong Kong nouvelle!); whole deep-fried chicken with shrimp chips and a slight savor of lemon; clay pots—not on the menu, you have to ask—featuring rare wild game and surprising combinations of dried delicacies and meats. 1416 Powell St, SF (415) 397-2290. Lunch and dinner daily. MC, V. Moderate.

• **MBE Restaurant** In the late '70s, Stanley Chan was the golden boy of gourmet Chinatown—an accomplished Hong Kong chef at 22, he was heading up his own San Francisco restaurant, Ocean Garden, by 25. A decade later, Chan and associate chef Marson Wong relocated

to Clement Street, where they now dish up some of the most spectacular food in town at the MBE. That's live sturgeon swimming in the large tank at the back of the dining room: sold by the pound, it goes into one of Chan's signature specialties, filleted and gently panfried with chives. His quail braised in Shaoxing wine with lily buds in a clay pot is equally sensational. A blackboard on the wall announces the day's available seafood, often including items as unusual as the sturgeon. The emphasis here is all on the food; the setting is utilitarian. Postmidnight closing hours make this a great stop after a play at the nearby Asian American Theatre (Clement at Arguello). 239 Clement St, SF (415) 688-1688. Lunch and dinner daily. MC, V. Moderate.

• **Ming's Villa** The Bay Area's most important Asian business group, the Asian American Manufacturer's Association, meets once per month here—and not just because the atmosphere is conducive to shop talk. Ming's is the top southern Chinese restaurant in the South Bay, a bona fide gold-cup establishment in every sense. Not the least of its accomplishments is a dim sum kitchen that may well be the finest in California. The setting is refined, and for those Santa Clara County residents who can't face the nightmarish parking of Chinatown, Ming's also boasts an enormous parking lot. 1700 Embarcadero Rd, Palo Alto (415) 856-7700. Lunch and dinner daily. Major credit cards. Moderate.

• **R&G Lounge** Although the name may conjure up a suburban cocktail bar, this is a small and wonderful walk-down eatery in the basement of a Chinatown commercial building. How good could it be? Suffice it to say that a leading association of Bay Area Chinese chefs is known to hold its business dinners here. We took a cue from them one evening and ordered a memorable platter of steamed winter melon, surrounded by greens and topped with shredded dried scallops, a Chinese delicacy that usually appears only on very expensive occasions. R&G, inciden-

Heung apart, however, is its big departure from the sweet-and-sour standbys many of us associate with old-time Chinatown eating. The regulars tend to order a couple of things here without fail. One is

Old-Time Chinese Restaurants

Before World War II, San Francisco's Chinatown was predominantly a bachelor society, populated by lonely workingmen whose families remained in Asia. These sojourners created a world-in-exile, with its own clubs, restaurants, and residential hotels.

Though in the main their customs remained distinctively Chinese, the bachelors were not immune to American influence—even at the lunch table. A wonderful echo of the Americanization of the Chinese palate persists in the **Sun Wah Kue Restaurant** (848 Washington St). It's a living museum of lost Americana: marble-topped tables set inside individual wooden booths, heavy porcelain mugs and creamers, a menu that dispenses honest portions of rare prime rib and custard pie at honestly blue-collar prices. Four-course meals at Sun

Wah Kue start at less than $5, and prices are about the same at its longtime competitors: **Ping Yuen Bakery Restaurant** (650 Jackson St), **New Woey Loy Goey Café** (699 Jackson St), and **Uncle's** (65 Waverly Place).

Sun Wah Kue and Ping Yuen both double as bakeries, producing their own rolls and many varieties of pie. (We recommend custard or apple at the former and strawberry cream at the latter.) Uncle's is a hangout for local pols, Chinese Six Companies officials, and import-export tycoons. The main draws are the biscuits, apple pies, and a three-quarter-inch-thick "extra-rib steak."

Vegetable lovers take note: the meats and baked goods at these places far outclass the garnishes, which can run to indifferent, over-cooked green beans or even canned corn.

tally, is one of those rare establishments that will happily translate its best dishes for those who cannot decipher Chinese ideograms. 631-B Kearny St, SF (415) 982-7877. Lunch and dinner, Mon–Sat. MC, V. Moderate.

• **Sun Hung Heung** This is old-time San Francisco Chinatown, right down to the cocktail bar off the foyer, the banquet room upstairs, and the padded booths in the main dining room. What sets Sun Hung

stuffed chicken wings, full of deliciously seasoned pork and deep-fried. Another is duck-sauce noodles. Added attractions are the late closing hours and proximity of picturesque Portsmouth Square. 744 Washington St, SF (415) 982-2319. Lunch and dinner Mon–Sat. MC, V. Moderate.

• **Sun Kong Seafood Restaurant** Sunset families gather here to eat steelhead—plucked live from a tank—served in "two dishes." The tender fillets are cooked with baby bok choy; the backbone, head, and tail portions are steamed with bean curd in a sauce of fermented brown beans and scallions. Seafood lovers can choose from a menu with nearly 50 fish and shellfish dishes or ask the chef to prepare virtually any denizen of the deep according to taste. A wonderful way to start is with bean-curd rolls stuffed with fat choy—thin strands of black seaweed. 1532 Noriega St, SF (415) 759-6997. Lunch and dinner daily. MC, V. Moderate.

Hakka Cuisine

When Wong Boon Chin and his wife, Ching Su, moved their family to San Francisco in 1969, they brought one of Asia's great culinary mysteries with them. The Wongs are Hakkas, descendents of a southern China subculture whose dishes were virtually unheard of in the United States until the family established the **Ton Kiang Restaurant** a decade after its arrival here.

Not even Chinese historians can agree on the origins of the Hakkas. Some trace their lineage to coastal Fujian; others contend they are descended from remnants of Genghis Khan's Mongol army. The most persuasive guess, according to Chine Wong, the scholarly daughter who now oversees the two Ton Kiang restaurants for her retired parents, is that the Hakkas were a nomadic northern tribe who wandered into the Canton region about a thousand years ago. It was there that they came to be called Hakkas, which translates as "strangers." Even today, the Hakkas remain distinct in language—they speak a

Secret Menus of Chinese Restaurants

Many Bay Area Chinese restaurants compare very favorably to the best dining houses in Asia. A few basic tips can dramatically improve your chances of ferreting them out:
• The first thing to search for is a restaurant crowded with Asians. A Chinese clientele indicates that a discriminating palate is being catered to.
• Classic menu entries, of the sort described in this chapter, reflect a traditional kitchen. Fortunately, most Bay Area restaurants post menus in their front window. But don't reject a place simply because it also offers the familiar foreigners' "family dinner" of sweet-and-sour pork, cashew chicken, and egg roll. Many restaurateurs feel they must include these items to attract non-Chinese.

• If you spot a water tank full of live fish, crabs, and lobsters, you've probably found a restaurant that meets the high standards for freshness that Chinese gourmets insist on.
• Stick with house specialties and items compatible with the chef's cultural identity. Even in the best Cantonese restaurants, ordering Hunan harvest pork is likely to produce a major disappointment. So, too, is a choice that makes no geographic sense; Sichuan-style fresh scallops are a contradiction in terms, since Sichuan is a landlocked province thousands of miles from any sea.
• Calligraphy-covered walls or blackboards suggest a changing repertoire of daily and seasonal dishes. There's often a valuable secret

dialect known as Kechua—and customs from their neighbors along the Ton Kiang, or East River, of Guangdong Province.

In Asia, the Hakkas are known for business savvy, self-reliant women, and rich, honest country cooking. Their classic creation is salt-cooked chicken. In Ton Kiang's version, whole birds are poached in a special broth to produce a succulent, silky texture and an unforgettable taste. Cut on the bone into bite-sized pieces and rearranged in their original shape, they await a final crowning touch of hot, fragrant oil and a dipping sauce based on crushed ginger and scallions. As two American anthropologists once wrote in an article on food and Chinese culture, "to describe this dish as chicken [flavored] with salt is as accurate and revealing as saying that Château Latour 1964 is fermented grape juice."

Other Hakka classics include stuffed bean curd, either braised or steamed; fresh bacon braised with

dried mustard greens; and fish balls—spheres of seasoned ground fish, usually pike or flounder, that are boiled and served in soup or stir-fried with greens. Notable, too, are the fermented wine flavorings used with various meats, poultry, and seafood: they are based on an

announced in such signs. It is known as a *wo choy*. Loosely translated, these two words mean "special banquet," and invoking them will bring to your table a selection of the chef's top recommendations—the best things available that evening from his kitchen, grouped in a carefully balanced composition and delivered at a price that will confound habitués of European restaurants.

Let's say, for example, that enthusiasm for Hakka food has whet your appetite. Just head for San Francisco's **Ton Kiang Restaurant** (Number Two or Number Three) with four or five friends, and order a Hakka *wo choy*. Within 15 minutes, your table will be groaning under the weight of a fish-ball-and-greens soup, a whole Dungeness crab or Boston lobster stir-fried with scallions and ginger, beef in wine sauce, the classic salt-cooked chicken,

bean curd stuffed with minced pork, braised Chinese bacon covered with preserved mustard greens, and a whole fish, fresh from the tank, steamed to perfection. In 1990, this entire meal would have set you back less than $60—for everybody.

Much more elaborate banquets are also available at scores of Bay Area Chinese restaurants. Normally, the tab is accounted by table, with 10 to 12 people accommodated.

• A last tip, one that we've exploited endlessly, is to build cordial relations with the staffs of good restaurants. With time, they'll learn that you mean it when you say you want "real Chinese food." They may not have time to translate complete menus for you, but friendly waiters and maîtres d' can be depended on for solid recommendations.

Star-Crossed Chopsticks

The pursuit of good fortune and good eating are among Bay Area Chinese-Americans' chief preoccupations. Their paths cross at every turn.

Many Chinatown restaurants will not serve a whole chicken without its head and feet because their absence suggests a break in the life cycle and can provoke a spate of very bad luck. No traditional Chinese diner will overturn a steamed fish; to do so symbolizes a capsized fishing boat and yet another tempting of fate. San Francisco's largest dim sum palace, **Ocean City**, keeps fresh bowls of water on its window ledge to slake the thirst of a dragon believed to reside in the basement garage across Broadway.

Further table wisdom for the cosmologically wary: If you find a pair of uneven chopsticks before you, expect to miss a plane, boat, or train. Crossed chopsticks mean generic bad luck—except in dim sum houses, where they mean you're done eating and are ready to settle your account. Pregnant women should eat chicken in moderation or their babies will be hoarse. Too much eggplant? That's a recipe for sterility. Pig's brain, on the other hand, leads to male impotence, and fish eyes make ladies lusty.

---

ancient family recipe, and personally aged in earthen crocks by Ching Su in the Wongs' Diamond Heights home.

Hakka Restaurants: The Top Choices

• **Ton Kiang** All the Hakka classics, as detailed above, are available in San Francisco's original Hakka restaurant. Superb *wo choy* banquets are also offered here, featuring either Hakka cuisine or Cantonese seafood. 3148 Geary Blvd, SF (415)

752-4440; 5827 Geary Blvd, SF (415) 387-8273. Lunch and dinner daily. MC, V. Moderate.

• **Dragon River** A former chef at Ton Kiang is now cooking in this warm little Richmond District spot. He brought an experienced touch with the wide repertoire of the tart Hakka "wine-braised" dishes, which are actually prepared with a traditional fermented rice-grain seasoning. If you order a meal 24 hours in advance, Dragon River can also produce a rarely available southern Chinese specialty, whole chicken stuffed with sweet rice. Ask the amiable waiters to introduce other unusual items that do not appear on the menu. 5045 Geary Blvd, SF (415) 387-6698. Lunch and dinner daily. MC, V. Moderate.

Chao Zhou Cuisine

Many Bay Area Thai restaurants live double lives: One is rooted in Saigon or Bangkok, the other some 180 miles northeast of Canton in the city of Shantou (aka Swatow), a faded museum of colonial architecture that was once among China's busiest trading ports and the home of the Chao Zhou people.

These names may not spark immediate recognition, but for local food lovers they ought to become household words. They announce San Francisco's emergence as the first Western capital of a major Chinese culinary tradition. Chao Zhou food comes our way via Thailand, Indochina, and the Malay peninsula, where generations of Shantou-born immigrants settled over the past century. In the 1980s, thousands of Chao Zhou immigrants moved on to California. First introduced in the Bay Area as a sidebar to Thai menus—a superb example is the estimable Narai restaurant on Clement Street in San Francisco—Chao Zhou cuisine is today fairly exploding on the local restaurant scene, openly declaring its identity, if you know how to look for it.

The literal translation of the Chinese characters for Chao Zhou is "people of the tidelands," an apt description for a population whose diet places great importance on the ocean's bounty. Spheres of ground fish afloat in a light broth, fine-textured crab rolls and prawn balls, turtle soups and braised eel are all favorites of the Chao Zhous. It's a healthful diet. That is why Chao Zhou women are said to have *dou fu* complexions— the best in China.

The tidelands people are especially ardent lovers of the oyster. Near Shantou they harvest them by thrusting long bamboo poles into the mollusk beds. When the sticks are thoroughly covered with mature oysters, they are promptly set over a hot fire to grill. In Chao Zhou restaurants throughout Southeast Asia, the most popular oyster preparation is a "cake" in which the shucked mollusks are mixed with an egg-and-tapioca-flour batter and minced green onions, and fried into a crisp round.

Another trademark of Chao Zhou restaurants is the pomfret, a spiny, round, flat fish related to the pompano, which is popular throughout Southeast Asia. It is most often deep-fried and served

with a brown-bean sauce or a shower of golden garlic. Prawn balls are yet a third source of pride at these establishments.

Still another tradition at Chao Zhou restaurants is the iron buddha, a round of strong, bitter black tea served in thimble-sized cups. The tea, brought at the beginning and again at the end of a meal, is said to aid the digestion. In the back streets of Kowloon, it is drunk with a gregariousness that reflects the tough, urban lifestyle with which many of the colony's Chao Zhous are identified. In San Francisco, you can have it at the Fortune Restaurant in Chinatown or at the relatively fancy Chiu Chow Restaurant on Powell Street.

Chiu Chow? If you cannot read the Chinese ideograms announcing a Chao Zhou menu, be forwarned that the translation (when it appears at all) is not uniform. In their own dialect, the tidelands people are called the Teochew, the term used in Singapore, Malaysia, and Thailand. In Cantonese, they are referred to as the Chiu Chow.

The sizable Chao Zhou soup lexi-

Ginseng and Tea

The finer points of ginseng can be fully explored at San Francisco's **World Ginseng Center, Inc.** (801 Kearny St), where the revered root is available in every conceivable form, from candy to soft drink. The healing and energizing properties of ginseng belong to a larger category of lore associated with teas. This is a realm in which no place is better informed—or supplied—than the Taiwan-based **Ten Ren Company** (949 Grant Ave). Stop by to sample a few of the dozens of brews they stock, which include everything from the poetic "iron goddess of mercy" to the practical "relaxing tea bag." While you're there, pick up a copy of *The Chinese Art of Tea* by John Blofeld (Shambala), a handsome, informative guide to buying and brewing.

con—their chefs are regarded as experts in all varieties of "wet cooking"—includes both pricy shark-fin preparations and the inexpensive rice porridge called *congee* (a name inexplicably derived from a south Indian Dravidian word). In a Chao Zhou meal, this neutral preparation will often replace steamed rice as the counterpart to "oily" dishes. With the addition of fish or meat to the bowl, it can be the total repast, sometimes accompanied with small portions of pickled vegetables and salted duck egg.

In Hong Kong, where Chao Zhou restaurants traditionally stay open until 3:00 a.m. to accommodate their regular patrons' late-night habits, one unmistakable sign of a Shantou cook is a fat, cold braised goose hanging in the front window. Delicate slices of the bird are often served on a bed of livers, with a dipping sauce of vinegar and garlic on the side. Given the realities of the poultry marketplace, Chao Zhou chefs in the Bay Area have compromised: they serve cold sliced duck, prepared with plump, fresh birds from Petaluma's Reichardt Duck Farm.

Chao Zhou Restaurants: The Top Choices

• **The Chiu Chow Restaurant** Every market town in Guangdong Province has at least one: a "wedding restaurant." That's not the establishment's sole purpose; but the combination of large banquet rooms and a top-notch kitchen does suit the southern Chinese taste for culinary celebration, nuptial or seasonal. The Tran family, owners of the Chiu Chow—Cantonese dialect for a Chao Zhou restaurant—hails originally from north Guangdong, from which they emigrated to Saigon and later to Los Angeles, running dinner houses in both cities. Late in 1988, they opened their wedding restaurant in San Francisco, where legions of brides and grooms begin their lives together over such Chao Zhou favorites as water spinach with garlic, deep-fried prawn balls, and an excellent fried pompano. 1326 Powell St, SF (415) 397-8634. Lunch and dinner Wed–Mon. MC, V. Moderate.

• **Fortune Restaurant** In our estimate, this is the best of the Bay Area's Chao Zhou restaurants—and arguably the best of the genre east of Hong Kong. Owner Jack Lai and his father-in-law, chef Lin, a Chao Zhou from Laos, consistently produce extraordinary dishes for their understandably faithful clientele. No one serves a finer oyster cake, the shellfish omelet that is virtually a signature of this cuisine. Chef Lin fashions an exquisitely thin, crisp pancake loaded with plump oyster meats and Chinese chives. Prawn balls are intricately prepared: finely minced prawns, crab, pork, and water chestnuts are mixed with spices, formed into walnut-sized rounds, wrapped in a bean-curd sheet, individually tied with string, and then deep-fried. The ambience here is Chinatown basic; Jack plans a slightly more decorous new branch at the southwest corner of Portsmouth Square. Be sure to try chef Lin's clay-pot dishes, some of which are traditional herbal preparations available nowhere else this side of the Pacific. 675 Broadway, SF (415) 421-8130. MC, V. Lunch and dinner daily. Inexpensive.

• **Narai** Kietisak and Supar Komindr, along with their four children, opened this extraordinarily successful Richmond District establishment after stints as restaurateurs in the Serramonte Mall and Kietisak's native Bangkok. They are Chao Zhou Chinese from Thailand, and the dual legacy gives Narai's menu great diversity without sacrificing a bit of authenticity. Chef Supar—herself China-born—turns out a superb braised duck, served at room temperature, to be dipped in garlic and vinegar. Deep-fried pompano is also showered with browned garlic. If Thai is your mood, try the squid salad, but be sure to finish up with Chao Zhou taro pudding filled with gingko nuts and dates. 2229 Clement St, SF (415) 751-6363. Lunch and dinner Tues–Sun. Major credit cards. Inexpensive.

• **Pho Hoa Ky** The 19th century saw thousands of Chao Zhou Chinese emigrate to Cholon, a suburban district of Saigon that became the cultural—and culinary—center of Vietnam's large ethnic Chinese community. One of its more talented residents was the chef who now runs this modest restaurant in the Avenues, which features both Chao Zhou and Vietnamese dishes. Among his stellar accomplishments is a variation on the popular shrimp ball, a mixture of finely minced white fish, shrimp, and water chestnuts formed into spheres, wrapped in dried bean-curd sheets, and deep-fried. Also exceptional is his steamed crab in the style of the city of Shantou—ancestral capital of the Chao Zhous. It's simply tossed with green onions and bound in a light egg sauce, with the rich crab butter left smooth and intact in the Dungeness carapace. 4012 Geary Blvd, SF (415) 387-9600. Lunch and dinner daily. MC, V. Moderate.

Shanghainese Cuisine

Chin Ming-chien, the chef at **Fountain Court**, was a pioneer in bringing authentic Shanghainese cuisine to the Bay Area. In Shanghai, that cosmopolitan giant lying at the mouth of the Yangtze River, cooks rely chiefly on braising instead of steaming or stir-frying, exceptionally rich sauces, copious amounts of garlic, sweet Shaoxing wine, vinegar, and oil.

The Richmond District's Fountain Court got its start in the early 1980s, with the aim of providing for upwardly mobile Asians where they live, rather than where they work. The ambience is considerably more refined than the Clement Street norm, befitting the urbane metropolis Fountain Court represents. The dining room is split-level, with brass railings, parquet floors, low lighting, and a subdued fountain.

We began one memorable meal there with a plate of assorted chilled appetizers that held chicken poached in Shaoxing wine, "smoked" fish (which is actually braised in flavored soy), marinated jellyfish, and a vegetarian "goose" made of soy-braised sheets of bean curd. Shanghai people always begin a meal with such chilled plates; ours was outstanding—the mock goose, in particular, had the silky texture and sharp, mildly sweet taste that characterize a properly prepared Shanghainese dish.

More remarkable yet was a whole catfish braised in wine, again lightly sweetened, and surrounded by roasted garlic cloves. We were momentarily distracted by the arrival at a neighboring table of a platter of *shi zi tou*. Literally "lion's head," this dish is to meatballs what caviar is to eggs—it revolves around spheres of seasoned, hand-minced belly pork that have been fried, then braised in a brown sauce. The lion's mane is composed of fresh greens.

All of these Shanghai classics and more are to be had at the upscale **Wu Kong** in the stunning Rincon complex, including braised pork, stir-fried slivered eels, and bean-curd whey tossed with broad beans. Take note, however, that some of these treats do not appear on Wu Kong's menu, which mixes in some Cantonese ringers. (The flagship Wu Kong is in Hong Kong.) Insist that the waiter tell you about the evening's Shanghainese specials.

One thing that is always available—and not listed on the evening menu at all—is Shanghai's favorite appetizer/snack. It is the *nanxiang xiao long bao*, named for the suburban town of Nanxiang and translated literally as "little dragon packets." They are superbly juicy wheat dumplings, stuffed with seasoned pork, steamed in a bamboo basket, and served with a dip of black vinegar and ginger. Wu Kong makes one of the most successful versions of this dish we have ever tried.

• **Fountain Court** 354 Clement St, SF (415) 668-1100. Lunch and dinner daily. MC, V. Moderate.

• **Wu Kong** Rincon Center, 101 Spear St, SF (415) 957-9300. Lunch and dinner daily. MC, V. Moderate.

Other Shanghainese Restaurants: The Top Choices

• **Four-Five-Six Restaurant** The name refers to a lucky combination of numbers in Chinese lore and was borrowed by chef-owner David Wang from a famous Shanghai restaurant. What brings Silicon Valley's northern Chinese engineers here at lunch is Wang's deft hand with such Shanghai dishes as the steamed little meat buns called *xiao long bao*, duck braised in brown sauce, and the full array of room-temperature appetizers that China's largest city so enjoys, including wine-cooked chicken, "smoked" fish, and salted shrimp. On weekends at lunchtime, northern dim sum is featured. Don't expect palatial surroundings; this is a pretty bare-bones joint, and much busier at noon than at 8:00 p.m. But for real food lovers, it's a great find, especially those who know Shanghai classics and order them. 2362

Pruneridge Ave, Santa Clara (408) 985-8456. Lunch and dinner Wed–Mon. MC, V. Moderate.

• **House of Nanking** Peter Fang, scion of a family that ran a celebrated ginseng shop on Shanghai's Nanjing Road, could use a restaurant four times this size, so popular have his

Secret Names of Chinatown

Many San Franciscans know that Cantonese old-timers still call Grant Avenue (Chinatown's restaurant Main Street) by its original name, Dupont Street. Fewer are aware that the Chinese ideograms chosen to express it amounted to a critique of early San Francisco's jerry-built architecture; *Du Baan Gai* means "Street of the Slatboard Capital City." Scores of San Francisco's pioneer-era wooden buildings, relates architect Philip Choy, were prefab structures, built in Canton and shipped across the Pacific. They came in a variety of Oriental and Occidental styles.

The Grant/Dupont phenomenon is not unique. In fact, most of Chinatown's byways have two names, with the Chinese version often providing rich insights into local history. Sacramento Street, the first street on which Asians were allowed to settle, is *Tang Yahn Gai* (Chinese People's Street). Waverly Place is *Tin How Hong* (Lane of the Heavenly Queen), named for a venerable temple. Jason Alley, a favorite prostitution quarter for Chinese gold miners, remains *Gum Ohk Hong* (Lane of the Golden Chrysanthemums) long after its flowers have wilted.

Beckett Street, a small lane to the east of Grant, was phoneticized to *Bak Wah Dien Gai*, which translates as "Plain-Language John Street," in honor of the interpreter who once lived there. Washington Street, as several restaurateurs will confirm, is quite appropriately rendered as *Wah Sheng Dun Gai* (Way Station to Chinese Prosperity). It's a great place, incidentally, to look for Chinese restaurants open after midnight.

Just below Stockton Street are two of the narrow alleys where early Christian settlement workers did much of their rescue work. Old Chinatown Lane was once another prostitutes' quarter that the Cantonese called *Ma Fong Hong* (Horse Stable Alley) for the livery that stood on it. Nearby were an opium den and cigar factory. Ross Alley was known as *Gau Leuie Sung Hong* (Old Spanish Alley) because its demimonde was heavily patronized by Latinos. Arnold Genthe, the 19th-century photographer, referred to Ross as "Gambler's Alley" in the caption of his most famous image of early San Francisco. An 1885 map of the district shows no fewer than 18 separate gaming rooms on Ross; today, it resounds to the humming bobbins of sewing factories.

San Francisco itself bears two Chinese names: the old-fashioned descriptive *Gum Shan* (Golden Mountain) and *Sam Faan See*, a more formal modern phoneticization that reads "City of Three Shores"— the Pacific, the Golden Gate, and San Francisco Bay.

Shanghainese dishes become. He's a stickler on authenticity, staying at work into the late hours just to prepare the yeast dough for the next day's batch of panfried meat-stuffed buns, a specialty few other chefs have the patience to offer. The same care goes into several dishes that employ Shanghai's technique of braising meat or poultry in Shao-xing wine; the tripe and chicken versions are especially good. 919 Kearny St, SF (415) 421-1429. Lunch and dinner daily. No credit cards. Inexpensive.

• **Star Lunch** This is the simplest of simple lunch counters; there aren't even any tables. But the warm and pleasant couple who welcome a maximum of eight diners produce exactly what the Shanghai office worker or bus conductor would sit down to at noon. A perfect example is the stir-fried pork and greens with rice cakes. Another is noodle soup with "pork chop," a quick-fried loin nicely offset by the flavor of salted mustard greens in the broth. 605 Jackson St, SF (415) 788-1552. Lunch only, Mon–Sat. No credit cards. Inexpensive.

Northern Chinese Cuisine

A rule for the dining road: Beware of Chinese restaurants promising mandarin food. Put bluntly, the promise may mean nothing. Despite a widely held misconception, "mandarin" does not equal "north-ern" in the Chinese culinary lexi-con. Indeed, as the familiar Cantonese inflections rising from most local "mandarin"—and most allegedly "Sichuan"—kitchens demonstrate, their chefs are from China's deep south.

There is, of course, a true mandarin cuisine, developed by the palace chefs of dynastic China to

meet the sophisticated tastes of its high-level bureaucrats, or manda-rins. These chefs turned out master-pieces from all the country's regions, not just the north—creations so elaborate that you are not likely to find them in any Ameri-can restaurant.

The same could long be said of genuine northern Chinese food in San Francisco—you weren't likely to find it here. Alas, that's still largely true for most northern cuisines; apart from the modest Four-Five-Six in Santa Clara, we lack good, authentic Sichuan dining opportu-nities in the Bay Area—and even that example offers just a few chili-laced Sichuan specialties on a larger north-ern menu. We're doing better on Shanghainese food in general, as this chapter points out.

But the really good news is that recent immigration has introduced another set of northerners to the Bay Area whose origins lie in or above the Yangtze basin, China's Mason-Dixon line. Gastronomically, the north is bordered by a rough rectan-gle, with three corners resting on Beijing, Sichuan, and Shanghai. It is the fourth corner, which falls on the Shandong peninsula just across the Yellow Sea from South Korea, that provides us with our brightest northern lights.

Shandong is a region as legendary to the Chinese as it is unknown to most Americans. Confucius was born and died there; Tai Shan, one of the four sacred mountains of Taoism, soars from its western flank; its central plains are a cornuco-pia of fruits and vegetables; and its major port, Qingdao (aka Tsingtao), is the home of China's finest beer. More to the point, the 16th-century Ming emperors imported hundreds of cooks from the area to man the woks of the Forbidden City—in effect, to cook the imperial mandarins' meals. Ever since, the term "Shandong chef" has been a synonym for kitchen genius in China. Now one such genius is hard at work out on Geary Boulevard near Second Avenue, in the **Happy Family** restaurant. To his admiring staff, he is known only as Master Han.

What Han has mastered is not the rarified menu of the Ming emperors but rather the fare of the northern Chinese common man, a fare we grew fond of during assignments in China through the '80s but resigned ourselves to forgetting each time we returned to San Francisco. Then we discovered Happy

Northern Dim Sum

San Francisco's **Golden Palace** (1830 Irving St) is one of a growing number of Bay Area restaurants that each weekend serves up a northern version of dim sum, the traditional morning repast that Mandarin speakers refer to as *zhao dian*, roughly meaning "light breakfast." (The restaurant's Chinese name is *Jing Chuan Fan Dian*, a contraction for Beijing and Sichuan Rice House.)

A visible departure from Cantonese dim sum style in these restaurants is that the dishes don't circulate on dim sum carts; you have to order from a handwritten list. The Golden Palace proprietors are among the few who have translated the complete *zhao dian* menu—but make sure you ask for it or you may simply be handed the English dinner menu, even at 11:00 a.m.

It also pays to be aggressive; survey the room and ask for what looks good on surrounding tables, or engage the waiter in a fact-finding mission. No matter how you finally unlock the mysteries, some dishes shouldn't be missed. Start with a bowl of hot *dou jiang* (soybean milk) and *you tiao*, a kind of deep-fried cruller—the coffee and doughnut of north China. The invention of a 19th-century American missionary, soybean milk is now the mainstay breakfast opener in Beijing and other north-

ern cities, especially on cold winter mornings. It comes either sweetened with sugar or "salty" with pickled vegetables.

Certainly you should order *shao bing*, sesame-topped unleavened bread that the Golden Palace uses to sandwich slices of five-spice beef (described on the menu as a "Chinese hamburger"), and *shui jiao*, boiled dumplings filled with shrimp, pork, or greens. Alternately, these dumplings are available steamed in bamboo baskets as *jing jiao*. Bowls of noodle soup are deservedly popular here; wheat noodles and beef or cellophane noodles and bean curd are just two of the many combinations available. Half a dozen fried noodle dishes are also offered; the Shanghai-style *zhao mian* of rough-cut flat noodles fried in fragrant oil with just a bit of scallion is unforgettable.

In addition to the Golden Palace, you can find authentic weekend *zhao dian* in the Bay Area at many of the better northern restaurants, among them San Francisco's **Wu Kong** and **Fountain Court**; the **Taiwan Restaurants** in San Francisco and Berkeley; **Golden Wok** in Mountain View; and **Four-Five-Six** in Santa Clara. In addition, Mountain View's **House of Yee** (160 Castro St) offers some 30 items on its weekend *zhao dian* menu, from wonton with hot red oil to jelly fish with sesame butter.

La Mian: Pulled Noodles of the North

A thick sauce sets many northern Chinese noodle dishes apart from their more lightly dressed south China equivalents, but that is not the only thing. The noodles themselves, called *la mian*, or "pulled noodles," are made by a unique centuries-old method refined in Shandong and nearby Hebei provinces. In only a few minutes, a master of this extraordinary art transforms a mound of ordinary flour-and-water dough into extraordinarily long, uniform strands. The dough is never touched by a knife; the strands magically emerge as the chef performs a repetitious series of swinging, stretching, and doubling actions, punctuated by sharp slaps against a wooden table.

The thickness of each noodle is determined by the number of times the dough is "pulled" through the time-honored ballet. For one famous appetizer in Beijing, *la mian* as fine as violin strings are deep-fried and then folded into a paper-thin pancake. Even the non-northern Chinese find the phenomenon amazing; in far western Kunming a few years ago, we saw a huge crowd gather outside a newly opened "Shandong Specialty Restaurant," gazing spellbound as the chef made his pulled noodles in the front window.

You can find *la mian* in at least half a dozen Bay Area restaurants, including San Francisco's **Happy Family** and the two **San Wang Restaurants** (see "Northern Chinese Restaurants") and at **Chef Wang's** (212 Castro St, Mountain View) in the South Bay.

Family and its wonderful *shui jiao*, delicious "boiled dumplings" that arrive filled either with shrimp and chives, pork and cabbage, or beef. In the wheat-oriented north of China, such dumplings often comprise a whole meal; a single lunchtime helping in the Beijing railway station delivers no less than three dozen *shui jiao*. Another wheat-based northern specialty is the potsticker, a pan-fried dumpling that many Cantonese menus include to attract Western diners, who seem to love them. Happy Family's put most southern copies to shame.

Not that Shandong chefs are beyond similar marketing ploys. Many have an ersatz Cantonese *chow mein* on their menus because diners expect to find it. But no resemblance to southern fare can be found in their genuinely northern noodle dishes: most notably, a hearty wheat "pasta" generously topped with thick, ingredient-laden sauces, sometimes with a extra bowl of sauce on the side. One such dish envelopes shrimp, slivered pork, and sea cucumber in a sauce of sesame paste, ginger, and chili pepper— a concoction to fight off the biting cold wind of a Beijing winter (or the bone-chilling fog of a San Francisco summer). Another blankets meats and seafood in an intense, deep-colored black-bean gravy. One way to beat the heavy sauce problem is to order the same noodles in soup, usually a rich seafood broth without any thickening agent added.

When money is no object, northerners (like their southern cousins) treat themselves to seafood but prepare it in their own characteristic styles. A classic example is sea cucumber with garlic, which illustrates the special skill Shandong chefs accord this prized delicacy, its velvety, rather gelatinous nature set off by a rich brown sauce.

In the inland north, which relies more heavily upon freshwater fish, the approach is directly related to topography. Because the long Yellow River drains thousands of square miles of high desert, it is thick with silt; thus, Beijing chefs traditionally put live fish in a clear-water tank for five days before cooking and then deep-fry them to purge any remaining muddiness. Their counterparts in the Bay Area omit this extra swim. But they prepare their whole fish, usually rock cod, in the two styles encountered most frequently in northern China: with a sweet-and-sour sauce that lacks the Hawaiian Punch look of many similarly named Cantonese-American dishes, or a thick soybean paste laced with garlic.

One dish on many of the Bay Area's authentic northern menus often appears only in Chinese and Korean, which instantly makes every adventurous English-speaking-only diner want to try it. Some waiters offer the unencouraging translation "pork salad" for what proves to be a memorable creation. At the edge of a large platter are small mounds of carrot, shrimp, wood ear fungus, egg, squid, jellyfish, cucumber, pork, and other ingredients. In the center rests a mountain of hot stir-fried pork strips and coarsely shredded mung bean sheets. The waitress expertly tosses together the hot and the cold, coating them with a nose-tingling mustard sauce.

Why does the dish appear in Korean? Why, moreover, does a bowl of fiery *kimchee*, the classic "pickle" of Korean cuisine, accompany every meal at several Bay Area northern Chinese establishments? The answer, as is so often the case,

lies along an immigration road to California that has more than one stop. "Our chef was born in Shandong, moved to Korea, then to Japan, and now he is here," the Korean-born, Shandong-descended waitress at Happy Family explains. "Many people from Shandong have spent time in Korea, often running restaurants. So Koreans know this food, and come here to eat it."

Northern Chinese Restaurants: The Top Choices

• **Golden Wok** Located just off Castro Street, the Grant Avenue of Mountain View's booming suburban version of Chinatown, Golden Wok is one sign that the South Bay may turn out to be the Bay Area's northern Chinese dining capital. With weekend northern dim sum (see description elsewhere in this chapter) and a full menu of classics from north of the Yangtze, Golden Wok certainly aims to please fussy Beijing palates. There are a few top dishes you have to ask for—they're not on the menu. One is a delicious bean-curd preparation seasoned with shrimp roe; a second is yellow fish, imported from the Yangtze, braised in a vinegary sauce. 895 Villa St, Mountain View (415) 969-8232. Lunch and dinner daily. MC, V. Moderate.
• **Gou Bu Li** Chef David Sung, who learned his trade in Taipei, runs a

modest little spot, squeezed inconspicuously into a suburban shopping mall, that excels at several northern Chinese cuisines. This is where the chili and bean curd lover should try Sichuan's fiery *ma po dou fu* or the flaky scallion cakes beloved of Beijingers. Sung also turns out delicious boiled dumplings filled with pork and cabbage. Moeser Lane Shopping Center, 10684 San Pablo Ave, El Cerrito (415) 525-5362. Lunch and dinner daily. MC, V. Moderate.

• **Happy Family** The kitchen of Happy Family, featured in the essay on northern Chinese food above, interprets the sophisticated cuisine of Shandong Province. This standby is famous for its hand-pulled noodles, served with a variety of sauces, and for such unusual specialties as cold seaweed salad tossed with garlic, pig's ear salad, and braised sea cucumber. 3809 Geary Blvd, SF (415) 221-5095. Lunch and dinner Thur–Tues. MC, V. Moderate.

• **Her Nan Restaurant** The north-central province of Henan (pronounced "Her Nan" by its residents) was the heart of Chinese civilization during the Shang dynasty 3000 years ago. Today, it's off the beaten path, which is one reason this small, friendly restaurant is probably the only one of its kind in America. Two Henan mainstays to try here are glutinous rice balls, served in a full-flavored broth with spinach and pork, and a long-simmered duck, boned and presented with feathery light wheat rolls. Virtually nothing on the specials menu will seem familiar; this is esoteric regionalism of the highest order. 3420 Balboa St, SF (415) 752-4009. Lunch and dinner daily. No credit cards. Inexpensive.

• **San Wang Restaurants** The two San Wangs are like night and day. The Post Street branch in Japantown, which opened first, is a noisy, boisterously friendly place. By contrast, the Clement branch is extremely reserved and takes its tone from the quiet foyer bar where a wood fire blazes in the hearth. What links the two is an exceptional Shandong menu. It offers not only the hand-pulled *la mian* that made the provincial name in noodle circles, but also a fabulous Shandong "salad" of pork, spun bean-flour ribbons, and mixed seafood tossed in a tart mustard dressing. We're addicted to the *jiao zi*, or boiled dumplings, here, particularly the ones stuffed with chives and shrimp. 1642 Post St, SF (415) 982-0471; 2239 Clement St, SF (415) 221-1870. Lunch and dinner daily. MC, V. Moderate.

Dim Sum

Dim sum, that ever-popular Cantonese morning ritual, has been handed down to the contemporary era from a venerable teahouse tradition. Originally, its intention was to provide a place to sip and chat. With time, small dishes of food, both savory and sweet, were added to the scene. Today, in both Asia and the Bay Area, the entire scene has become big and brassy, with enormous dim sum palaces competing to produce the largest variety of dishes—some cooked right at the table on portable grills and steamers.

It helps to study the glossary provided here, unless you want to limit yourself to the conventional pork buns and shrimp dumplings that tend to be offered to non-Chinese. The way it works is that dim sum waitresses who push carts through the palaces are de facto salespeople. They walk around the dining room, hollering out the names of their dishes and occasionally a few ribald jokes. The jokes, alas, will be beyond all but the accomplished Cantonese speaker, but the more dish names you recognize, the better you'll eat.

Begin advertising your expertise the moment you sit down. Passivity in the opening minutes of a dim sum meal will often bring you a pot of indifferent tea. Remember, this is a teahouse; your fellow diners are picking their brew from a list that may boast jasmine, oolong, litchi, lok on, daffodil, dragon well, gunpowder green, and more. Our own invariable preference is a black tea with a measure of chrysanthemum blossoms. Ask for *pooneh guk fah cha* and you'll get it, plus some respect.

The best of the local teahouses include such gold-cup dinner houses (listed elsewhere in this chapter) as Harbor Village, the Hong Kong

A Select Dim Sum Glossary

Savories

App gwal jaat: Steamed, stuffed duck feet.

Char siu bow: Steamed bread stuffed with barbecued pork.

Chong fun: Steamed rice-flour pancake filled with beef (*ngau yuk*), barbecued pork (*char siu*), or shrimp (*har*).

Gai bow: Steamed bread stuffed with chicken.

Har gow: Steamed shrimp dumpling.

Jing joon: Glutinous rice flavored with dried shrimp, sausage, and/or other meats steamed in lotus leaf. Commonly called "Chinese tamale."

Jar woo kwok: Fried taro turnover.

Juk: Rice porridge.

Laap chong guan: Steamed pork sausage roll.

Lo shoy ngau jap: Braised, seasoned beef tripe.

Lu bak go: Fried turnip squares, usually seasoned with dried shrimp.

Ngau yuk siu mai: Steamed beef meatballs, usually on a bed of greens.

Ng heung ngau: Braised beef shank.

Pai gwat: Steamed spareribs.

See jiu fung jow: Chicken feet cooked with black beans.

Shan juck guen: Meat wrapped in dried bean-curd sheet.

Shu app: Roast duck.

Shu yuk: Crispy-skin roast pork.

Siew gai: Soy-braised chicken.

Siu mai: Steamed meat dumpling.

Yue chee gow: Steamed shark's fin turnover.

Yu-ju gun tang gow: Large dumplings that encase soup and bits of meat and vegetable.

Teahouses also specialize in noodle dishes, usually found on a written menu with English translations. Order from the waiter/waitress who brings your tea, not from the cart pushers.

Sweets

Dan tar: Custard tart.

Gee mar guen: Black sesame roll.

Gin doy: Deep-fried rice-flour puff.

Jap gaw ja lee: Mixed fruit gelatin.

Lin yung bow: Steamed lotus bun.

Ma lye go: Steamed sponge cake.

Ma tay go: Water chestnut pudding.

Flower Lounges, Ming's Villa in Palo Alto, East Ocean in Emeryville, Fook Yuen in Millbrae, and San Francisco's Wu Kong (a Shanghai restaurant that serves both Cantonese dim sum and northern-style *zhao dian*). Other accomplished establishments specializing in dim sum follow.

Dim Sum Restaurants

• **Hong Kong Seafood Restaurant**
On weekend mornings, Sunset District Chinese families crowd this comfortable dining room. Although the chef doesn't offer the wide variety prepared by some of his larger competitors, everything is good here, from delicate steamed dumplings and spareribs in black-bean sauce to eggplant slices stuffed with ground fish and noodle-and-rice-stuffed dumplings in soup. 2588 Noriega St, SF (415) 665-8338. Daily. MC, V. Inexpensive.

• **Hong Kong Teahouse** This was one of the first Hong Kong-style dim sum restaurants in San Francisco's Chinatown, and it still has a loyal following among both local residents and suburban Chinese-Americans in for a day of shopping. Aficionados cite the *har gow* and *jing joon* served here. 835 Pacific Ave, SF (415) 391-6563. Daily. MC, V. Inexpensive.

• **Jade Villa** Oakland's Chinese restaurant scene is growing like Topsy, but for the moment Jade Villa is still the number one choice for dim sum. Sample any of the steamed dumplings or the chicken and mushroom wrapped in bean-curd sheets and you'll know why. Go early to avoid the noontime crush, when Oakland Chinatown's movers and shakers take over the room. 800 Broadway, Oakland (415) 839-1688. Daily. MC, V. Inexpensive.

Hong Kong Breakfast

The **Hong Kong V.I.P.** restaurant and bakery (671 Broadway, SF) is a coffee shop where the ambience, customers, and menu are Crown Colony to the core. It is definitely real, and the proof lies in its steaming bowls of elbow-macaroni-and-ham soup.

Believe it or not, that's exactly what the Kowloon common man eats over his *Ming Pao* or *South China Morning Post*. In a century and a half of British rule, Hong Kong has borrowed plenty of things from Anglo culture, but none so peculiar as this soup, which has been shifted from London lunch to Asian breakfast and made part of a standard combination that also includes orange juice, coffee, or milk-infused tea and a *ngau yau bau*. This last item, which translates literally as "cow-oil container," is in some ways the best part of the legacy, and when eaten alone with coffee, amounts to Hong Kong's version of the continental breakfast. Baked right on the premises and served piping hot, V.I.P.'s *ngau yau bau* is a superb wheat roll, delivered with two pats of cow oil, aka butter.

• **King of China** Richmond District residents regularly stop by this silver-sheathed restaurant, where the portions and variety reflect the teahouse taste for big, while the prices are a minimalist bargain. It's a homey, boisterious place with sturdy food—a villager's brunch despite the monarchist moniker. 939 Clement St, SF (415) 668-2618. Daily. MC, V. Inexpensive.

• **North Sea Village** Housed in a dockside building overlooking the Richardson Bay marina, this outpost of a Hong Kong restaurant empire delivers a first-class view with its first-class dim sum. When you're flush with cash, try the bird's-nest–filled dumpling in soup. Less pricy but equally delicious are the chive-stuffed dumplings, braised chicken feet with chili, and deep-fried taro turnovers. 300 Turney St, Sausalito (415) 331-3000. Daily. Major credit cards. Moderate.

• **Tung Fong** A Chinatown favorite that offers a cozy retreat from the more glittery dim sum emporiums. Many serious dim sum students believe that the overall quality here is superior to that of the competition—no matter what their size.

Try the shrimp dumplings, fried turnip cake flecked with dried shrimp, and spareribs in black-bean sauce and judge for yourself. 808 Pacific Ave, SF (415) 362-7115. Thur–Tues. No credit cards. Inexpensive.

• **Yank Sing** Located on the edge of the Financial District, this stylish dining room caters to the three-piece-suit set five days a week. Weekends, however, belong to the rest of us. The personable staff always makes lunch here a particular pleasure. The original Yank Sing, which was located on Broadway in Chinatown, is reputed to have been the first dim sum restaurant in San Francisco. 427 Battery St, SF (415) 362-1640. Daily. Major credit cards. Inexpensive.

Chinese Vegetarian Food

"It softens the sharp, it loosens the tangled. It harmonizes what is brilliant and assimilates itself to what is worldly. How tranquil it is!"

Of all the claims made for vegetarianism, none reached further than these words of Lao-tze, the mystic sage of sixth-century-B.C. China who founded the movement known as Taoism. Tao—literally "the Path"—prescribed a route to human perfection that abjured all strife. In its purest form, it also abjured meat eating. Carnivores, in Lao-tze's scheme, were hopelessly caught up in the worldly tangles that Taoism sought to unravel.

Over the centuries, Lao-tze's beliefs have gradually been absorbed into the larger universe of Chinese thought. Their culinary reflection is an almost obsessive preoccupation with balance and harmony. Taoism, in the temple and at the table, is about the reconciliation of opposites—the marriage of *yin* and *yang*. At their best, Taoist cooks aim for subtle contrasts in color, texture, and taste, pleasing sensations in their own right that also mesh "cold" (*yin*) with "hot" (*yang*), descriptions that refer not to temperature or spiciness, but rather to spiritual and medicinal properties.

Too philosophical for restaurant chitchat? Not when the restaurant in question shares its quarters with Ching Chung Temple, a California outpost of Hong Kong's most famous Taoist shrine. **Lotus Garden**, a serene oasis one floor above the hectic streets of San Francisco's Chinatown, is more than a restaurant. It's a way station on the Path.

One of our own journeys at Lotus Garden began with pickled Chinese cabbage and preserved bean cake, a wonderful mélange of green, pale gold, orange, honey-brown, and black shreds, tossed in aromatic spices and oils that imparted an unusual smoky flavor. In addition to the cabbage and preserved bean cake—a pressed tofu that has the bite of meat—there were shreds of bamboo shoot, snow pea, carrot, and black fungus. Their *yin-yang* targets, we were told, range from measles and diabetes to ulcers and hangovers.

Type A personalities would do well to order another entrée: eggplant sautéed with bean-curd sheet. We tried it in a black-bean sauce recommended by the waiter. Healthwise, it was addressed to heart and digestive problems, but its chief appeal for us was less clinical. The squares of bean-curd sheet had been deep-fried and then steamed; they were crêpelike on the outside and almost custardy inside. Placed over purple cylinders of steamed Japanese eggplant, they suggested surrealist sculpture—an essay in form and shape that tasted as intriguing as it looked.

It was a kind of illusion: vegetables presented as geometry. And it was followed by an even more whimsical illusion: vegetables in the guise of seafood and meat. The first of these looked for all the world like a deep-fried whole fish, though its composition was actually taro root, a starchy tuber widely consumed in East Asia and the Pacific. (Good for relieving inflammation, according to our guide in these matters, the Vancouver Chinese medical scholar Dr. Henry Lu.)

Another example of the Lotus Garden's expertise in culinary illusion is the black mushroom with sliced gluten puff. The puff is a wheat-flour dough frequently used in mock meat dishes. In this preparation, it is cooked in a sauce similar in color to that used for *cha siu*, "barbecued pork," which it resembles to a startling degree.

After our repast, we repaired to the temple, just upstairs from the dining room, to meditate on the snares of all such illusions.

Just a few blocks away, the bright, airy **Kowloon Vegetarian Restaurant** has become the latest pioneer out to win the hearts of the cholesterol watchers. Its menu runs to scores of items, including some two dozen dim sum selections. Try the crispy mushroom-stuffed turnover, made with rice flour, or the steamed dumplings filled with either bamboo shoots or mixed vegetables. Bean thread noodles stand in for the shark's fin in soup, and bean-curd sheets double for fowl in a wonderful plate of "roast goose." Or forgo such fakery altogether and order a plate of Kowloon's straightforward—and delicious—black mushrooms with thread fungus.

Lotus Garden 532 Grant Ave, SF (415) 397-0130. Lunch and dinner Tues–Sun. Major credit cards. Moderate.

Kowloon Vegetarian Restaurant 909 Grant Ave, SF (415) 362-9888. Lunch and dinner daily. MC, V. Inexpensive.

Chinese Food Glossary

Chinese menu entrées are usually expressed in a series of three or four ideograms that indicate cooking method, ingredients, and sometimes seasoning. Thus, a diner can order items that do not appear in an English translation simply by mixing from various categories listed in the very elementary glossary provided below, with their pronunciation in Cantonese and Mandarin. Remember that Chinese dialects are inflected; if your effort fails the first time, try different tones. The accompanying ideograms will help you to decipher the dishes that appear only in Chinese. A comprehensive guide—translating thousands of wonderful dishes—is James D. McCawley's *The Eater's Guide to Chinese Characters* (University of Chicago Press).

中文	牛肉	辣醬	炸
English **Cantonese** **Mandarin**	beef **ngauh** **niu**	chili sauce **lah jow** **la jiao**	deep-fried **jau** **zha**
雜	豆豉	塊	丁
assorted (mixed) **jaap** **za**	black bean **dou see** **tou chi**	chunks **faai** **kuai**	diced **ding** **ding**
豆腐	菜心	切	乾炒
bean curd **dou fu** **dou fu**	cabbage hearts **choi sum** **cai xin**	bite-sized **chit** **qie**	dry-fried **gon chow** **gan chao**
腐乳	冷	蜆	鴨
fermented **fu yu** **fu ju**	cold **laahng** **leng**	clam **heen** **ge li**	duck **aap** **ya**
粉絲	鷄	螃蟹	魚
bean threads **fen see** **fen siu**	chicken **gai** **ji**	crab **pong haai** **pang xie**	fish **yuh** **yu**

鮮
fresh
sin
xian

油
oil
yau
you

砂鍋
sand (clay) pot
sa wo
shao guo

蒸
steamed
jing
zheng

辣
hot (chili)
laaht
la

蠔
oyster
houh
hao

臘腸
sausage
laap chang
xiang chang

炒
stir-fried
chow
chao

羊
lamb
yeuhng
yang

豬
pork
jyu
zhu

海鮮
seafood
hoi si
hai xian

釀
stuffed
neuhng
niang

龍蝦
lobster
lung haah
long xia

蝦
prawn
hai
xia

絲
shredded
see
si

甜酸
sweet-sour
tihm syun
tian suan

肉
meat*
yuhk
rou

紅燒
red-cooked
huhng siu
hong shao

片
sliced
pin
pian

肚
tripe/innards
touh
du

菰
mushroom
gu
ku

飯
rice
faahn
fan

湯
soup
tong
tang

菜
vegetables
choi
cai

麵
noodle (wneat)
mein
mian

燒
roasted
siu
shao

瓜
squash
gwa
kua

水
water
sui
shui

粉
noodle (rice)
fun
fen

鹽
salted
yihm
yan

魷魚
squid
yau yuh
wu zei yu

蕹菜
water spinach
ong choy
weng cai

Always pork unless otherwise specified.

Japan: Tradition at the Table

I n the '60s, the Bay Area em-braced the burrito. In the '70s we abandoned beef. The '80s will surely go down in history as the sushi decade. It would have been easy to conclude that the Japanese never cook, except for rice.

Easy and wrong. The truth—which could turn out to be the describe it.

Let us consider the humble noodle. We stand at the window of **Mifune**, the San Francisco Japan-town branch of a famous restaurant owned by the Miwa family of Osaka. Lined up before us is a battery of models, a sculpted version of the menu inside: plastic shrimp and

theme of the '90s—is that raw fish is usually no more than a supporting player in a Japanese meal. In the culinary Japan that lies beyond sushi (as in all of Japanese society), everything has its orderly, immuta-ble group life. No cuisine on earth is more obsessed with categories, formal customs, and exactingly detailed definitions, ruling *everything* from the size and the shape of the serving dish to the alphabet used to chicken floating in plastic broth, clumps of plastic pickled plums, plastic egg, and plastic seaweed. (Take it on faith, incidentally, that good-looking models mean good food; Japanese windows seldom lie.)

Mifune is the real thing, a genu-ine *soba-ya* (noodle house), represent-ing one of Japan's most prolific restaurant categories. It's the kind of place the Honshu middle class goes to for lunch, and the working class

People and Their Neighborhoods

Where they live: Until World War II, central San Jose, along Jackson Street, and the Nihonmachi District of San Francisco's Geary Boulevard corridor had large, thriving Japanese-American residential communities. Thousands of Japanese-Americans returned from their forced internment in wartime camps to find that their homes and businesses had been confiscated. Into the 1980s, some of the older, first-generation Japanese immigrants still hang on in the traditional prewar districts. But today the residential community is largely dispersed, and Japanese—both American-born and business expatriates—live all over the Bay Area.

Where they gather: Nihonmachi, bordered by Geary Boulevard and Bush Street on the south and north and Fillmore and Octavia streets on the east and west, offers America's closest approximation of an authentic Japanese commercial district. It's home to everything from first-rate markets and Soko Hardware, chockful of imported woodworking tools, to the local Japanese newspaper and the recently expanded central Buddhist Church. In San Jose, Jackson Street's old Japantown has shrunk to a tofu manufactury, a couple of stores, and half a dozen restaurants, but it retains a nostalgic glow.

Estimated Bay Area population: 80,000

for dinner. It offers an array of noodle possibilities that makes the menu of some Italian *trattorie* seem anemic. At Mifune, you can have *soba* (buckwheat) or *udon* (wheat) noodles; the

first is associated with Tokyo, the second with Kyoto and Osaka. Both come hot or cold, in more than 20 combinations each, in soup or out, with toppings that range from grated mountain yam to herring.

No matter which of these options you exercise, the presentation follows a protocol that can only be called rigid. The tempura and cold *soba* combo known as *tenzaru*, for instance, is always served on a *zaru*, a bamboo lattice rack in a square frame. *Nabeyaki udon*, a fish broth full of chicken, tempura shrimp, vegetables, and egg, must arrive in an iron pot, in allusion to the country setting it is supposed to recall. By the way, loud slurping of hot noodles is encouraged in Japan as a means of cooling the mouth, a necessary habit in a country where office workers customarily down their lunch in less than five minutes.

The alphabet? Depending upon context, Japan employs no less than three competing systems, and all three appear on the Mifune menu. Because the basic concept of noodle soup was imported from China centuries ago, Chinese characters are still used to represent it. But the Japanese claim *udon* specifically for themselves, so *it* is represented in the *hiragana* syllabic alphabet, which is reserved for truly Japanese phenomena. The idea of dessert, on the other hand, is Western to the core. Thus, Mifune's dessert section is headed in another syllabic alphabet, *katakana*, which is used for non-Chinese foreign ideas. Translated, one of its entries reads "a-i-su kurimu." Say it aloud quickly and you'll get the point.

As Mifune's noodle-o-pedic approach suggests, genuine Japanese restaurants are phenomenally specialized. In Tokyo, no one can tell you the best all-around place to eat Japanese food, because no such place exists. Instead, every Japanese has a favorite *sushi-ya*, *soba-ya*, and *shokuji dokoro* (traditional bistro), to cite just a few of at least 18 major categories in the national restaurant repertoire.

The range can be hinted at with a survey of a single site: a shopping center in San Francisco's *Nihonmachi*, or Japantown—the focal point of an old-line ethnic neighborhood that is everything to the Bay Area's 80,000 Japanese-Americans that North Beach is to Italians. The shopping center is named the Kinkei-Kintetsu Mall, after the Honshu Island railroad line that built it. And it is exactly the kind of place that Honshu commuters would flock to for their dinners. Indeed, Mifune is located here.

Next door to Mifune is **Misono**, a cozy little *shokuji dokoro* prepared to serve you a genuine Tokyo sukiyaki. It was religious vegetarian minimalism that allegedly drove rebellious eighth-century farmers to the pleasures of one of Japan's most famous—and most abused—

creations. According to legend, *sukiyaki*, or "plowshare cooking," came about when a born-again Buddhist emperor forbade the eating of meat. The rural folks engaged in carnivorous civil disobedience, but they did it in secret, grilling their beef on the metal blades of their plows.

In America, the term sukiyaki has come to be identified with the worst sort of kitchen atrocity, often producing nothing more than a syrupy beef stew. At Misono and other genuine Japanese establishments in the Bay Area, it is a different matter. First the waiter carries out a special cast-iron cooking plate, the descendent of those plowshares. In accordance with custom,

the plate is greased with suet, before being carefully filled with wedge-shaped piles of bamboo shoots, *shirataki* noodles made from the so-called "devil's tongue" root, onions, mushrooms, watercress, bean curd, scallions, and an enormous measure of thinly sliced sirloin. The entire arrangement is doused with a broth

Unagi (eel) builds stamina, says Japanese lore. It's eaten during the hottest summer days to avoid exhaustion and anytime as an aphrodesiac.

of rice wine, soy sauce, and fish stock, then cooked at the table. Unlike its forgettable namesakes, this real sukiyaki is a complex composition of individually identifiable elements.

Misono is also the only place we know that serves *wappa-meshi*, a rustic preparation of meat or vegetables steamed over rice. Both of these dishes, when properly done, are bistro classics, rooted deep in Japan's culinary memory.

A bridge crosses into the Japan Center's west building. At its end stands tiny **Kame-sushi**, where a husband-and-wife team holds court over the freshest, highest-quality sushi imaginable. Tiny is no exaggeration; Kame-sushi can handle no more than eight customers at a time—perfect for a neighborly *sushi-ya*.

A final note on raw fish: Sushi may not be all there is to the cuisine, yet its symbolic importance to Japan cannot be exaggerated. Historically, Japanese culture has been defined by two things: the presence of the sea and the physical limitations of its island home. The sea has isolated Japan, yet at the same time has been the gateway for foreign influences. The population has long been too large for the Japanese archipelago, yet Japan's ability to adapt to confined spaces has always been its greatest strength.

These two paradoxes are also at the heart of the Japanese culinary aesthetic, in which purity and restraint coexist with adaptation and invention. So don't object to fussily arranged portions that may strike the American eye as insubstantial; the idea is to savor each element of a meal. If you're still hungry after your meal, ask for more rice—or finish up with an eclair. The brilliantly adaptable Japanese make Asia's best European pastries.

Japanese Restaurants: The Top Choices

• **Akasaka** A touch of authentic Japanese custom: Above the bar that lines one wall of this traditionally decorated *shokuji dokoro* stand half-emptied Suntory whiskey bottles, each bearing its owner's name. The combination of private-club atmosphere and Japan Central Bank credit-card stickers on the front door means this is a restaurant frequented by Tokyo's overseas salarymen, who know a first-rate broiled *unagi* when they taste one. Indeed, that's what we always order here—broiled fillet of eel, brushed with a teriyaki sauce and served atop rice in a lacquer box. 1723 Buchanan Mall, SF (415) 921-5360. Lunch and dinner daily. Major credit cards. Moderate.

• **Benkay at the Nikko** An impeccably restrained dining room, a panoramic view of downtown San Francisco, and a menu to suit a shogun (with prices to match): this is the Japanese traveler's home away from home. The kitchen excels at *kaiseki* dinners, the elaborate Japanese banquet form, changing the meal's composition constantly to assure that the finest seasonal ingredients are used. According to custom, however,

Japanese "Foreign Food"

For centuries, the Japanese have been devising ways to incorporate "foreign food" into their domestic diet. One result is the *shokudo-ya*, a specific variety of restaurant that offers Western dishes and food from other Asian countries. The Bay Area has dozens of these establishments, serving Japanese versions of foreign dishes that are as intrinsically part of Japan's daily diet as pizza—an Italian import—is in America's.

A case in point is the longtime San Francisco Japantown favorite **Sapporo-ya**. The house specialty is a gargantuan bowl of homemade *cha su ramen*, nothing more than a version of China's *char siu lo mein*, wheat noodles in broth with barbecued pork. Chinese *jiao zi*, or "dumplings," have become Sappora-ya's *gyoza*. There's also *kare raisu*, "curried rice," adapted from Anglo-India and thus forgoing the word *gohan*, Japanese for "rice."

A more unusual offering is *okonomiyaki*. Literally, it means "as-you-like-it grill," and it dates back no further than the postwar American occupation of Japan. Created by Osaka street vendors, *okonomiyaki* is Japan's notion of a Yankee pancake, a rice-flour-and-egg batter that is grilled with contents of the customer's choice, usually beef or shrimp. After-ward, the pancake is dusted with bonito flakes, and bathed in that all-purpose Anglo-American sauce, Worcestershire.

In sum, virtually nothing that Sapporo-ya offers is by origin Japanese, which is precisely what makes it a genuine *shokudo-ya*. Another of this genre is **Niji**, a funny little downtown establishment that has carried the *gai-jin* theme to its logical extreme. From the nation of McDonald's, Niji has imported chicken nuggets.

Incidentally, Japanese don't regard tempura—a standby on the menu of virtually every Japanese restaurant—as indigenous. For the record, Portuguese Jesuits introduced the concept of deep-fried battered fish and vegetables to Nagasaki in the 16th century. Japanese historians claim that Ieyasu, the founder of the Tokugawa shogunate, died from over-eating tempura—an early warning against the dangers of too much Western influence. This is not to say that tempura doesn't have an authentic place in Japan; it is to say that the group to which it belongs, even after 400 years of residence, is still *gai-jin*, "foreign."

• **Sapporo-Ya** West Wing, Japan Center Building (second floor), 1581 Webster St, SF (415) 563-7400. Lunch and dinner daily. MC, V. Inexpensive.

they will always include some variety of sashimi, tempura, grilled fish, and braised vegetables. Both Benkay and the hotel it crowns are owned by Japan Airlines. Nikko Hotel, 222 Mason St, SF (415) 394-1105. Lunch and dinner daily. Major credit cards. Expensive.

• **Dojima-an** Handmade *udon* and *soba* in a no-frills atmosphere. Dojima-an is owned by an Osaka-based hotelier who attracts Japanese lodgers from the hotel district in search of a familiar breakfast or a bowl of noodles. Most of the latter come in a tasty bonito-based broth, with the diner choosing from a list of "toppings" that includes herring, tempura shrimp, and various vegetables. The resident American staffers are sent periodically to Japan to refresh their grasp of the traditions and methods of Osaka noodle making. 219 O'Farrell St, SF (415)

Robata: Realm of the Grill Master

Maybe it's the garish wall posters of Hakodate at night. Maybe it's the guy in the Delta Force jacket seated next to us at the *robata* bar, silently pondering a quart of Kirin and a bowl of crispy-fried salmon skin and onions. Maybe it is the Tokyo salarymen, already half-looped, stumbling past on their way to the nearby Sunshine Pub, where a torch singer is painfully resurrecting the ghost of Billie Holliday.

Maybe it's our imagination that makes **Mitoya** seem vaguely sinister at midnight. More likely, it's everyone's imagination, working overtime to deliver on the ambience that distinguishes any good *robata-ya*: innocence in the guise of sin. Hakodate is a provincial capital on the rustic island of Hokkaido; at night it's about as racy as Lincoln, Nebraska. Mr. Delta Force scowls endlessly into his Kirin, but when his sleeve accidentally brushes against one of us, he dissolves into a litany of *sumimasens*: "Excuse me! Excuse me! Excuse me!" The souses are noticeably sober when it comes time to negotiate the long stairway down to Post Street. The torch singer is strictly an amateur, accompanied by taped orchestration and crooning into a karaoke amplifier.

In short, a *robata* bar is where the Japanese go to act out a kind of film-noir fantasy. Foodwise, it's their equivalent of the Western grill—a place that serves meats, vegetables, and seafoods broiled over a charcoal fire, plus a selection of Japanese classics ranging from tempura to sushi. At Mitoya, the possibilities run to more than six dozen separate items, not including 16 sushi choices and an array of nightly specials. They're small plates—the idea is to order several, aiming for a variety of tastes and textures.

The grill items are spread out on an ice-covered counter between the *robata* master and his seated clients. On a typical night, the counter holds mackerel, smelt, river trout, cuttlefish, clams, chicken liver, beef, eggplant, mushrooms, leeks, and peppers. Overcoming our indecision, we point to a sleek, razor-toothed fish. "*Hai, dozo!*" the grill man exclaims, interrupting a practice golf swing. "One barracuda coming up." Removed from the coals a few minutes later, it is firm yet flaky and garnished with lettuce, grated ginger, and *daikon*.

956-0838. Breakfast, lunch, and dinner daily. MC, V. Inexpensive.

• **Iroha** The house-made *ramen* is a strong draw here; tempura, *yakitori*, and sashimi are also specialties. The ambience couldn't be more authentic, with the restaurant installed in the Buchanan Mall that might have been lifted whole from a provincial Japanese town. Iroha is under the same ownership as the always-crowded Mifune, but it emphasizes *ramen* noodle soups rather than the *soba* and *udon* its sister establishment is famous for. 1728 Buchanan Mall, SF (415) 922-0321. Lunch and dinner daily. Major credit cards. Moderate.

• **Mifune** This highly popular San Francisco Japantown *soba-ya* is a branch of the famed Miwa family restaurant in Osaka, which is more or less to Japanese noodles what Emilia-Romagna is to Italian pasta. Thick bleached wheat *udon* and thin buckwheat *soba* are made on the premises. Our favorites here are *nabeyaki udon*, served in an iron cooking pot filled to the brim with bonito-based broth, shrimp tempura, fish cake, and chicken; and *tenzaru soba*, a lacquer tray that carries cold *soba*, tempura, and soy-ginger dipping sauce. West Wing, Japan Center Building (first floor), 1737 Post St, SF (415) 922-0337. Major credit cards. Inexpensive.

• **Misono** Misono is an authentic *shokuji dokoro*, or "traditional bistro," where waitresses prepare sukiyaki in the proper manner right at your table. This is a reserved, mannerly establishment in the classic Japanese style, perfect for visiting guests who have a yen for a Tokyo experience but lack the yen to get there. West Wing, Japan Center Building (first floor), 1737 Post St, SF (415) 922-2728. Lunch and dinner daily. MC, V.

• **Mitoya** On a typical night, the counter at this *robata-ya* holds at least a dozen grill possibilities. For a thorough description of the genre and this restaurant, see "Robata: Realm of the Grill Master" in this chapter. West Wing, Japan Center Building (second floor), 1855 Post St,

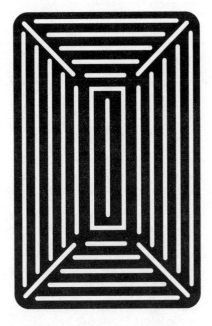

SF (415) 563-2156. Dinner daily. Major credit cards. Moderate.

• **Niji** An eccentric joint much frequented by Japanese young people and downtown junior executives, Niji recalls tiny establishments tucked away in the back streets of provincial Honshu towns. There is a little of everything here, from sushi to curry, all at minimal prices. The dining room is also minimal, seating no more than a dozen people. 311 Grant Ave, SF (415) 398-1690. Lunch and dinner daily. No credit cards. Inexpensive.

• **Okina** A Richmond District sushi bar, Okina was the closely kept secret of the staff of the nearby Asian Art Museum until we blew the whistle in *San Francisco Focus*. Now we're the ones who are sorry, because we, too, dislike sharing this intimate little gem, high on quality and low on pretension, with more than a few select friends. 776 Arguello St, SF (415) 387-8882. Dinner Wed–Sun. No credit cards. Moderate.

• **Sanppo** A longtime San Francisco favorite, decorated to resemble the interior of a rustic Japanese home, with a casual ambience and a big menu that covers all the best-

Kaiseki: Tea and Simplicity

In the 15th century, Yoshimasa Ashikaga, the most refined of all shoguns, had a small teahouse built on the grounds of his Kyoto estate; there the Japanese tea ceremony was refined. In time, a light meal constructed around carefully selected delicacies was added to the drinking ritual. The minimalist repast was called a *kaiseki*, for the heated stones (*seki*) that Buddhist holy men carried in the folds of their robes to help them forget their growling stomachs (*kai*).

Today, in the age of Toyota and Sony, a *kaiseki* still adheres to its founding principles: the best seasonal foods prepared in the simplest manner and presented with uncluttered elegance. One of the most refined versions to be had in the Bay Area is the pricy *kaiseki* at the Nikko Hotel's **Benkay Restaurant**. There in an impeccably restrained dining room painted in rich shades of gray, kimonoed waitresses pad softly about while their clients gaze at a panoramic view of Union Square.

Less expensive—though never cheap—*kaiseki* are available at dozens of other establishments, from San Jose to Santa Rosa.

known fare. Grilled seafood is especially good here, as is the tempura, dumplings in broth, and *chirashi-zushi*, a selection of raw fish atop seasoned rice. This would be the place to bring a guest who is new to Japanese cuisine and wants to pick from the widest array of possibilities. 1702 Post St, SF (415) 346-3486. Lunch Tues–Sat, dinner Tues–Sun. Inexpensive.

• **Shimo** This attractive *sushi-ya* also includes a few standard dinner items. But sushi is definitely the main attraction, and Shimo has a reputation for stocking the widest variety around—and that's no mean feat in a town with more sushi bars than San Antonio has chili parlors. For a departure from the conventional, try the raw sweet-water shrimp bodies on *nigiri-zushi* followed up by their crunchy tempura-cooked heads. 2339 Clement St, SF (415) 752-4422. Dinner Tues–Sun. Major credit cards. Moderate.

• **Wasabi Sushi** Sushi as high art: Taki, the owner of this wonderful hangout on Haight, has made his sushi bar into a postmodern gallery—or is it vice versa? For more on the man and his utterly idiosyncratic approach to Japanese dining, see the section on sushi that begins below. 553 Haight St, SF (415) 626-4632. Dinner Tues–Sun. No credit cards. Inexpensive.

Sushi

Two schools of thought exist on how to choose from the long, long ranks of Bay Area sushi bars: the traditional and the hip.

Traditional establishments, many of which cater to the large numbers of Japanese tourists and business people who sojourn here, duplicate the look and atmosphere back home. They have the requisite blue *noren* cloth hanging in the doorway, a white cypress counter, and a sushi master who never fails to yell out *"Irashaimase!"*—"Welcome!"—as diners enter. The sushi bar at the venerable **Yamato Sukiyaki House** (717 California St, SF) is a good example of this genre. So is the little **Kame-sushi**, on the second floor of the Japan Center's West Building, with just half a dozen stools, two small tables, and a single master. In true Tokyo custom, it doesn't even allow tipping. Downstairs in the same building is **Iso Bune**, with a water-lane conveyor belt that runs sushi-loaded boats right past the diners. The design is an import from Japan, where such fast-food sushi houses are popular for quick snacks at low prices.

A good way to spot the best of these traditional Japanese sushi bars is to look for the JCB sticker. The JCB—Japan Central Bank—credit card is the meal ticket of traveling Japanese executives, and the sign of an establishment that curries their discriminating favor. The sticker appears on the door of one of our favorites, the superb **Shimo** at 2339

Oden: Mountain Soup

Few places in the Bay Area serve *oden*, a wonderful mountain specialty. *Oden* is a hearty soup, almost a casserole, filled with tubers, ferns, bean curd, fish cake, and dozens of other highlights from Japan's rural cuisine. When winter comes to the Japan Alps, the *yatai*, or "*oden* vending wagon," is a common sight on village lanes. Each wagon is a portable restaurant: The vendors unfold a canvas shelter accommodating four or five diners, who sit down to steaming bowls of oden inside. There are, of course, no *oden* wagons here. Still, a pretty decent version of this hearty dish can be tried at San Francisco's oddly named, modest **Globos' West** (419 Grant Ave), near the gated entrance to Chinatown.

Clement St, SF.

Those who frequent the hipper establishments can remember that, in Japanese cities, sushi bars are neighborhood institutions, with personalities that reflect the area's character. Hence, the second school—the San Francisco sushi bar—is no less authentic just because

it is often hip and eccentric. A marvelous example is **Wasabi Sushi**, in the booming neobohemian Lower Haight. Its owner, Taki, is an artist, and Wasabi is both his restaurant and a gallery. Every so often, he redoes the decor to suit his mood, and he exhibits some of the most interesting new art in town on his walls. Not far from Wasabi stands **Nippon**, which doesn't even have a sign marking its entrance at 314 Church Street. The lines outside will alert you that you are nearing it. Inside, the walls are covered with everything from magazine cutouts to samurai swords, the furniture is decidedly rustic, and the staff is delightfully offbeat.

Whichever school you choose, never fail to apply the general rule: Freshness is all. Take a gander at the cubes of raw fish in the glass counter case before you take a seat. Some of the more dependable sushi stops, in our experience, are included in our list of the top Japanese restaurants.

A Select Sushi Glossary

Although most sushi bars give the customer the opportunity to just point at what looks good, there are times when you will want to request something in particular. Here are some standard sushi items and the Japanese names for the most popular fish and shellfish. (A note on methodology: The cognoscenti always dip the fish into the *wasabi*—horseradish—and soy, rather than the rice underneath it.)

Aji: Horse mackerel.

Ama ebi: Shrimp, prawn (raw).

Awabi: Abalone.

Chirashi-zushi: Assorted raw fish arranged atop vinegared rice in a lacqueur container.

Ebi: Shrimp, prawn (boiled).

Fugu: Blowfish.

Hamachi: Young yellowtail.

Hotate gai: Scallops.

Ika: Squid.

Ikura: Salmon roe.

Inari-zushi: Minced vegetables and vinegared rice packed inside a fried tofu pouch.

Kaki: Oyster.

Kani: Crab.

Kazunoko: Herring roe.

Kohada: Sardinelike fish (marinated).

Maguro: Reddish tuna.

Maki-zushi: Slender strips of seafood or vegetables rolled with vinegared rice inside a sheet of *nori* (seaweed); *tekkamaki*, tuna roll; *kappamaki*, cucumber roll; *unakyu*, grilled eel and cucumber roll.

Mirugai: Variety of surf clam (boiled).

Nigiri-zushi: Small oval mounds of vinegared rice topped with fish, usually raw, of choice; also, a standard combination of this type, usually consisting of seven pieces.

Saba: Mackerel (marinated).

Sake: Salmon (cured).

Shako: Mantis shrimp.

Suzuki: Sea bass.

Tai: Red snapper.

Tako: Octopus (boiled).

Temaki: Seaweed-wrapped cornets of rice surrounding tuna or other fish.

Tobiko: Flying-fish roe.

Torigai: Cockle.

Toro: Pinkish tuna.

Unagi: Eel (grilled).

Uni: Sea urchin.

Korea: Delicacies Fit for a Dynasty

Young Hong remembers when the Bay Area's Korean community could be summed up in one slightly adjustable wedding image. Its fixed elements were one eternally beaming prelate and the front portal of a single Chinatown church. "There were so few of us here in the old days," says Young, who arrived in California as a student in 1964, "that we were all married at the same altar by the same minister—so we all have essentially the same wedding picture. The faces of the bride and groom are the only things that change."

The portal belongs to the Korean Methodist Church on San Francisco's Powell Street, the first—and for many years the sole—Korean church in America. Those were the old days. Today, Korean brides can choose from more than 100 Bay Area churches that speak their language, serving a community of 100,000 people. Koreans have been among the nation's fastest-growing immigrant groups since the dawn of the 1980s.

The culinary evidence of the boom ranges from ranks of Seoul-style barbecue houses along El Camino Real and Geary Boulevard, to the arrival of pickled garlic, fermented cabbage, and marinated meats as standard items at Safeway. Korean food is happening.

Nowhere is it happening with more taste than at Young's **Sorabol Restaurant** on the east shore of Oakland's Lake Merritt. On a typical evening there, diners are presented with the kind of feast that would have delighted Korea's Silla dynasty warlords in their brilliant capital of Kyongju 1200 years ago. From end to end, the table is literally covered with food, in dishes large and small, bubbling in ceramic pots, steaming from a collection of

People and Their Neighborhoods

Where they live: There is no concentrated Korean residential district, though large numbers of Koreans have been settling in San Francisco's Sunset and Richmond districts.

Where they gather: Geary Boulevard in San Francisco's Richmond District, with its *bulkogi* grill houses and bustling Korean markets, is emerging as the key commercial street of the Bay Area's Korean community—but hardly the only one. In recent years, these aggressive entrepreneurs have become a major force in San Francisco's Japan Center, and in the center of downtown Oakland and in Hayward. Fussy shoppers also know that Korean green grocers all over the Bay Area offer some of the region's highest quality produce at its lowest prices.

Down south amidst the silicon plantations, Korean high-tech workers are also building a community for themselves—its size reckoned at approximately 40,000 members—along El Camino Real and San Carlos Avenue, primarily in Santa Clara.

Estimated Bay Area population: 100,000

of Korean turnip (sometimes called radish); fresh whole leaves of the sesame bush; a "salad" of raw squid; a caramelized cluster of dried squid. Several of these delicacies are fermented and laced with chili in the manner of the cabbage. Others are cool and mild. Yet others are somewhat sweet. Many belong to the *kimchee* family, the array of room-temperature prepared foods, served with every meal, that are synonomous with Korean dining.

An enormous ceramic casserole, which bubbles atop a burner, holds *sukuh jjige*, a mixture of cuttlefish, pork, bean curd, scallions, onions, squash, dried red chilies, fresh green chilies, and egg, in a broth so fierce that Young, who created the recipe, has felt obliged to describe it as "very, very hot" on her menu.

Beside it sits a platter of apple, carrot, and lemon slices arrayed around two generous fillets of broiled eel brushed with a house sauce. In the remaining space are crowded *beandae-duk*, "pancakes" of ground mung bean, pork, and vegetables, plus those steel bowls, respectively filled with simple soup and steamed rice. Not to mention a constantly replenished supply of blessedly cold water and soothingly hot tea. As Young puts it, "The mark of a successful Korean meal is variety—in flavor, in texture, in cooking style."

Back in 1976, when Young and her husband were driving home cross-country from the Montreal Olympics with their three children, they found themselves daydreaming about such variety. "All the way, we kept stopping in the big cities, looking for Korean restaurants," she recalls. "The Korean population was beginning to grow already, but the result was Korean-owned grocery stores, dry cleaning shops, and fruit stands—no Korean restaurants."

When they got back to Oakland,

stainless-steel bowls.

The small dishes hold eight separate delicacies that the waitress refills upon request: napa cabbage fermented in brine, chili, and garlic; the pickled stems of garlic plants; fresh mung bean sprouts and spinach, both tossed in sesame oil; cubes

Young Hong was determined to do something about that; three years later, Sorabol opened its doors in a Grand Avenue building whose interior had been transformed into an elegant facsimile of a Silla-era royal courtyard, complete with carved wooden panels and ceramic tile roofs. If anything, the food outdid the decor, accomplishing a feat that few other Korean restaurants have yet managed: by the mid-'80s, Sorabol had acquired a dedicated clientele that ran the gamut from Korean consular officials to white-gloved Piedmont matrons.

It was quite an accomplishment for somebody whose professional background was a then-unfinished ethnic studies degree from Mills College. But Young's sheer energy and culinary instincts are a match for anything Stanford Business School and Cordon Bleu could possibly offer. Today, thanks to one of the finest Korean kitchen staffs east of Seoul, Sorabol's barbecued pork and fish casserole are legendary

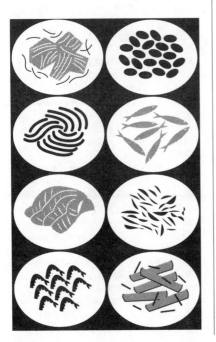

(Occidentals favor the first item, Koreans the second), and Young herself is marketing pickled garlic and cabbage in area supermarkets.

Korean Restaurant Types

It was about 1985 that smoke began to rise over San Francisco's Geary Boulevard. The fire burned in the braziers of the straightforwardly named **Wooden Charcoal BBQ** restaurant near Tenth Avenue, and it signaled a quantum leap in the authenticity level of the Bay Area's Korean dining.

Hitherto, the grilled, marinated meats that play a central role in a special Korean meal were cooked over gas jets. But as the Korean community grew, so did its taste for real wood-fired barbecue—the kind you can find in the narrow streets of Seoul or Pusan, where a good *bulkogi-jip*, or "meat house," is often so thick with charcoal smoke that the diners resemble characters in William Blake's vision of *The Inferno*. Today, the Bay Area's supply of *bulkogi-jips* is at least a dozen strong and growing. Fortunately, in addition to charcoal, they have invested in ventilation fans whirring over the hibachis at each table. (Los Angeles is apparently less sensitive to cultural authenticity; the city fathers there have declared the wood-fired grills fire hazards and closed them down.)

The meats—your choice of beef ribs, beef fillets, chicken, pork cutlets, various innards—have been marinated in soy, sesame, garlic, ginger, scallion, and black pepper. Plucked sizzling from a grill, they taste superb. The drill is to wrap a piece of the meat in lettuce leaf with a small amount of rice, slivered scallion, and hot bean paste.

Our own favorite *bulkogi-jip* is

Brothers Wooden Charcoal Barbecue Restaurant on Geary Boulevard, which prompts a word about names: these restaurants *seem* to have essentially the same one. That's not because they are franchises of a chain called "Wooden Charcoal BBQ." It's because the actual name is often noted only in Korean Hankul characters, and the English sign merely states the obvious—there's charcoal grilling going on inside.

In any case, distinguishing between *bulkogi-jips* isn't easy, especially for the layman; the menus are as similar as the English signs—which is not to say that they are necessarily simple to decode. A case in point is *panch'an*, usually translated as "side dishes," which refers to small portions of such things as spiced dried fish, salted black beans, and *kimchee* that are served at the beginning of a meal.

Take note, however, that *panch'an* are not to be confused with the category of "side dishes" that appear on the translated English menus of many Korean restaurants, including the *bulkogi-jips. These* tend to be full entrées that don't precisely fit the grilled, broiled, casserole, or panfried categories into which Korean menus are divided.

The divisions, incidentally, reflect full-fledged restaurant types in the old country. Like the grill-oriented *bulkogi-jips*, specific establishments there specialize in specific cooking styles. In Seoul, you would go to a *mandoo-jip*, or "dumpling house," for dumplings, and a *saengsan hoe-jip* for raw fish dishes.

Like the *bulkogi-jip*, the *poonsik-jip*—"noodle house"—is making its appearance in the Bay Area, usually in smaller storefront lunchrooms that dot Santa Clara County and San Francisco's Richmond District. They serve three kinds of noodles: wheat (*kuksu* or *ramyon*), usually in a hot soup; buckwheat (*naengmyon*), usually cold, tossed with chili paste,

meats, and vegetables; and potato flour (*tangmyon*), mixed into rice dishes or soups. Oddly, the cold noodles are favored in Korea's frigid winters, when they are thought to generate body heat.

Korean Restaurants: The Top Choices

• **Brothers Restaurant** There is no mistaking what makes this Geary Boulevard barbecue house popular with the local Korean community: wood-fired hibachis at the tables; a mile-long list of grill possibilities, from short ribs to beef heart; superlative *kimchee*; and some of San Francisco's most powerful ventilation fans. If you're not up to cooking, order *yuk-hweh*, half a pound or so of raw beef, tossed with raw egg, sesame oil, pine nuts, and slivers of fresh apple. Or sample any of the big bowls of hot or cold noodles 4128 Geary Blvd, SF (415) 387-7991. Lunch and dinner daily. MC, V. Moderate.

• **King Charcoal Barbecue House** One of San Francisco's early wooden charcoal barbecue restaurants, this smoky stop offers preset dinners that are a good way to crack the usually lengthy Korean menu. Depending on which meal you choose, you will sit down to such Seoul standards as barbecued short ribs, pork, and beef, grilled fish, meat-stuffed dumplings in soup, shrimp tempura, and *jap chae* (bean thread noodles tossed with beef and vegetables). 3741 Geary Blvd, SF (415) 387-9655. Lunch and dinner daily. MC, V. Moderate.

• **Kyung Bok Palace** By 1989, it seemed that Geary Boulevard couldn't possibly sustain any more Korean restaurants. That didn't stop Kyung Bok Palace from opening, and whatever the supply-demand curve suggested, there were enough customers around to make it an instant success. The rigors of competition being what they are, the Palace had to offer all the usual inducements plus something more. The usual part includes 10 *kimchee* items and the live-coal burners for grilling meat and fish that makes San Francisco's Korean restaurants so much more authentic than their L.A. rivals. The something more is a number of dishes no one else offers. One stellar example is a deep iron pot of broth, placed over a fire at the table, in which are pieces of lamb, chrysanthemum leaf, and assorted vegetables. It comes with a dip of scallion, sesame paste, garlic, and chili. There's a specific method to be followed: As the diners make their way through the lamb and vegetables, the broth becomes ever richer, cooking down until it is an intensely flavored sauce. At that point, the waitress arrives with steamed rice, which is promptly stirred into the pot, where it produces a delicious lamb fried rice of sorts. Like many Korean restaurants, incidentally, this is a night

Kimchee: Cabbage as National Treasure

"The real test of a Korean restaurant is the *kimchee*," says Tom Kim, executive director of Korean Community Services in San Francisco, whose grandfather helped build the first Korean church in the United States. "If the *kimchee* is bad, business will be bad."

Kimchee is a lot more than a dish of spicy cabbage to Koreans—it's a way of life. A museum is dedicated to it in Seoul, and it has been designated a national treasure by the Korean government. Each fall, virtually every family in the old country puts up its own in a ritual known as *kimbang*, which involves salting the cabbage, seasoning it to taste, packing it into earthenware jars, and burying them behind the house, to be dug up in the spring.

One result, for those of you who haven't experienced it, comes in the form of bracing layers of cabbage leaves, laced with the chili, ginger, and garlic to which Koreans ascribe warmth-giving properties in winter and medicinal miracles year-round. The recipe? Everybody has his or her own. Some *kimchee* experts claim the taste comes from the fingertips of the maker.

It also comes from things like Korean turnip, garlic stems, and sesame leaves. For the term *kimchee* isn't limited to cabbage, although that is what it means when it appears alone. In combination with another word—*mu kimchee* (turnip *kimchee*), for instance—it applies to any fresh food that is fermented in salt brine. Most (but not all) of the small dishes set on the table before a classic Korean meal are some type of *kimchee*. As for the cabbage version, it not only appears at the opening of a meal, but also turns up in soup, and mixed with rice and beef. Both of these dishes are often found in a menu category called *il poom yori*, roughly translating as "one-dish dinners."

owl's treat, open until 3 a.m. 6314 Geary Blvd, SF (415) 221-0685. Lunch and dinner daily. MC, V. Moderate.

• **Mun's** Unlike many Korean restaurants, Mun's has a small menu. In fact, the menu is nothing more than wall-hung banners in Hankul and English. There are about half a dozen offerings in all, including noodles in soup, *bulkogi*, *kalbi*, and a mixed-beef plate. The latter, which comes in two sizes, is a lettuce-lined platter topped with separate mounds of thinly sliced brisket, tongue, and tripe. A dynamite dipping sauce of soy, garlic, chili, sesame seed, and scallions accompanies the meats. This no-frills place is part of a small

Korean commercial strip in the Richmond District; a Korean-run video store and a Seoul-style café are just steps away. 401 Balboa St, SF (415) 668-6007. Lunch and dinner Mon–Sat. No credit cards. Inexpensive.

• **New Korea House** Decorated with ginseng posters and advertising Korean breakfasts (strictly in the Hankul alphabet), this branch operation of the nearby Korea House nightclub draws a clientele of Korean businessmen, families, and courting couples. Aficionados of Japanese-style sashimi will find this kitchen's approach to raw fish a satisfying substitute: A large bowl holds an elaborate pyramid of tuna, octopus, clam, seaweed, cucumber, carrot, scallion, *daikon*, and omelet strips; pine nuts dot the construction. A few quick tosses and it's ready to eat. For a bit of Korean surf and turf, try the menu listing called *bul ko ki* (aka *bulkogi*) *sang chu sam*, an inspired pairing of grilled beef and deep-fried fish fillet. 1620 Post St, SF (415) 931-7834. Breakfast, lunch, and dinner daily. MC, V. Moderate.

• **Secret Garden Restaurant** The "secret" can be taken literally. There was no name in English over the door on our first visit, just a sign reading "Authentic Korean Food." That promise is met with some of the fieriest fare in the South Bay. The menu includes a sidebar of Chinese dishes, but our advice is to stick with the Korean items, especially the *jungol*, or casserole, which arrives crowded with abalone, octopus, shrimp, squid, clam, sea cucumber, beef, and tripe. For less complexity at the table, try grilled kingfish or the tongue-scorching chilied skate wing noodles, served at room temperature. 3430 El Camino Real, in Rancho Shopping Center, Santa Clara (408) 244-5020. Lunch and dinner daily. MC, V. Moderate.

• **Seoul Garden** Although this handsome dining room is tucked away on the top floor of San Francisco's Japan Center, it is strictly Korean. Beyond the exterior's blue-tiled roof is a small bar and two booth-lined rooms that recall an upmarket Seoul establishment. New items are regularly inked in on the very large menu of barbecued, panfried, and casserole items. A serving of steamed *mandoo* delivers a platterful of hand-wrapped dumplings. The caviar-and-bean-curd

Korean Food Glossary

There is no standard translation of Korean Hankul into Roman letters, although the McCune-Reischauer system is the most widely accepted. Romanized food terms, however, continue to appear in wildly different spellings from one restaurant menu to the next. We have tried to choose the most common spellings and the ones that make phonetic pronunciation the easiest.

Beandae-duk: Egg "pancakes" made of meat and vegetables.

Bibimbop: Rice topped with beef strips, vegetables, and egg; to be tossed together with chili paste.

Bibim gook soo: Noodles with beef slices and *kimchee.*

Bulkogi: Thinly sliced beef marinated in garlic, chili, sesame, green onions, and soy and then grilled. *Kalbi* (beef short ribs), *yumtong-guyee* (sliced beef heart), *dweji-guyee* (sliced pork), *gobchang-guyee* (beef intestine), and *dak* (sliced chicken) are prepared for grilling in the same marinade.

Dubu-jjige: Bean cake and pork in broth flavored with hot bean paste.

Hweh-naengmyon: Raw skate wing with cold noodles in hot sauce.

Janguh-guyee: Grilled eel.

Jungbok-hweh: Raw abalone.

Jungol: Casserole dishes; *gopchang-jungol,* beef intestine; *nakiji-jungol,* octopus; *uhmool-jungol,* assorted seafood.

Ke-jjige: Crab in broth flavored with hot bean paste.

Mandoo: Dumplings; *mandoo gook,* dumpling soup; *dukmandoo gook,* dumpling soup with rice cakes.

Modum-hweh: Mixed raw seafood.

Naengmyon: Buckwheat noodles in cold beef broth.

Ojinguh-guyee: Squid grilled with hot sauce.

Sengsun-hweh: Raw tuna.

Soon dae: Sausages.

Sengsun-jjige: Casserole of fish in broth flavored with hot bean paste.

Yuk-hweh: Seasoned raw beef served with condiments; *yuk-hweh bibimbop* combines raw beef with vegetables, egg, and rice.

---

casserole delivers whole sacks of cod roe simmered with bean curd and scallions in a broth of unadulterated liquid chili. The grilled bean-curd appetizer is topped with slivered seaweed and spices, and paper-thin slices of beef brisket are partnered with a garlicky soy dipping sauce. East Wing, Japan Center Building (second floor), 22 Peace Plaza, SF (415) 563-7664. Lunch and dinner daily. Major credit cards. Moderate.

• **Sorabol** Young Hong is indisputa-bly the Bay Area's best-known Korean restaurateur. Her Sorabol restaurant, discussed at length in the introduction to this chapter, serves the Seoul version of dim sum, called *cham maat,* for weekend brunch. This is also a good spot to host a Korean banquet: Sorabol has a private dining room that will accommodate a party of up to 30 people. 372 Grand Ave, Oakland (415) 839-2288. Lunch and dinner daily. Major credit cards. Moderate.

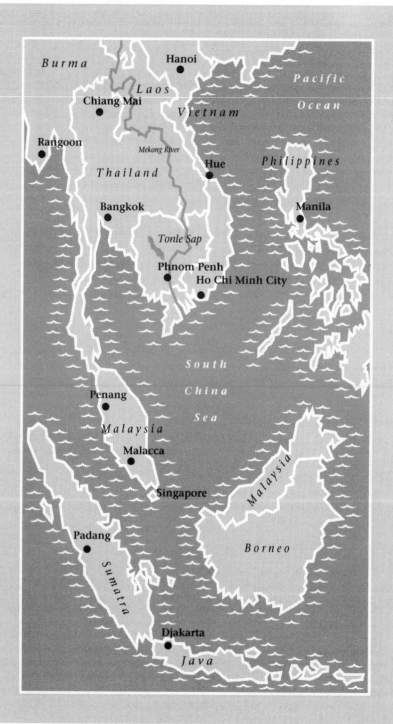

Southeast Asia: Culinary Melting Pot

We Americans—North, South, and Caribbean—renowned for our culturally mixed cuisines, often presume to have a monopoly on the notion of a culinary melting pot. Yet the Western Hemisphere is far from the sole place where different cultures have met to create exotic fares. The proof is unmistakable in Southeast Asia, one of the world's great maritime and commercial crossroads for 2000 years. There, in the vast tropical arc that sweeps from the Andaman Sea to the island of Luzon, kitchens draw inspiration from such diverse sources as Brazil, the Arabian peninsula, France, Spain, Portugal, China, and India.

The Portuguese, for example, introduced the searing chili pepper to Southeast Asia and are also responsible for carrying the peanut from South America to Indonesia, where it has become an indispensable pantry item. Crushed and mixed with spices and coconut milk, it forms the famous sauce used on *sate*—a chicken or beef "shish kebab" that has distinctly Middle Eastern origins—and on the vegetable-and-egg salad called *gado-gado* in Indonesia and Malaysia. Then there is *lumpia*, a spring roll borrowed from China, and *martabak*, a meat-stuffed pastry pancake derived from southern India's Tamils.

China's influence on dining habits in Southeast Asia is not simply a souvenir of the distant past, when many of today's independent nations there paid tribute to the powerful dragon throne. In most of these countries, Chinese residents are still the chief restaurateurs. But they

Southeast Asian Etiquette

There is a widespread misconception that the authentic way to eat Asian food is with chopsticks. In fact, chopsticks are used in much of Southeast Asia, but almost everywhere they are used primarily for one thing: noodles. For other dishes, the informed diner employs spoon and fork, though not in the way familiar to Europeans.

In most of Thailand, Indonesia, Malaysia, the Philippines, and Burma, the fork is used to push food into the spoon, which carries it to its destination. In Laos, the Golden Triangle, and northeastern Thailand, however, the staple grain is sticky glutinous rice, which the diner rolls into balls by hand and dips into sauces—dispensing with both chopsticks and silverware.

have moved considerably beyond the limits of their own ancestral cuisine to create something new. One of its defining traits is the use of fish sauce instead of China's soy, a custom that links the cuisines of Indochina, Thailand, Vietnam, Burma, Indonesia, and the Philippines (although the latter two also use a sweetened version of soy). A powerful appetite stimulant that may put off some Westerners with its salty, fermented nature, it's the closest thing to a Southeast Asian kitchen universal.

What makes these observations more than academic are numbers. Twenty-five years ago, the Southeast Asian population of the entire Bay Area was probably under 10,000 people—most of them Fili-pino sojourners, single men who came here as cannery workers or farm laborers and never returned to their island homeland. Today, marking one of the most profound demographic revolutions in American history, the Bay Area counts half a million residents from Southeast Asia.

The two largest communities by far are the Filipinos and Vietnamese, and it is they who offer the diner the most authentic ethnic experience. There are true Little Saigons and Little Manilas all over the Bay Area, from Solano County to Santa Clara County, with their own commercial streets, newspapers, and entertainment (including thriving nightclub scenes). More to the point, they are full of restaurants patronized primarily by Filipinos and Vietnamese, genuine in the most uncompromised sense. With the sort of guidance we offer here, you can find meals in these establishments that are precise facsimiles of what you would be served in Manila or Saigon, aka Ho Chi Minh City.

In other instances, the traditions we cover fall into the category of "cuisines without neighborhoods." There are no Thai districts in the Bay Area, no identifiable geographic communities, notwithstanding scores of Thai restaurants. The same is true of our restaurants representing Burma and the Malay archipelago: the food is real and the cooks are natives, but the streets outside the restaurant doors do not call Rangoon or Jakarta to mind. Like the Cambodian and Lao establishments of Northern California, these are restaurants, pure and simple, and not cultural gathering places for expatriate Asians. This reflects both numbers—none of these populations approaches the size of the Filipino and Vietnamese communities—and economics: Cambodian and Laotian refugees can't afford their own restaurants.

Vietnam: Seven-Jewel Beef and Other Miracles

Nobody really knows how many Vietnamese immigrants now live on the south flank of Nob Hill, near downtown Oakland, and in the heart of San Jose. Some estimates suggest that more than 130,000 former residents of Vietnam dwell in these three major "Little Saigons" of the metropolitan Bay Area.

In San Francisco's Tenderloin, their impact is self-evident: the neighborhood that housed generations of bachelor clerks along its upper streets and set the gritty scene for scores of detective potboilers in its lower depths, speaks a different argot today. From Larkin to Mason, between O'Farrell and Turk, a Southeast Asian city has materialized since 1980, amidst the rooming houses where Dashiell Hammett's gumshoes once slept.

A sign reading *"Pho Bo Ha Noi Dac Biet"* (or simply *"Pho"*) often appears over Vietnamese establish-ments. It means "Beef *Pho*, Hanoi-style, Specialty of the House," and it conveys a bit of history. In southern Vietnam, the classic morning meal is *hu tieu*, a noodle soup that combines shrimp, crab, and pork meat in a pork broth. But after Ho Chi Minh's victory over the French in 1954, northern war refugees—including the families of many Bay Area Vietnamese restaurateurs—headed in large numbers for the Mekong Delta. They launched a *pho* wave in Saigon, where the northern specialty soon attracted a wide southern following.

It wasn't the first time that *bo* (beef) had won disciples in this traditional stronghold of seafood and pork. Saigon was ruled by France from 1859 to 1954, and the natives noticed early on that their colonial masters were big *bo* eaters. One result was that northern Vietnam developed a modest cattle economy. Another was the adoption of

People and Their Neighborhoods

Where they live: San Jose, with approximately 75,000 Vietnamese residents, has the second largest concentration of immigrants from Indochina in the United States. Another estimated 55,000 Vietnamese live to the north, primarily in San Francisco and Oakland. Some 20,000 Cambodians and 20,000 Laotians are also spread across the Bay Area, chiefly in the same districts inhabited by the Vietnamese.

Where they gather: San Jose's Little Saigon, extending along downtown Santa Clara Street, is the most important Vietnamese commercial district, followed closely by San Francisco's Tenderloin. In Oakland, Vietnamese businesses are springing up around Lake Merritt and south along the East 14th Street corridor. In all three cities, the businesspeople tend to be ethnic Chinese from Vietnam—a group that is also increasingly making its weight felt in the Chinatowns of San Francisco and Oakland. One result is that Southeast Asian markets, overflowing with tropical exotica seldom seen in these parts before the 1980s, are now part of the normal fabric of Bay Area life.

Estimated Bay Area population: 170,000

French beef dishes by the Vietnamese themselves, but in guises that owed much to local inspiration.

The best-loved of these cultural hybrids is a cousin of *boeuf à la bourguignonne*, served complete with potatoes and baguette, and usually called *bo kho banh mi* (sometimes *banh mi bo kho*)—literally, "beef stew with bread." Like *pho*, it was originally a breakfast item; unlike beef burgundy, it calls into play such exotica as lemongrass, coconut, and curry powder.

The most celebrated Vietnamese beef offering is *Bo Bay Mon*, the "Seven-Jewel Beef Dinner." Pioneered by two famous Saigon restaurants, this ambitious banquet is now prepared, with minor variations, by many establishments around the bay, including San Jose's superb Quoc Te, and the Rose Restaurant in the Tenderloin.

First in this classic banquet comes a French-inspired fondue, but with major twists: the thin slices of meat are cooked at the table in boiling seasoned vinegar, then rolled up in rice paper with lettuce, basil, rice noodle, peanuts, and bean sprouts, and dipped in a pungent mixture of fermented anchovy and crushed pineapple. Next, in quick succession, are sizzling morsels grilled with lemongrass, three variations on shish kebab—the broiled meat wrapped around pineapple, around scallions, and in the form of sausage—and spiced beef-and-cellophane-noodle meatballs. Last is a thick rice soup with shredded ginger, ground beef, and slivered tripe.

Designed for a tropical climate, the Vietnamese menu includes many dishes that revolve around crisp, uncooked vegetables and light sauces. It's the perfect summer cuisine and a dieter's delight. For starters, there are the *cuons*, rice-paper rolls filled with rice noodles, mint, and small amounts of poached shrimp and pork (*goi cuon*) or other meats. Cold rice noodles also serve as a base for *nuong*, or "barbecued," meats or prawns. Lemon-accented beef salad and the wonderful *goi sua tom thit*, which mixes shrimp and jellyfish, round out the summery repertoire.

The Mekong River and its tributaries are fertile breeding grounds for many freshwater fish that have no exact American equivalent. But Bay Area Vietnamese chefs do wonders with Sacramento Delta catfish, which they often cut into steaks and simmer in a clay pot. The simmering liquid, composed of *nuoc mam* (fish sauce), soy, and caramelized sugar, is reduced to a near-glaze, imparting a concentrated sweet-tart flavor to the fish. Similar catfish miracles are performed in the form of a hot-and-sour soup called *canh chua*.

Like Filipino restaurants (and unlike most other Southeast Asian restaurants in the Bay Area), the best Vietnamese establishments serve a large and loyal clientele of their own people, which means that a premium is placed on authenticity. These are, in the truest sense, neighborhood institutions. It takes

an adventurous spirit and an inquiring mind to unlock their mysteries. But the rewards make the effort well worthwhile.

The Vietnamese Regional Table

Some people mistakenly dismiss Vietnamese food as a mere subset of French and Chinese. Although Vietnam was occupied by the Chinese for a thousand years and ruled by France for a century, its culinary culture has remained its own to an astonishing degree. Instead of soy sauce, that staple of the Chinese kitchen, the Vietnamese use *nuoc mam*, a fermented sauce made from small fish and salt. It is used in cooking and as a condiment, often arriving at the table in a small dipping bowl, mixed with vinegar and sugar and garnished with shredded carrots or chilies.

Other Vietnamese flavoring ingredients seldom seen in China include lemongrass, a tropical herb that has a distinctly citrus taste; several varieties of mint; purple basil; banana blossoms; coconut milk; shallots; and lime. The Vietnamese also serve fresh, uncooked vegetables—lettuce, cucumbers, carrots, bean sprouts—at every meal. In contrast, the Chinese almost always cook their vegetables.

As its noodle-soup repertoire suggests, Vietnam's table is complex with regional distinctions. In effect, it may be divided into three "styles." One is found primarily in the northern Red River Delta region, with Hanoi as its center. A second is based in the mountainous center of the country, where the ancient royal capital of Hue lies. The third revolves around the Mekong Delta and Saigon, now Ho Chi Minh City.

Thanks to its proximity to China, the north relies a bit more on stir-frying than does the rest of Vietnam and uses fewer hot chilies. Fish, too, is less important there, though the port city of Haiphong is noted for its crab dishes.

The center produces more pungent dishes, achieved through the inclusion of chilies and powerful fermented shrimp sauces. Foods there are decorated very elaborately as part of the monarchist legacy. The region also boasts what was in the past considered some of Southeast Asia's finest pork: Hue pigs are pampered on a diet of banana-tree trunks and rice.

The humid south, watered by the endless delta tributaries of the Mekong, grows an enormous percentage of the nation's rice and produce and is inordinately fond of fish. It is there that the French influence is strongest, as apparent in the presence of potatoes and asparagus. In addition, Thai and Indian influences are evident in an array of spicy curries.

> Vietnamese traditionally ate cold foods on the third day of the third lunar month, when lighting a fire in the kitchen was forbidden.

Vietnamese Restaurants: The Top Choices

• **Anh Dao** This is a favorite haunt of Vietnamese young people, located somewhat incongruously in a former Red Barn fast-food outlet in the heart of East Santa Clara Street's Little Saigon. In addition to the standard array of noodle and soup preparations, it boasts many untranslated menu items and, for a change, waiters who are willing to help sort out the mysteries. Vietnamese rock 'n' roll, by the accomplished likes of Elvis Phuong, keeps up a steady beat in the background. Try the squid with lemon and anchovy sauce on lettuce, sprinkled with crushed shallot. 250 East Santa Clara St, San Jose (408) 298-7076. Lunch and dinner daily. MC, V. Inexpensive.

• **Ba Le** Famed for its homemade charcuterie items, Ba Le—featured in our discussion of Vietnamese cafés—is also recognized as one of the best places in San Francisco to eat classic Vietnamese noodle and rice dishes. If you're new to these possibilities, the best way to start is with one of the many combination rice plates; an especially good one brings grilled marinated pork chop and seasoned sausage atop rice. The friendly Cathy Nguyen, one of Ba Le's owners, will explain the rest of the menu upon request. 511 Jones St, SF (415) 474-7270. Lunch and dinner daily. No credit cards. Inexpensive.

• **Garden House** This Richmond District mainstay has a more upmarket ambience than many local

carapace acts as roasting oven, retaining and circulating the cooking heat. The result is a delicious cache of steaming crab meat, to be dipped into fresh lemon juice, salt, and pepper. 133 Clement St, SF (415) 221-3655. Lunch Thur–Sun, dinner

Pho: Hanoi's Classic Soup

Almost any Sunday afternoon, you can find Vietnamese San Franciscans lined up near the corner of Larkin and Eddy, outside of Mrs. Ninh Nguyen's **Pacific Restaurant**. They are voters in the Great *Pho* Campaign.

Scores of the Bay Area's Vietnamese restaurants and cafés feature the dish at the heart of the campaign, which marks a special turn in the San Francisco lives of these refugees. *Pho* is what they typically ate for breakfast in the old country; and now that some of them have acquired a little pocket cash for dining out, *pho* is what they hunger for, even at lunch and dinner. Mrs. Nguyen, whose mother ran the popular Binh Dan restaurant next to the hospital of the same name on Ho Chi Minh City's Dien Bien Phu Street, is one of the leading nominees for *pho* champion.

It's a lot easier to describe *pho* than it is to order it. "Fa," "fo," "far," and "fuh" all come close to the pronunciation, but not close

enough to deliver a bowl to the table. "You must say 'faah-uhh-ahh'—first down and then up," Mrs. Nguyen explains, producing what sounds like a riff on a sliding trombone. "It's better, maybe, if you just say 'beef noodle soup.' "

Campbell's it isn't. Cooked for hours over a slow fire, the broth is an intense, fragrant mix of beef, star anise, ginger, cinnamon, shallots, and *nuoc mam*, the fermented fish sauce that is to Vietnam what soy is to China. It is ladled piping hot over a mound of thin rice noodles, cooked beef (*chin*), and, among several options, rare beef slices (*tai*) and/or beef meatballs (*bo vien*). The Vietnamese words are worth learning, because translations are not always provided in *pho* houses. With the soup arrives a fiery chili sauce and a side dish heaped with raw bean sprouts, onion, coriander sprigs, hot chilies, and lemon wedges, to be added according to the diner's taste. At Pacific Restaurant, a gigantic portion costs less than $4.

Southeast Asian restaurants and a decidedly fine touch with crab, of which Vietnamese are extremely fond. Chef Nguyen, the master of the Garden House kitchen, produces delicious crab *beignets* and curries. But his pièce de résistance is salt-roasted crab, which is actually dry-fried in a wok. In effect, the crab's

daily. MC, V. Moderate.

• **Pacific Restaurant** Many aficionados consider this the best place in town for *pho*, the much beloved Vietnamese soup. The clientele was so large by the late '80s that the small Larkin Street original had to expand into the space next door; just months later, a second branch opened on Jones. The reasons will be obvious when you sit down to one of Pacific's enormous bowls of *pho;* the broth alone, which has been steeping for many hours before it reaches your table, is worth the trip. 607 Larkin St, SF (415) 441-6722; 337 Jones St, SF (415) 982-4022. Lunch daily. No credit cards. Inexpensive.

• **Pho 84** East Bay residents needn't travel to the Little Saigons of San Francisco or San Jose to have an authentic bowl of Vietnamese *pho.* Downtown Oakland's Pho 84 turns out no fewer than 22 varieties of this classic noodle soup. As if that weren't enough, there is also a full dinner menu, offering such delights as grilled pork on skewers over

Vietnamese Word Games

Nuong is a word that appears repeatedly on every Vietnamese menu. It means "barbecue," and it can refer to everything from minced pork, shrimp, or beef to sliced meats, whole pieces of chicken, or pâtélike sausages, marinated and then grilled over coals. Look for *nuong* items wrapped in soft, moistened rice paper with raw vegetables and mint, served over steamed rice (*com dia*), or served with *bun,* sometimes translated as "rice sticks."

Another commonplace entry is the word *cuon,* which simply means "roll" and is always preceded by another word describing the roll's contents. The roll itself can be either fresh rice noodle or moistened dried rice paper. The premier roll, however, is not called *cuon* at all. Instead, it is *cha gio* or "imperial roll," the famous deep-fried rice-paper cylinder usually filled with pork, shrimp, and crab meat.

If *cuon* seems complicated, *banh* is Byzantine. Literally translated as "cake," it may be nothing more exotic than French bread (*banh mi*) or something as unusual as *banh xeo,* a kind of pancake-omelet stuffed with shrimp, bean sprouts, and pork. Another such pancake is the Hue-style *banh khoai.* Both use Western cake flour,

which is why Vietnamese markets stock shelves full of Swansdown. Confused? *Banh* also describes several varieties of rice noodle, and *banh chung* is a New Year's cake of mung beans, glutinous rice, and pork.

In choosing an entrée, check for meat, fish, and fowl words: *bo* (beef), *bi* (shredded pork skin), *ca* (fish), *cua* (crab), *ga* (chicken), *heo* (por), *tom* (shrimp), and *vit* (duck).

A genuine Vietnamese banquet includes a variety of textures and tastes, from the delicate to the spicy. A good way to sample the breadth of this cuisine is to order one of the classic regional noodle soups, a barbecue item, a rice-paper roll, and one or more of the *mon dac biet*—"the specialties of the house"—such as the firepots (look for the word *lau*); curries (look for *cari*); or quick-fried dishes. A platter of fresh greens and vegetables accompanies most meals.

Then there is the matter of beverages—or are they desserts? An infinite array of concoctions appears erratically under these labels, composed of ingredients that range from sweet red beans, green beans, "jellies," lemons, and soybeans to tropical fruits, usually but not always floating in coconut milk and crushed ice. They're delicious and extremely refreshing.

seasoned rice noodles, lemongrass chicken, and a complex and hearty dish called *com tay tom*, in which rice is cooked in a clay pot filled with chicken broth, crab meat, shrimp, and vegetables. 354 17th St, Oakland (415) 832-1429. Lunch and dinner Mon–Sat. MC, V. Inexpensive.

• **Quoc Te** If you could try just one Vietnamese restaurant in the Bay Area, the choice would have to be Quoc Te, which translates as "The International." Named for one of the most celebrated dinner houses in old Saigon, this sensational establishment, located in a former Mexican-Chinese restaurant, has a menu that, on our most recent visit, ran to an astounding 281 items. Like the kitchen staff and the ownership, the Quoc Te menu is divided between Chao Zhou Chinese (see the China chapter) and Vietnamese selections. The latter category will stagger the gourmand in you, offering such exotic possibilities as noodles tossed with escargots, a firepot of catfish in tamarind broth, and broiled shrimp-wrapped sugarcane. We find it hard to believe that the chef was a file clerk in the U.S. Embassy in Saigon. 155 East San Fernando St, San Jose (408) 289-8323. Lunch and dinner daily. MC, V. Moderate.

• **Rose Vietnamese Restaurant**
This comfortable Tenderloin restaurant is a favorite lunch spot for staff members of the nearby Center for Southeast Asian Refugee Resettlement. It serves an excellent *Bo Bay Mun*, the seven-course beef dinner that is a classic banquet feature in Vietnam. Instead of Hanoi-style beef *pho*, however, the Rose emphasizes *hu tieu*, the seafood noodle soup of Saigon and the lower Mekong Delta. At night, try the enormous fondue pot of fresh seasonal fish and shellfish. 791 O'Farrell St, SF (415) 441-5635. Lunch and dinner daily. MC, V. Inexpensive.

• **Thang Long Larkin Restaurant**

Located on the edge of the Tenderloin, this bright, airy restaurant has one of the most ambitious Vietnamese kitchens in the Bay Area. Unfortunately, its really unusual choices appear on an untranslated card that sits atop each table and not on the menu the waiter brings over. Unusual is no exaggeration. One choice is a "salad" of crisped veal skin and meat, tossed in roasted rice

powder and spices, to be dipped into a chili-laced dish of fish sauce. Another is a sort of Vietnamese *carpaccio*, built around paper-thin slices of raw beef; the diner wraps the slices around boiled shreds of beef tripe, along with several varieties of mint and basil leaves, then dips the packet into yet another spiced fish sauce. There are also three goat dishes—including one called "goat according to a recipe by Mao Zedong"—and a panoply of preparations involving frog, eel, and, for the truly adventurous, duck's blood, a genuine Vietnamese delicacy. 500 Larkin St, SF (415)

665-1146. Lunch and dinner daily. Major credit cards. Moderate.

• **Vietnam I and II** The saga of this two-branch establishment began with a minuscule Chinatown Vietnamese diner, barely accommodating 15 people (including the two cooks), that was so immensely popular it gave birth to the Tenderloin's largest banquet house. At number one, which still does a land-office business, the bill of fare is necessarily restricted to grilled pork, rice, and noodle dishes. Number two, however, offers a menu to suit the wedding parties it often hosts; the long, long list of specialties covers all three of Vietnam's regional cuisines (southern Mekong,

Vietnamese Food Glossary

Unlike most Asian cuisines, the Vietnamese table is generally divided into courses—appetizers to desserts—in the European manner. (Note: A precise understanding of Vietnamese requires accent marks, which are not used in this text.)

Appetizers

Banh xeo: Soft, southern-style pancakelike omelet, filled with shrimp, pork, and vegetables and seasoned with turmeric.

Cha gio: Deep-fried rice-paper roll, filled with pork, crab, and vegetables.

Chao tom: Ground shrimp formed around lengths of sugarcane and grilled.

Cuon: Stuffed fresh rice-paper or rice-noodle roll; *goi cuon* is stuffed with shredded pork, shrimp, mint, and chilled rice noodles; *banh cuon* uses minced pork; *bi cuon* uses pork skin.

Goi sua tom thit: Salad of jellyfish, shrimp, and vegetables.

Nem nuong: Grilled pork meatballs.

Soups and Noodles

Bun bi: Rice vermicelli, topped with shredded pork skin seasoned with roasted rice powder.

Bun bo Hue: Spicy Hue noodle soup with pork and beef.

Bun thit nuong: Rice vermicelli, topped with barbecued, marinated pork slices and fish sauce.

Chao: Rice porridge, often served with pork tripe, shrimp, or duck.

Hu tieu: Southern-style noodle soup with shrimp, crab, and pork.

Pho: Hanoi-style noodle soup with beef.

Sup mang tay cua: French-inspired asparagus and crab soup.

Haiphong-Hanoi). Large tanks near the front door hold live fish, crabs, and other shellfish. 620 Broadway St, SF (415) 788-7034; 701 Larkin St, SF (415) 885-1274. Lunch and dinner daily. MC, V. Number one, inexpensive; number two, moderate.

Vietnamese Cafés

Three boulevardiers sit idly chatting over their *cafés filtres*. At the next table, a shopkeeper grabs a quick lunch of *pâté maison* with baguette and salad. Behind the counter, young women prepare sandwich plates of *fromage de tête, épaule de porc,* and *terrine de canard.*

Paris? *Non.* Montreal? *Pas de tout.* The scene is Stockton Street in San Francisco's Chinatown, and though the food has a decided French connection, the conversations—and the prices—are 10,000 miles away from the Champs Élysées. This is a Western bastion of the Far East's greatest café culture: almost unknown here in 1980, the Vietnamese coffee shop/deli has become a Bay Area mainstay, from Chinatown to the Tenderloin in the city, across the Santa Clara Valley, and around the periphery of Lake Merritt in Oakland.

For Northern California's thousands of Indochinese immigrants, these establishments are homes away

Main Courses

Bo kho banh mi: Vietnamese-style beef bourguignonne (stew), served with French bread.

Bo la lot: Highly seasoned minced beef rolled in tropical lot leaf.

Bo xao xa ot: Beef slices quick-fried with lemongrass.

Ca kho to: Fish steaks and pork pieces stewed in earthenware pot.

Com tay cam: Rice topped with chicken and mushrooms, cooked in earthenware pot.

Cua rang muoi: Fried crabs with salt, pepper, and fish sauce.

Ech xao lan: Quick-fried frog legs, usually prepared in curry sauce.

Ga kho xa ot: Chicken quick-fried with lemongrass.

Ga rut xuong nhoi nep: A whole chicken, boned and stuffed with seasoned glutinous rice.

Vit quay: Crisp-skinned roast duck.

Firepots

Lau canh chua: A metal cooking pot, heated by charcoal held in a chimney in its center, and filled with a sour-hot broth, vegetables, and pieces of meat or fish. The firepot may be served with eel (*luon*), shrimp (*tom*), catfish (*ca*), or a combination of seafood and meat (*lau thap cam*).

Bo nhung dam: A firepot served with slices of raw beef and vegetables, to be added to the broth at the table.

Dessert Beverages

Dau do banh lot: An iced drink containing sweet red beans and coconut milk.

Dau xanh banh lot: An iced drink made with sweet green mung beans.

Sam bo luong: An iced drink concocted of coconut milk and assorted sweets.

these establishments are homes away from home, de facto community centers—much like their original inspirations in France—that buffer the pressures of urban life. For

the rest of us, they offer a chance to sample a fascinating menu that blends some of the best café fare from Paris and Saigon.

Stockton Street's aptly named **Little Paris** (939 Stockton), for instance, offers a full range of what the Vietnamese call *banh mi thit*, literally "meat on bread rolls," stuffed to the brim with ham, head-cheese or pork shoulder, shredded carrot, onion, cucumber, and tomatoes, topped with mayonnaise and a sprig of coriander. So far, the meal is mostly French—a *sandwich au viande* by another name. But as likely as not, the second course will be *dau xanh banh lot*, an iced dessert of sweet green mung beans. Alternatively, you can open with *cha gio*, deep-fried imperial rolls, and finish off with cream puffs.

There's a ready explanation. By the time the French left Vietnam, the *charcuterie*, *boulangerie*, and *patisserie* had become central to the lifestyle of Indochina. Saigon, especially, was blessed with cafés serving superb pastries and pâtés, as well as the Vietnamese version of café food—chiefly rice noodle dishes.

Eating isn't necessarily the point in a Vietnamese café, but coffee almost always is. Alas, drinking coffee there is no simple matter. *Ca phe den nong*, usually translated as French filtered coffee, is brewed at the table in a metal contraption that may take up to 30 minutes of agonizingly slow dripping to secure a small cupful of strong java. Jostling and shaking the equipment barely affects the speed; forget *ca phe den nong* if you're looking for an instant rush.

There are many good Indochinese cafés in the Bay Area, including the small **Café Tai** (410 Ellis St) in the Tenderloin and San Jose's more spacious **Dac Phuc** (198 West San Clara St), a favorite hangout of the South Bay's Vietnamese journalists. But the finest café, for our money, is **Ba Le**, with branches at 511 Jones St in San Francisco and at 225 East Santa Clara St in downtown San Jose. (The name is the Vietnamization of the French pronunciation for Paris, or "Par-ee.") Under the stewardship of Hung and Cathy Nguyen, the San Francisco Ba Le offers pâtés, sausages, cold meats, and a host of other impressive Southeast Asian savories and sweets.

A homemade French-style pork-liver pâté is sold alongside three decidedly Vietnamese varieties, one fried, one boiled, and the third baked with cinnamon. There is pale pink ham that recalls a mild French *jambon*, and the exotic *gio thu*, or headcheese, is a mix of pig's ear and head to rival your favorite *fromage de tête*.

All of these delicacies are among the best buys in town, each coming in at less than $5 per pound.

Cambodia and Laos: Royal Fare and Village Cuisine from along the Mekong

Cambodians share a certain point of view with the French who once ruled them: they regard themselves as heirs to a seminal culture. Their Southeast Asian neighbors, in the Cambodian frame of reference, were mere borrowers, fortunate beneficiaries of Khmer civilization.

Nothing, over the 14 centuries since the Khmer classic era opened, has shaken that conviction. Not conquest at the hands of latecomer Thai and Vietnamese empires. Not the French *colons*, with their European notions of imperial destiny. Not the American bombs of the Indochina war. Not even the awful nightmare of Pol Pot and his killing fields.

The contemporary world tends to think of the Cambodians as victims. The 20,000 Cambodian refugees in the Bay Area prefer to remember the great Buddhist temples of Angkor Wat and the ancient royal city of Angkor Borei. They dream, still, of Rajendarvarman II, the guiding light of the 10th-century Khmer heroic age and builder of the great temple of Baksey Cham Krong.

Today, Angkor Wat, Angkor Borei, and Baksey Cham Krong are likely to put San Franciscans in mind of the dinner houses that bear their names. Along with a few others, they add up to one of the most unusual developments in the lengthy annals of local cuisine. To the Cambodians' own surprise, the Bay Area has become the undisputed world capital of Cambodian restaurantdom.

Cambodian menus can be extensive. (Angkor Palace's runs to more than 60 dishes.) One way to cope with such a selection—and a useful principle in any unfamiliar restaurant—is to consider geography. The best things on most ethnic menus reflect the strengths of the land that originally produced them, even when the cooks have expatriated.

In Cambodia's case, that means two things: products associated with the Mekong River and the Tonle Sap, a vast lake that covers the heart of the nation, and the exotic bounty of a fertile tropical countryside.

These basic elements— freshwater fish, snails, frog legs— tend to be combined with extremely complex and delicate sauces, especially at such top-of-the-line establishments as Sony Sok's Angkor Palace and Lim Su Ke's Cambodiana's. Although the emphasis in the sauces is tropical, with extensive use of coconut milk, lemongrass, galangal, lime leaves, and fish sauce, don't be surprised to encounter such European touches as butter and parsley.

One omnipresent and unquestionably native staple of Cambodian cuisine is *prahok katih*. The *prahok* itself is a small, anchovylike fish (the best are from the Tonle Sap) dried and fermented in an earthen crock. It is not exported, so local Cambodian restaurants use a Thai alternative. *Katih* is ground pork in coconut milk and spices. Together, fermented *prahok* and *katih* make a thick, pungent sauce eaten in Cambodia with raw vegetables and rice.

You will find a version of *katih* in the specialty known as *trob trung kor*, eggplant topped with spiced pork and shrimp; every Cambodian cook has his or her own approach to this dish. At its best (in our opinion, the offering at Cambodiana's), the eggplant takes on a wonderfully smoky flavor.

Cambodians also are skillful barbecue cooks, producing their own counterparts in pork and chicken to Thailand's and Indonesia's *sate*. Similarly, the national dish—a chicken in red curry sauce known as *kary morn*—bears evident links to Burma's *panthe kaukswe* and Thailand's many curries.

Cambodian Restaurants: The Top Choices

• **Angkor Borei** This popular Mission District stop is the second effort of Sonn Pok and his Thai wife, Wemonrat, who founded and still run the pioneering Cambodia House. Angkor Borei is named for the site of an ancient Khmer capital, near the Vietnamese border, where archaeologists found a sixth-century Khmer inscription, the oldest known record of a Southeast Asian written language. On a more contemporary note, Pok offers a lengthy menu that includes *nohm ban jok*, mild fish

curry and rice noodles served at room temperature. His *prahok katih* and *such jrouk aung* (grilled marinated pork) are also Cambodian country favorites. 3471 Mission St, SF (415) 550-8417. Lunch and dinner daily. MC, V. Inexpensive.

• **Angkor Palace** Owner-chef Sony Sok offers exquisite food in a royal Khmer setting. "Royal" is no exaggeration. Diners rest luxuriously on deep, plush cushions. At one end of the dining room the formal silver service of the last Cambodian princely court is mounted in a display case. At the opposite end stands a red velvet throne—just in case a bona fide blue blood shows up. Elaborate "palace suppers" featuring such exotica as roast guinea fowl and fried goat with ginger and lime leaves can be ordered in advance. But even the daily menu lists plenty of royal fare, including chicken-and-fruit soup, crispy ox-tripe salad, sautéed pork with banana blossoms, whole deep-fried fish, and stuffed chicken legs. 1769 Lombard St, SF (415) 550-8417. Dinner daily. Major credit cards. Moderate.

• **Angkor Wat** This old favorite was one of the first Cambodian restaurants in town. Keav and Joanna Ty built their success on such marvelous dishes as banana blossoms doused with lime, lemongrass-scented charbroiled rabbit, and whole boneless chicken cooked in a coconut. The Tys have always been trendsetters, having helped to launch the upscaling movement that resulted in fancier decor and more sophisticated presentation throughout the Cambodian restaurant community. Their own very attractively decorated dining area includes a small stage for the performance of traditional Cambodian dancing. 4217 Geary Blvd, SF (415) 221-7887. Dinner Tue–Sun Major credit cards. Moderate.

• **Baksey Cham Krong** This spot is

Khmer civilization gone Haight Street hip. It's ensconsed in a second-story Victorian flat that probably did duty as a crash pad during the Summer of Love. Back then tofu burgers and vegetarian moussaka were the kitchen standards. But all memory of those meals will pass when you sit down to an order of shredded duck in red curry with fresh spinach, or a crispy deep-fried whole fish topped with tiny nuggets of chili and garlic. 1770 Haight St, SF (415) 387-9224. Lunch Wed–Sun, dinner Wed–Mon. Major credit cards. Moderate.

• **Cambodia House** Within just a few months of opening this restaurant in 1985, Sonn Pok and his kitchen staff had won an enthusiastic following for their traditional Khmer fare. One of our favorite dishes here is *trei phrat*, a subtle blend of fried slivers of sun-dried fish tossed with garlic, sugar, and salt that is served with lettuce and grapefruit chunks. The chef can be equally proud of the *noum am beng*, a crisp crêpe stuffed with pork, shrimp, and vegetables; *morn aang*, grilled chicken with chili sauce; and *char seang*, spinach with shrimp paste. The table-linens atmosphere is a comfortable mix of formal and friendly. 5625 Geary Blvd, SF (415) 668-5888. Lunch and dinner daily. MC, V. Moderate.

• **Cambodiana's** This is an absolute gem of a restaurant, one of our favorite dinner houses of any ethnicity. Lim Su Ke and his chef and wife, Bopha Pol, offer an exquisite array of inspired, French-

Cambodian Restaurants? Not in Cambodia.

There's more than artful packaging at work in the ornate decor favored by Cambodian restaurateurs. The truth is, in Cambodia you could *only* eat this kind of food in the royal palace or, barring that, in the home of somebody with royal kitchen aspirations.

Put simply, in prewar Cambodia there were no Cambodian restaurants. That's the biggest reason why their emergence here is such a profound anomaly.

Almost everywhere in rural Southeast Asia, the dining-out trade has historically fallen to the families of immigrants from China. The restaurant topography is slowly changing now, as the region's indigenous ethnic traditions begin to assert themselves in the business realm. But until recently, when local farmers traveled to the market towns of Thailand and Burma, as well as

Cambodia, they invariably stopped at a Chinese teahouse for a bowl of noodles—usually the Chao Zhou rice noodle expressed in Cambodian as *guey tiow*—or the rice porridge called *bobor*.

The Cambodian situation was further complicated by the hand of European imperialism. Indochina's French overlords, who remained in power from the mid-19th century until 1954, weren't about to settle for *chow fun*. They wanted *blanquette de veau* and *côtes d'agneau*, and they built restaurants—and the boulevards of Phnom Penh—to provide an agreeable setting for them.

Opening a dinner house, in short, was something that the foreign oppressor tended to do. Getting over that bias was a considerable hurdle for Cambodians. The leap began for many of them with stints in Bay Area French kitchens.

influenced Khmer classics just steps from the UC Berkeley campus gate. Dinner opens with a complimentary appetizer that epitomizes the East-West table: French bread drizzled with warm coconut milk sauce. Bopha, a master of sauces and marinades, prepares Cambodian-style garlicky escargots; crisply cooked marinated stuffed quail; and fish mousse steamed in banana leaf. Lim Su and his daughter Bora are the extremely gracious dining room hosts. 2156 University Ave, Berkeley (415) 843-4630. Lunch and dinner daily. Major credit cards. Moderate.

Lao Cuisine

There is no strictly Laotian neighborhood in the Bay Area, and the number of Laotians residing here is only half that of the Central Valley, where some 40,000 Hmong tribespeople from Laos now live. But here's an inside tip: in Oakland, you can get the most faithful rendition of Laotian haute cuisine you will find in America.

The secret lies in **Sang Thong**, a little gem of a restaurant right downtown on Broadway. Although it bills itself as Thai, proprietors Keovythone Sang Thong and his wife, Phaphaiphone, aka Key and Elli, are natives of Laos. With two days notice, they will move back across the culinary border from Thailand (which shares many culinary traditions with Laos) and prepare a 10-course Laotian banquet that matches the best memories of old Vientiane. It goes for $15 per person, and can be enjoyed weekends along with traditional Laotian dancing.

Key and his sister Bang are the geniuses behind the Sang Thong kitchen. They grew up in the village of Banhom, on the Mekong River, where they learned to cook one of the banquet's key dishes, fish with

herbs steamed in a banana leaf. In Laos, this delicately flavored preparation is only made for special occasions, such as New Year's Day or the visit of an honored guest. Another Keovythone family culinary triumph is handmade fresh pork sausage that comes with a sweet-sour dipping sauce.

Some of the dishes are very intensely flavored mixtures—prawn and grilled eggplant in one case, pickled vegetables in another—meant to be taken in small amounts with the sticky rice that is the staple grain of Laos. Key instructs the uninitiated in the ways of Laotian dining, insisting that to enjoy the meal fully, one must eat as the Laotians do, with the hands, rolling the rice into balls and dipping them into sauces.

His own introduction to American table customs was more haphazard. The first day here, unable to read English, he went to a supermarket in search of a bottle of fish sauce—and came home with maple syrup.

• **Sang Thong** 850 Broadway, Oakland (415) 839-4017. Lunch and dinner Mon–Sat. Order special Lao banquet a day in advance. MC, V. Moderate, for banquet meal, inexpensive for everyday menu.

• **Malai Lao Restaurant** A quiet oasis amidst the wild and woolly streets of the north Mission. The catfish steamed in banana leaves and the grilled quail with a dipping sauce of garlic, chili, and lemon juice are both good bets. So, too, is *larb gai*, minced chicken flavored with roasted rice powder and spices. These dishes, as is the case with many Lao specialties, will remind you of Thai preparations. The imprint of history has left solid culinary links between the two nations, but Malai Lao owner Lai Khammoungkhoune will be happy to point out the distinctions. 3189 16th St, SF (415) 626-8528. Lunch Tues–Fri, dinner Tues–Sun. Major credit cards. Inexpensive.

The Philippines: East Indies with a Spanish-Chinese Accent

I f cuisines came into fashion based on quality, complexity, and imagination, Filipino food would be the next wave. In a world infatuated with cultural crossovers, the Philippines table offers an exquisite blend of Spain, the East Indies, and China. For those who crave variety, its menu is encyclopedic with possibilities. Of all the culinary hybrids spawned by the conquistadores in their far-flung global empire, it is the most highly developed.

It is also the least recognized. Except for Filipinos themselves, few people in America have the faintest idea what Filipino cuisine is, even though the United States succeeded Spain as the islands' colonial ruler—and the San Francisco Bay Area is the largest Filipino metropolis east of Manila.

Even in a simple place like **Goldilocks**, a lunch stop in the center wing of Daly City's Serramonte Mall, the complexities of Filipino cuisine are evident. To one side of the counter, mothers wait patiently before a profusion of brightly decorated custards, confections, tropical sweets steamed in banana leaves, and multilayered European cream cakes. At the other end, school kids, secretaries, and truck drivers on their lunch breaks are pointing out their choices: helpings of lechon kawali, sliced from a whole roast pig; pancit sotanghon, mung-bean noodles tossed with chicken, leeks, and shrimp; sate baboy, highly seasoned, skewer-broiled pork.

The words alone tell a fascinating tale. In effect, this short menu selection encapsulates a millennium of Filipino history, which commences with the islands' ancestral Malay-rooted language and culture, picks up additional elements from Javanese and Chinese traders around A.D. 1000, and acquires an Iberian accent after Miguel Lopez de Legazpi's arrival from New Spain in 1565. Lechon is Spanish for suckling pig; pancit is derived from faan si, a Hokkien Chinese noodle term; baboy is adopted from babi, Malay for pork. Then there is lumpia, a word that's a bit difficult to pin down because it is vaguely related to the Hokkien po pia, literally "thin pastry," but is also a standard part of the Indonesian vocabulary.

Whatever its etymological origin, fresh lumpia is a quick dish to shame any hamburger. Essentially, it is a large, paper-thin, eggless wheat crêpe filled with a "salad" of garbanzos, tofu, bamboo shoots, carrots, green pepper, and pork, topped by a slightly sweet sauce laced with garlic and dusted with crushed peanuts. Don't confuse it with Shanghai lumpia, a miniature version of the familiar deep-fried Chinese spring roll.

And don't confuse Goldilocks with an Americanized rendition of the Filipino real thing. Back in Manila, shoppers line up for the same lumpia their cousins are enjoying at Serramonte, because Goldilocks is an enormously successful Philippines chain with outlets from Mindanao to Luzon. Now it's a West Coast chain, too—as are Barrio Fiesta, Max Fried Chicken, and Josephine's of the Islands, equally famous Manila outfits that have opened outlets in the Bay Area. In addition to its Daly City food center stand, Goldilocks has bakery/restaurants in South San Francisco, Vallejo, and Vancouver, British Columbia.

A more ambitious approach to the Filipino creole table is available at **Tito Rey of the Islands**—if you can find it. This Bay Area dinner house, a branch of another Manila chain, is hidden away in Daly City's truly obscure St. Francis Square. (Take I-280 from San Francisco to the Pacifica spur, exit at Clarinada, turn right on St. Francis Boulevard, drive north several blocks, and keep your eyes peeled.)

It's definitely worth getting lost for, because Tito Rey is to Filipino culinary hopes what Caesar was to Roman ambition. He's out to conquer an overseas empire. So far, the beachheads include Washington, D.C., and Los Angeles, as well as Daly City.

Actually, Tito Rey is two people, Rey Bautista and Larry Cruz, whose expansive notions started with Kamiyan, an upscale restaurant in Manila's Makati business district. The original restaurant specializes in fresh fish grilled in banana leaves, a traditional Filipino preparation that Tito Rey's also offers in Daly City. A classic variation on this theme is their *kinulob na pampano*, a whole spiced pompano stuffed with onions and tomatoes, wrapped in banana leaves, and steamed rather than grilled. The flavors utterly permeate the fish.

The legacy of *España* is especially obvious at Tito Rey's, where *paella* and *puchero* grace a menu that calls on tomatoes, olives, and other allusions to the Iberian world. "We consider *adobo* our national dish," our Filipino gourmet acquaintance, Wigbert Figueras, says of this extraordinary chicken and/or pork stew. "But we recognize that, like so many of us, it is of Spanish descent, a grandchild of *adobo*."

Still, *adobo*'s accent is distinctly Tagalog: tart and lively in a Southeast Asian manner that characterizes many of the islands' classic plates. One genre of Filipino soup dishes, called *sinigang*, owes its tanginess primarily to tamarind, which plays a similar role in Thailand. In other instances, including *adobo*, the tartness comes from a generous use of vinegar, either in cooking or as a dipping-sauce ingredient. Figueras says there are two major vinegar varieties in his homeland: one is a strong, rich, red brew made from sugarcane in the Ilocano region of northern Luzon; the second, which is clear and milder, is a product of fermented palm fronds.

Filipinos, by the way, are the premier popular musicians of Asia; their rock, jazz, and blues artists can be found in lounges from Singapore to Beijing. Tito Rey's is their easternmost Pacific gig. Every evening except Sunday and Monday, the house resounds to outstanding combos and the dulcet tones of a singing waiter.

Turo-Turo: Fast Food, High Quality

The Tagalog phrase *turo-turo* literally translates as "point-point," and refers to a popular variety of restaurant in the Philippines that displays daily specialties for public viewing in a row of platters and open pots. Diners simply point to their choices. Dozens of *turo-turos* have appeared in the Bay Area in the past few years.

At most, every dish is carefully made from scratch, according to traditional methods and recipes. That gives the *turo-turos* a big edge in quality over the fast-food joints with which they compete for bargain-hunting diners. Many *turo-turos*, incidentally, fall short of being bona fide restaurants; they are operated as stands in the multi-ethnic "food centers" of downtown San Francisco, especially along Mission and Market streets, and also in suburban shopping malls. They provide a facsimile of the typical dining experience in the old country.

Filipino Restaurants: The Top Choices

• **Alido's** The Alido family's popular Mission District *turo-turo* is as tiny and modest a diner as you'll ever come across. The menu changes daily, but there's always a *sinigang*, a *pancit*, and an *adobo*. Point to the *kare-kare*; it's a specialty of the Alido home province of Pampanga on Luzon, regarded as the birthplace of the best cooks in the islands. The Alido's version is an inspired match of oxtail, honeycomb tripe, eggplant, and long beans braised in a rich peanut sauce. The cognoscenti season it to taste with the fermented shrimp condiment called *bagoong*. The homemade *bibingka* is the perfect sweet finish to a meal. 2186 Mission St, SF (415) 863-9144. Lunch and early dinner Mon–Sat. No credit cards. Inexpensive.
• **Barrio Fiesta** Inside an enclosed gazebo-style building that captures the tropical warmth of the islands,

People and Their Neighborhoods

Where they live: Daly City, South San Francisco, and the outer Mission corridor of San Francisco house the largest single community of Filipinos outside of the Philippines. There are also large communities in Vallejo and in Alameda and Santa Clara counties.

Where they gather: Filipino businesses are not as commercially concentrated as those of the Bay Area's Vietnamese communities. But there are identifiably Filipino stores and shops sprinkled widely across the Mission, from 17th Street south, and in small shopping centers that dot northern San Mateo County.

Estimated Bay Area population: 350,000

waiters clad in the native *barong tagalog* were already scrambling to accommodate a full house just a week after Barrio Fiesta opened in late 1988. That's because its flagship restaurant in Manila is an islands' tradition, a place where families flock for Sunday dinner. What Filipinos order at Barrio Fiesta on both sides of the Pacific are enormous helpings of crispy *pata*, *pinakbet bangus*, and *kare-kare*. 909 Antoinette Ln, South San Francisco (415) 871-8703. Lunch and dinner Wed–Mon. No credit cards. Moderate.
• **Café Glenda** The kitchen here serves what we call Filipino food, Berkeley-style: chicken *adobo* flanked by boutique vegetables. In other words, Glenda's, which sits at the east end of Solano Avenue's

restaurant row, offers a nouvelle treatment of classic Manila fare. You can see it in its *inihaw* plate, where the grilled prawns, mussels, squid, chicken, and pork are neatly arranged alongside a hillock of those tiny vegetables. The servings are small by Filipino standards, and the crowd is mostly Birkenstock-clad gringo. Still, the native touch is present in the moderate use of coconut milk, hints of tamarind, garlic rice, and subtle allusions to the blending of Spanish, Chinese, and Malay words and culinary influences. 1897 Solano Ave, Berkeley (415) 527-7499. Lunch Tues–Sat, dinner Tues–Sun. Major credit cards. Moderate.

• **Filipinas** This venerable *turo-turo*, which for years was the best lunchroom within sight of San Francisco's Transbay Terminal, relocated some time back to a space in the shadow of the *Chronicle* clocktower. Filipinas caters to a downtown San Francisco workforce in search of a first-rate chicken *adobo* or a classic *pinakbet*, the mixed-vegetable dish that makes every Ilocano dream of home. No matter what you order from the selection of at least nine daily specials, you will receive a large portion delivered with a friendly smile and a modest tab. 953 Mission St, SF (415) 543-0232. Lunch Mon–Fri. No credit cards. Inexpensive.

• **Goldilocks** The most famous bakery chain in the Philippines has opened three branches in the Bay Area. Alongside a full line of custards, confections, and European

Filipino Food Glossary

Adobo: Chicken and/or pork (and sometimes other foods) braised in vinegar, soy sauce, garlic, and bay.

Adobong pusit: Braised squid, often cooked in its own ink.

Baboy: Pork.

Bagoong: Shrimp, or occasionally small fish, fermented in brine and served as a sauce.

Bangus: Milkfish; *rellenong bangus*, stuffed milkfish.

Bibingka: Sweet rice cake usually cooked inside banana leaves.

Crispy pata: Pork hock boiled with spices and then deep-fried.

Dinuguan: Pork blood and innards stewed in vinegar, garlic, and seasonings.

Goto: Thick rice soup with tripe.

Halo-halo: A dessert made of sugar, milk, ice or ice cream, and beans, jackfruit, banana, corn, and/or other fruits and vegetables.

Hipon: Shrimp; *hipon sa gata*, shrimp cooked in coconut milk.

Inihaw: Grilled meats or fish (sometimes called *ihaw-ihaw*); *inihaw na pusit*, grilled squid.

Kalderata: Goat stew.

Kangkong lechon: Water spinach simmered with roast pork.

Kare-kare: Oxtails braised with vegetables and sometimes tripe and/or calf foot in broth thickened with peanuts and ground rice.

Karne: Beef; *karne mechacho*, beef pot roast.

Kilawin: A preparation, similar to ceviche, in which raw fish or cream cakes, Goldilocks (covered in detail in this chapter's introduction) has a *turo-turo* counter filled with *sate baboy, pancit sotanghon, paksiw na lechon,* and more. The sweets chefs make an excellent version of one of our favorite indulgences. It's called *polveron* and is a kind of Filipino version of a shortbread cookie, rich with butter, milk, and sugar. 92 Serramonte Shopping Center, Daly City (415) 992-2537. Lunch and early dinner daily. 3565 Callan Blvd, South SF (415) 873-0565. Lunch and early dinner Tues–Sun. 3885 Sonoma Blvd, Vallejo (707) 557-9977. Lunch and early dinner Tues–Sun. Inexpensive.

• **Kenkoy's Diner** Two of the best *turo-turos* in San Francisco, Filipinas and Kenkoy's, are within a block of each other, so it's always hard to choose between them. Kenkoy's, however, clearly gets the nod for ambience. Run by a former boxer and a stand-up comedian, it's decorated with 1940s photos of the Manila entertainment and sports scenes, plus license plates and grills from that city's celebrated jeepneys. As with any true *turo-turo,* the menu varies daily, offering all the classics of the owners' homeland. Their *lechon* is a match for anyone's in town. 54 Mint St, SF (415) 957-0404. Breakfast and lunch Mon–Sat. No credit cards. Inexpensive.

• **Manila Sunset** A bright and cheery *turo-turo* and bakery, this sister operation of a Los Angeles establishment excels at *pancit mala-*

shrimp is marinated in vinegar and seasonings.

Laing: Taro leaves cooked in coconut milk with chilies.

Langonisa: Pork sausage.

Leche flan: Egg custard, usually caramelized.

Lechon: Crispy-skinned roast pig; *paksiw na lechon,* roast pork in a slightly sweet-sour sauce.

Lechon manok: Roast chicken, sometimes served with liver sauce.

Lomi: Flat noodles cooked with meat and vegetables and served with broth.

Lumpia: Meat, shrimp, and/or vegetables wrapped in a thin wheat pancake and served fresh or deepfried.

Mami: Wheat noodles with condiments.

Pancit: Noodles; *pancit molo,* pork-stuffed wontons in soup; *pancit malabon,* noodles prepared with seafood; *pancit palabok,* rice noodles with pork, bean curd, and egg in shrimp sauce.

Pinakbet: Braised mixed vegetables—eggplant, okra, green beans, pumpkin—with *bagoong.*

Puchero: Spanish-inspired stew of beef, chicken, and chick-peas.

Sinigang: Meats or seafood in a tamarind-infused broth.

Sotanghon: Mung-bean noodles; *sotanghon guisado,* noodles cooked with chicken, pork, shrimp, and/or vegetables.

Tapa: Philippine-style jerky, usually beef, deep-fried and served with vinegar and soy sauce.

Tinola: Chicken and green papaya simmered in broth.

Tocino: Bacon.

bon, goto, and *bibingka.* The practically outfitted dining area won't win any design awards, but the spirit of the place is warm and easygoing, in true Filipino tradition. Don't leave without taking out some *ensaimada,* sweet rolls dusted with sugar that are ideal partners for your morning java. 269 El Camino Real, South San Francisco (415) 952-3844. Lunch and dinner daily. No credit cards. Inexpensive.

• **Max Fried Chicken** It will come as no surprise that this bustling South San Francisco outpost of a Manila empire is famous for its fried chicken. The crispy-skinned birds come with biscuits and salad, just as they do back home. Max also serves a memorable crispy *pata* and a delicious *dinuguan,* the pork-innards stew that most folks consider an acquired taste. If you've acquired it, be sure to order a few *puto*—steamed savory rice cakes—

to go along with it. *Dinuguan* aficionados consider them an obligatory accompaniment. 2239 Gellert Blvd, South San Francisco (415) 878-0610. Lunch and dinner daily. No credit cards. Inexpensive.

• **Tito Rey of the Islands** Once you're past the Daly City shopping center parking lot, the experience at this attractive dinner house is pure Manila, right down to the live music rising from the corner of the dining room. It's no wonder the place rings authentic: proprietors Reynaldo Bautista and Lorenzo Cruz own nine dinner houses in the Philippines' capital and two others on this side of the Pacific. (This sizable restaurant operation is looked at in detail in the introduction to this chapter.) St. Francis Square, 3 Southgate Ave, Daly City (415) 756-2870. Lunch and dinner Tues–Sun. Major credit cards. Moderate.

Filipino Breakfast and Merienda Brunch

Filipinos like to say that their history was molded by 400 years in a convent followed by 50 in Hollywood. That description sums up the islands' Spanish and American colonial experience. Add to it their original Malay culture and centuries of Chinese influence, and you have the classic Manila breakfast: Malay-style panfried dried fish, Chinese-inspired garlic fried rice, Spanish *langonisa* sausage, and Yankee eggs, scrambled or over easy.

Show up sometime before 8:30 a.m. at downtown San Francisco's **Cora's Coffee Shop** (or Kenkoy's Diner on Mint Street behind the old U.S. Mint) and you'll see how that rich mixture powers the engine in San Francisco's office economy. Hidden away at

number 5 on Stevenson Street, a glorified alley under the towers that soar around First and Market, Cora's is where dozens of Filipino clerks and managers start their workdays. It isn't Postrio by a long shot; at Cora's, the atmosphere suggests a buffet gathering in somebody's basement.

Many of the Bay Area's modest Filipino lunchrooms also feature *merienda*—Manila's counterpart to Los Angeles brunch or London high tea. This meal between meals (usually served around 10 a.m. or 3 p.m.) is built around leftovers, simple snacks, and sweetcakes. It is as much a social experience as a nutritional one, meant to provide an excuse to gather for the lively conversations that Filipinos love.

Thailand: Fashionable Package, Fiery Content

Thai restaurants were to food in the late '80s what fax machines were to the office. A few years ago, they barely existed; today, you're nowhere if you don't have at least three to choose from inside a five-minute walk.

Our own San Francisco Western Addition neighborhood, once a most unlikely site for any culinary boom, is a case in point. It used to be tough to buy a decent hamburger nearby. Now we can sample *tod mun* (deep-fried fish cakes) and *gai yang* (barbecued chicken) at five separate local establishments. How many Thai restaurants are there in the Bay Area? It's a moot point: today's guess will be an underestimate tomorrow. You have to wonder how the state's chili-pepper farmers cope.

Blame Pathama Parikanont and Phonchai Wongsengam—better known as Kai and Paul to the many admirers of their **Thep Phanom** restaurant—if the chili supply runs out. They have come closer than any restaurateurs we know to perfecting the basic formula behind the great Bay Area Thai-food boom.

"First and foremost, there's the taste of the food itself," says Kai. Thai food has caught on because its essential flavors—wrought by a mixture of fiery chilies and lively herbs—met a popular taste hereabouts that was addressed first by Mexican and Sichuan restaurants but not entirely filled by them.

The case is made more compellingly by one of Kai's meals than it is by words. Start with *larb ped*, a warm, minced roast-duck salad tossed with mint leaves, chilies, red onion, and lemon. Proceed to a delicious catfish stuffed with a stalk of lemon grass and infused with the flavor of the banana leaf in which it had been wrapped and then charbroiled. Its dipping sauce is composed of chili, lime, red onion, and fish sauce. Move on to *paksa vehok*, deep-fried quail marinated in garlic and black pepper before cooking, then served on a bed of fresh coriander and alfalfa sprouts arranged to resemble a bird's nest. Alongside sits a dipping sauce of lightly sweetened rice vinegar, garlic, chili, and fish sauce.

You'll get the point. "In their own homes, Thai people insist on dishes that blend many different flavors—complex recipes, even for everyday meals," Kai says. "An American hamburger has almost no taste for us. But Thai food has every kind of taste. Hot, tart, salty, sweet. Every kind. When we opened our restaurant, we consciously set out to deliver that experience to our customers."

Adds Paul, who himself learned the finer points of the food trade in a French kitchen on Union Street: "What has happened in the last decade is that Americans also began to want such complex tastes."

The complexity is most evident in the phenomenal array of Thai curries, *kaeng*, usually divided on a menu according to their predominant "color"—red, green, or yellow. (*Kaeng*, however, means more than curry. The word literally means "liquid" and can refer not only to a curry but also to a soup or any dish that is prepared with a lot of sauce.) The first and second mixtures, both explosively hot, employ scores of ingredients around a base of red or green chilies; yellow curries rely heavily upon turmeric and are milder. All three add coconut milk. There are also dry curries that drop the coconut milk in favor of a sharp tamarind sauce.

A few more tips, based on cultural geography: Thailand, like Vietnam, is rice country, full of lovely green paddies and slow-flowing rivers. Over there, we take our cues from the presence of grilled rice birds and fried frog skins on a menu. (These latter items, which are exactly what they sound like, eerily suggest miniature business suits. So far, we haven't found them on a California Thai menu.) Remember, too, that the Gulf of Thailand is one of the globe's richest shellfish beds. Thais are unequaled masters of dishes with prawns, clams, and mussels.

A heavy emphasis on grilled marinated chicken, especially if it is available with sweet, or so-called sticky rice, is the sign of a northeastern Thai cook.

A negative buzz term is "stir-fry"; all Thai restaurants will have some stir-fry dishes, but a stir-fry surfeit means too much Chinese, too little Thai. Warning bells should also sound if you see repeated references to oyster sauce.

Which brings up the sole problem with the great Thai restaurant boom for those in search of authentic ethnic experience—not enough Thais have come to town. Informed guesses on the size of the community run to only a few thousand people, almost all of whom seem to own or work in restaurants. That makes the Thai phenomenon different from most of the Bay Area's Asian restaurant explosions. Unlike its Korean, Chinese, and Vietnamese counterparts, it doesn't reflect an immigration wave. Most Thai restaurants are opened for you and me, not for Thais.

Thai Restaurants: The Top Choices

• **Bangkok 16** Most Thai restaurant menus in the Bay Area are facsimiles of each other. Toy "Terry" Lilittham hasn't fallen into that trap. His attractively appointed Bangkok 16 offers such intriguing concoctions as northern Thailand's *meang kom*—a platter with small mounds of ginger, lemon, sweet pepper, red onion, dried shrimp, roasted peanuts, toasted coconut, and a bowl of slightly sweet coconut sauce. You mix the ingredients together in a spinach leaf and eat the packet in one bite. Succulent fried duck fillets arrive atop a bed of deep-fried shredded greens in *ped-tod-kana-grob*. Lilittham grew up in a family of restaurateurs in a southern Thailand town famous for its sweets. His family still runs a restaurant there— as well as the local boxing stadium. Lilittham shares his considerable knowledge of Thai cuisine in cooking classes at the restaurant. For the moment, he has no boxing lessons planned. 3214 16th St, SF (415) 431-5838. Lunch Mon–Fri. Dinner daily. MC, V. Moderate.

• **Chiang Mai** Named for the premier city of the Golden Triangle, this Richmond District restaurant offers a handful of northern specialties amidst the best-known dishes of the country. Among the most interesting are *kao soy Chiang Mai* (noodles and beef in coconut-milk sauce) and *num plik onge* (pork with chili and tomatoes). You can really spot the Bay Area's chief demographic trend when you walk out the door here: up and down the nearby blocks of Geary are ranks of Thai, Chinese, Korean, and Vietnamese restaurants. 5020 Geary Blvd, SF (415) 387-1299. Lunch and dinner Tues–Sun. Major credit cards. Moderate.

• **Linda's Thai Noodle** The name doesn't quite say it all, for Linda serves a couple dozen rice dishes, too, at this elaborate version of a Bangkok back-street food stand. Try the steamed chicken with garlic rice, spicy chicken with mint leaf and rice, or chili-laced fish-ball noodles with spinach. Located just across Mission Street from the Transbay Terminal, Linda's is among the most popular lunch stops downtown frequented by Southeast Asian office workers. 510 Mission St, SF (415) 546-7376. Lunch Mon–Sat, dinner Mon–Fri. No credit cards. Inexpensive.

• **Manora's** When cozy, attractive Manora's set up shop on Mission Street in early 1985, it was the first establishment in what was to become a little Southeast Asian

Thai Style

The Bay Area has always boasted great Asian cuisine at moderate prices. But the trade-off, before the Thais came to town, usually was two hours in one of those noisy linoleum palaces. They were not the places to wine and dine visiting in-laws or prospective clients.

All that has changed with the arrival of the Thais. Instead of the familiar garish flocked wallpaper and echoing linoleum, San Francisco's **Thep Phanom**, for example, is appointed with linen tablecloths, art on the walls, fresh flowers on each table, and soft lighting. From their decisions on haircuts to their preferences on paint and carpeting, owners Kai Parikanont and Paul Wongsengam are hip and elegant, but in an idiom so natural that they seem to have been born to it. And so, to an astonishing degree, are Thai restaurateurs across the Bay Area.

At **Chiang Mai**, out on Geary Boulevard, the centerpiece is a lovely glassed-in Oriental garden, complete with a restrained waterfall, that suggests the view through a Fabergé egg. **Siam Lotus**, on lower 24th Street, features a simulated temple scene with a beautiful gilded altar. At the **Royal Thai** in San Rafael, the staff wears delicate Thai silks.

Even **Racha**, a Tenderloin establishment whose generous portions and overall consistency has made it one of our regular haunts for years, has upscaled its look. In the late '80s, owner Bo Dong moved from his original tiny storefront to brighter, airier quarters on Ellis Street and invested in a contemporary decor accented with a forest of polished oak.

Thai aesthetics extend far beyond decor, to food presentation and a great sense of style in all things. The dishes at most local Thai establishments are composed as much as they are cooked, with garnishing tomatoes carved into roses and orange slices arranged in graceful twists. As for the staffs, they often look as though they have walked the runway of a new-wave fashion show. No wonder the Bay Area is having a love affair with Thai dining.

restaurant strip. It was also the first—and remains one of the best—of the establishments whose combination of white tablecloth ambience and carefully prepared food made Thai cuisine the leading food fad of the Bay Area in the late 1980s. Both the Mission District and somewhat fancier SoMa branch offer a full menu of Thai national dishes. Among the more notable are: *poh-pier-sod* (crab, shrimp, sausage, and black fungus in rice paper), *moo kra tiem* (pork with garlic and pepper), *hor muk* (minced fish steamed in banana leaf), and *panaeng-sam-ros* (fried beef, chicken, and pork with coconut-lemongrass sauce). 3226 Mission St, SF (415) 550-0856; 1600 Folsom St, SF (415) 861-6224. Lunch Mon–Fri, dinner daily. MC, V. Moderate.

• **Narai** Run by ethnic Chinese from Thailand—as are most restaurants in Thailand—Narai delivers both Thai dishes and the specialties of southern China's Chao Zhou people. A description of chef Supar Komindr's Chinese highlights can be found in our China chapter. As for her Thai delights, the *pad woon sen*, silver-noodle salad, is sensational, as is her fried pomfret with an almost startling sauce of garlic and chili. 2229 Clement St, SF (415) 751-6363. Lunch and dinner Tues–Sun. Major credit cards. Moderate.

• **Racha Café** A steady stream of Thai food lovers forced owner Bo Dong to move his popular Racha from its original tiny storefront to larger quarters up the street a few years back. Now he has the same problem there—too many diners and too few tables for the largest portions of Thai food in town. Regulars swear by the tangy squid salad. This is also the place to order *tod mun*, the deep-fried fish cake Thais dip into a sweet-and-sour sauce, or the fried rice-noodle classic called *pad Thai*. 771 Ellis St, SF (415) 885-0725. Lunch and dinner daily. MC, V. Moderate.

• **Siam Cuisine** Before there was a Thai restaurant in almost every Bay Area neighborhood, there was Siam Cuisine. It continues to hum right along, dishing up some of the Bay Area's favorite Thai specialties to a loyal fan club. Among the things that keep them loyal are fabulous curries. These are often the least satisfactory dishes on make-do Thai restaurant menus, especially disappointing because in Thailand the curry genre is highly developed, boasting a dozen or more variations based on the color of the chili pepper used, the nature of the meat, poultry, or seafood it laces, and the thickness of the cooking sauce. In the East Bay, Siam Cuisine comes closest to doing justice to a curry science second only to India's. 1181 University Ave, Berkeley (415) 548-3278. Lunch Mon–Sat. Dinner daily. Major credit cards. Moderate.

• **Thep Phanom** There's no mystery as to why we selected Thep Phanom to introduce Thai food at the beginning of this chapter. From the day it opened in the mid-'80s, this Haight-Fillmore establishment was a sensational success. Don't miss the *kinnahree sod sai* (chicken wings stuffed with silver noodles, mushrooms, and chicken), *plah-muk sod sal* (stuffed calamari), or *paksa vehok* (deep-fried quail with chili-garlic dipping sauce). 400 Waller St, SF (415) 431-2526. Dinner daily. MC, V. Moderate.

Indonesia: Myriad Variations on a Tropical Theme

Indonesia, that immense island nation straddling the equator across 4000 miles of ocean, was the historical Asian meeting ground of Christian Europe and Middle Eastern Islam. Firman Symasu, who runs the **Padang Restaurant** on San Francisco's Post Street just north of the downtown theater district, is an heir to that meeting. He is a member of the Minangkabau tribe, inhabitants of the mountainous central region of Sumatra, one of the largest of Indonesia's 13,600 islands.

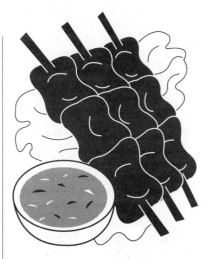

The tribe's chief city, Padang, sits on a gorgeous tropical coast backdropped by smoking volcanoes. Aside from their spectacular landscape, the Minangkabau are famous for two things: they are among their country's most devout Muslims and unquestionably its best chefs, thanks to Islam and Europe alike.

Their cooking prowess is so universally acknowledged that the phrase *nasi padang*—essentially meaning "Padang rice house"—is virtually synonymous with "restaurant" all over Indonesia. The European touch comes from the Portuguese, who were the 16th-century allies of Firman Symasu's ancestors against the principality of Aceh in Sumatra's north. The same source accounts for a great deal of Symasu's kitchen vocabulary. In modern Indonesian, the Portuguese words *bolo, caldo, queijo, couves,* and *mesa* survive as *bolu, kaldu, kedju, kabis,* and *medja* (in English: cake, broth, cheese, cabbage, and table).

You might assume from this list that the gastronomic influence on the Minangkabau is primarily a European matter. But it's not, even though a genuine Indonesian banquet at the Padang Restaurant carries yet another European name. The banquet in question is the *rijsttafel* (rice table in Dutch), a kind of grand combination meal that Indonesian cooks invented to please the Hollanders who succeeded Portugal as the region's major European imperial power around 1610. It makes a good way to sample the complexities of the *nasi padang*.

One evening at Padang we started out our *rijsttafel* with *soto ayam*, an intensely flavored *kaldu* full of bean thread noodles, fried onions, and ginger. It was followed by *ayam panggang*, chicken rubbed with spices and coconut oil and grilled; a mound of sweet spiced coconut flakes; *gado-gado*, a salad comprised of potatoes, cucumbers, hard-boiled egg, and bean sprouts, covered in a chunky peanut sauce; and the rich dry beef "curry" known as *rendang*.

There was a blistering hot *sambal*, in this case, a chili-based condiment. Despite a widespread misapprehension to the contrary, not all *sambals* are chili sauces; the term applies to almost any intensely flavored dish—fried shrimp with shallots is a famous example—served at room temperature to be mixed in with rice or other foods.

The supreme treat in our banquet was *sate sapi*, a strong candidate for the title of Indonesia's national passion. Every street and every village has its *sate* man, fanning a tiny bed of coals over which he turns a recognizable counterpart to the Persian kabob. At Padang, this tradition yields a deliciously marinated spit of beef chunks served in a pool of crushed peanut, sweetened soy, and chilies, the classic *sate* sauce.

What apple pie is to America, *sate* is to Indonesia. And yet it wouldn't exist at all without the two determined rivals who circled

Sate

Sate—not just the dish, but even the word itself—is today served in virtually every country within 2000 miles of Indonesia, with which it is most closely associated. Go to a Thai restaurant and you can order *moo satay*, skewered pork in a peanut-and-chili sauce. A Malaysian will recommend *satai ayam* or *satai kambing*, using chicken or lamb. In a southern Chinese Chao Zhou restaurant featuring the specialties of the city of Shantou, the choices include *sa dai zhu rou*, thin strips of grilled pork, beef, or chicken in the familiar peanut sauce. Similar grilled skewered meats are also among the most popular items on the menus of the Philippines, Burma, and Vietnam.

the globe in the 15th and 16th centuries and transformed the entire world's eating habits in the process. The Persian merchants and Arab conquerors who brought Islam to Sumatra also introduced kabobs and curries. Soon afterward, European adventurers discovered the peanut and the chili pepper in South America and ferried them to the kitchens of Aceh and Padang. *Sate* was the happy result.

There are only a few more places in the Bay Area to sample Indonesian cuisine. The dearth is not surprising, given the small number of Indonesians who have emigrated to the United States. The largest colony in the Bay Area is probably the Indonesian student community at the University of San Francisco. So homesick are they for their native fare that the good Jesuits allow a special catering service at the student dormitory, with specialties prepared and delivered by the Indonesia Restaurant, a modest kitchen just down the street from the Padang.

• **Padang Restaurant** 700 Post St, SF (415) 775-6708. Dinner Mon–Sat. Major credit cards. Moderate.

• **Indonesia Restaurant** This homey little spot would indeed be right at home on a side street in Jakarta. More a coffee shop than a full-fledged restaurant, the Indonesia offers less than a dozen dishes, all for surprisingly low prices. Order *nasi rames*, Indonesia's traditional combination plate, and you'll get a taste of three of the archipelago's down-home preparations that the kitchen has cooked up that day. A typical order includes curry chicken, coconut beef, and fried fish around a hill of steamed rice. Spice up the whole thing with a little *sambal oelek*, an explosive brew of red chilies that Indonesians find irresistible. 678 Post St, SF (415) 4026. Lunch and dinner daily. No credit cards. Inexpensive.

Burma: Mild Curries and 16-Part Salads

urma, which straddles the cultural dividing line between India and China, was once the epicenter of a Buddhist civilization that enthralled both of its enormous neighbors. Remnants of that glory are still to be seen on the upper flood plain of the Irrawaddy River at Pagan, where a vast city of abandoned temples slowly returns to the soil. Today, Burma's influence on the rest of Asia is minimal, but it is still a cultural referee at the table. The Burmese have negotiated between the various claims of Chinese, Thai, and Indian food traditions to produce their own wonderful cuisine.

They have been far less successful in negotiating their internal political and cultural conflicts, alas—and since the mid-1960s, thousands of Chinese Burmese and other minority peoples of Burma have been forced to emigrate. The Chinese Burmese, in particular, have been greatly attracted to the Bay Area. And it is to them that we owe the distinction of enjoying what is probably the world's largest number of Burmese restaurants.

Chinese though they may be, the owners of San Francisco's Mandalay, Burma's House, and On Lok Yuen, Oakland's Nan Yang, and Millbrae's Ray's Place are true to the dishes they learned to love as children in Rangoon and Mandalay. The most notable are the two great classics of the Burmese table, *panthe kaukswe* and *moo hing nga*. The first of these is a curried chicken noodle, rich in the nuances of the Southeast Asian spice trade. The second is a thick fish soup, replete with noodles. In both cases, the mixed legacy is palpable: Chinese noodles in the coconut sauces favored by India and Thailand. They're the dishes to order first in any Bay Area Burmese establishment—the true measure of its credentials.

More demanding tests can be applied to the range of unusual "salads" that highlight Burmese meals. At the Mandalay, for instance, there is a remarkable version that has as its centerpiece green tea leaves, which are tossed with peanuts, ginger, sesame seeds, yellow peas, fried garlic, and coconut shreds to produce a symphony of tastes and textures. A similar preparation at Philip Chu's Nan Yang features no less than 16 separate players, with fresh ginger in the starring role.

Curries are mainstays of the Burmese table. Almost without exception they contain onion, garlic, chilies, ginger, and turmeric, and are often less fiery than those of neighboring kitchens. Both chicken and prawns frequently turn up in curried coconut-milk gravies; a tamarind-based curry is usually favored for fish balls, pork, and beef.

Confirmed Asiaphiles also know that they can find strictly Indian and Chinese dishes in most Burmese restaurants. On Lok Yuen, for instance, serves very good—and very inexpensive—Indian *parathas* (fried flat bread) listed on its menu under the Burmese pronunciation *plada*. Look also for chili-laced Chinese meat and poultry salads in the style of Yunnan Province, just across the border from Burma on the northern side of the Golden Triangle.

Burmese Restaurants: The Top Choices

• **Burma's House** When Burma's House first appeared in the late '80s, it experienced some unevenness in the kitchen and a dearth of clientele. Both situations have improved, giving this unpretentious little restaurant a chance to succeed. Chinese dishes are sprinkled throughout the menu, so search out what Rangoon natives crave. The *nga pe dok*, fish cake tossed with coriander and fried garlic, and *chin hinyee*, fish soup seasoned with chili and lemongrass, are good places to start. Finish up with an order of *shwe gyi mok*, deep-fried wheat puffs flavored with coconut. 720 Post St, SF (415) 775-1156. Lunch Mon–Fri, dinner daily. MC, V. Inexpensive.

• **Inlay Burmese Food** Back in Burma, street-side food stalls are the best way to sample the everyday fare of the people. Now two charming Burmese women have opened a stall in an Ellis Street food pavilion, in quarters shared with purveyors of Korean *bulkogi* and Mexican burritos. For only pennies, they offer the downtown lunch bunch a delicious alternative to the usual fast-food options. Try the noodles with curried chicken, in soup or out, or any of their other dishes, from beef curry to fish soup. San Francisco Food Center, 24 Ellis St, SF Lunch and early dinner Mon–Sat. No credit cards. Inexpensive.

• **Mandalay Restaurant** This is the granddaddy of San Francisco's Burmese restaurants. Opened in 1984 by a Chinese-Burmese family from Rangoon, the Mandalay continues to be a vital outpost of Burma's national table. In a dining room decorated with hanging lanterns, intricate artworks, and light woods, you can order up not only great *panthe kaukswe* and *moo hing nga*, but equally accomplished renditions of *chin mong kyaw*, a leafy, sour-flavored vegetable prepared with shrimp; tea-smoked duck; and satay. And Mandalay offers a truly exotic ice cream dish that blends tapioca and coconut. 4344 California St, SF (415) 386-3895. Lunch and dinner daily. MC, V. Moderate.

• **Nan Yang Restaurant** Rangoon native Philip Chu and his wife, Nancy, opened the Nan Yang in Oakland Chinatown in 1983. Their menu includes a banquetful of Burmese specialties, including shrimp curry, jellyfish and fishcake salad, curried chicken soup, and a 16-part ginger salad (described in this chapter's introduction) that Philip describes as a "glimpse of nirvana." 301 Eighth St, Oakland (415) 465-6924. Lunch and dinner Tues–Sun. MC, V. Inexpensive.

• **On Lok Yuen** David Chou and his family satisfy diners with a large menu of Burmese specialties offered at unbelievably low prices. Burmese pig's-ear salad is a dish that will never be taken up by fast-food chains in search of a new twist, but it's one you shouldn't miss. Its dressing of fresh chilies, fish sauce, lime, garlic, and scallions overcomes whatever queasiness the general concept might prompt. Also recommended are *nan gyi dok*, noodles tossed with chicken, coconut, fried garlic, and sesame seed; and fish-ball curry. 3721 Geary Blvd, SF (415) 386-6208. Lunch and dinner daily. MC, V. Inexpensive.

Nan Yang Asia:
Kitchens of the Southern Ocean

The Chinese communities on the Straits of Malacca boast one of the most distinctive cuisines on earth—a rich mixture of their own ingredients and cooking methods with pungent spices indigenous to Malaysia. The idea, according to legend, was inspired by the 15th-century marriage of a Malacca sultan to a princess from Beijing. Their legacy is the centerpiece of the culinary tradition called in Mandarin *nan yang*—literally "southern ocean," referring to the Chinese-descended residents of Southeast Asia.

The *nan yang* capital is the city-state of Singapore. The major reason its cuisine doesn't ring bells in the West is that Singaporean cooks seldom emigrate to America. Chris Yeo, the Singaporean proprietor of a successful San Francisco hair salon, saw that as a grand opportunity and opened the **Straits Café**.

The strait in question is the Malacca, which separates peninsular Malaysia from Sumatra; its coastal cities, including Malacca, Penang, and Singapore, harbor one of the world's most fascinating melting pots. The region's culture—and cuisine—blends influences from Europe, India, south China, and the Malay archipelago. The results, available at Chris' coolly understated bistro on Geary and a few other Bay Area restaurants, are as exotic as the equatorial Orient.

Take *nasi lemak*, a kind of blue-plate special that assembles chilied prawns, fresh tomato-cucumber salad, and *ikan bilis* (chili-fried whitebait and peanuts) around a mound of rice cooked in coconut milk. It

adds up to a startling mélange of textures, tastes, and colors. So, too, do *tahu goreng*, small cubes of fried bean curd, cucumber, and bean sprouts covered with a rich peanut sauce; and *laksa*, a tamarind-scented broth containing fish, chilies, onion, and rice noodles.

Tahu goreng, *laksa*, and several other Straits Café dishes are drawn from the cuisine of the Nonyas, a Southeast Asian subculture said to be descended from that 15th-century Malay-Chinese marriage. The same can be said for *rojak*, a medley of fresh fruits and raw vegetables tossed in a dressing of chilies, fermented prawns, and sesame seeds that is among the Nonya offerings of another straits establishment, the **Singapore Malaysian Restaurant** on Clement Street. Its proprietors hail from George Town, a picturesque Malaysian port on the island of Penang, which is the second city of Straits Chinese culture.

It's also a city infatuated with the possibilities of the rice noodle, a fondness responsible for the dish called *chow kway teo*, broad noodles sautéed with prawns, clams, and bean sprouts.

Two more dishes deserve special mention. One is *sambal kachang*, sensational green beans topped with a fiery mélange of spices. Another is *chendol* (spelled *cheng loi* on the menu), an exotic dessert drink of coconut milk, vegetable jellies, and crushed ice sweetened with palm sugar.

Many of these specialties are also offered by a small San Francisco Chinatown lunch place, the **Capitol Kim Tar**, run by *nan yang* Chinese from Indochina. Like Penang and Singaporean cooks, its chef is also a master of the *nan yang* world's favorite dish: *Hainan ji fan*, a poached chicken, served with rice cooked in chicken broth and a sauce of vinegar, chilies, garlic, and ginger.

Nan Yang Restaurants

• **Capitol Kim Tar** It's standing room only at high noon in this Chinatown noodle-and-rice house. In addition to Hainan chicken rice, the staff delivers big portions of fried fish cake, in the style of Thailand, and plates of braised duck, a specialty of southern China's Chao Zhou people. The menu reads like an international agreement, with separate pages devoted to English, Chinese, Cambodian, and Thai. 758 Pacific St, SF (415) 956-8533. Breakfast, lunch, and dinner daily. No credit cards. Inexpensive.

• **Monsoon** Bruce Cost, a highly respected chef and food scholar, has opened the Bay Area's first upmarket *nan yang* restaurant—within shouting distance of the Opera House. Cost relentlessly pursues only the finest ingredients for the Monsoon kitchen. The results are memorable meals that echo the time-honored culinary traditions of China and Southeast Asia. One of Cost's strong suits is a spectacular pork shoulder prepared in the "red-cooked" Shanghai style, a process of slow braising in a sauce of spiced soy and Shaoxing wine. Another is the Thai-influenced, chili-scented coconut-milk soup. And you can't top Monsoon's seafood for freshness: the chief ingredient in its Cantonese steamed catfish dish can be found swimming in a back-room tank moments before you see it showered with black beans, scallions, ginger, and chili in the dining room. Opera Plaza, 601 Van Ness Ave, SF (415) 441-3232. Lunch Tues–Fri, dinner Tues–Sun. MC, V. Moderate.

• **Nan Yang Restaurant** This wildly popular Oakland restaurant also appears in the Burmese chapter of this book. That's because owners Philip and Nancy Chu are natives of Rangoon, and their Burmese dishes are the reason for much of the restaurant's highly loyal following. But the restaurant's name tells the full story, and diners should try the *nan yang* specialties the Chus offer. Among them are a great Malaysian chicken curry, Thai garlic rice noodle, Hainan chicken rice, and Singapore satay. 301 Eighth St, Oakland (415) 465-6924. Lunch and dinner Tues–Sun. MC, V. Inexpensive.

• **Singapore Malaysian Restaurant** The Malaysian family that launched this modest Richmond District restaurant in 1989 are ethnic Chinese, but their menu reflects the region's cosmopolitan table. In addition to the dishes discussed in this chapter's introduction, look for such Malay archipelago classics as chicken in a red coconut sauce, panfried pompano with curry sauce, and one of our favorite equatorial desserts, *pulut hitam,* black-rice pudding topped with coconut milk. 836 Clement St, SF (415) 750-9518. Lunch and dinner daily. MC, V. Inexpensive.

• **Straits Café** Chris Yeo's Penang-born head chef creates delicious renditions of all the *nan yang* favorites in a dining room with one wall that re-creates the laundry-draped shophouse fronts of old Singapore. Try the *kway pai ti* (pastry shells with slivered vegetables and chili), *otak-otak* (ground fish steamed in banana leaves), *kari lembu* (Indian-style beef curry), and *patong kari ayam* (coconut curry chicken) for a true Singapore experience. 3300 Geary Blvd, SF (415) 668-1783. Lunch and dinner daily. Major credit cards. Moderate.

INDIA, MIDDLE
EAST & AFRICA

India: New Wave from the Subcontinent

We once spent the better part of a month in India sampling *thalis*. Every restaurant, train-station cafeteria, market stall, and snack shop on the subcontinent offers some version of this budgeter's special. Its signature is a large metal tray with a mound of rice or pile of *chapatis* (whole-wheat griddle bread) in the center and several metal bowls of savory meats and vegetables along the periphery. Perhaps it's shorthand-accurate to call the *thali* India's version of the "combo." But its characteristics and presentation are so genre specific that, in the end, the comparison doesn't quite work. Not just any Indian combo makes a *thali*.

What reminded us of these nuances was a conversation over a selection of *chaats* (snacks) at **Sujatha's Indian Café**, a wonderful little snack shop in Santa Clara. As an Indian friend wrapped a triangle of *bhatura* around some delicious *chole*, he alternated between expressions of pleasure and complaints about the difficulty he'd had finding good Indian food since his emigration here a decade before. "Not just any curry makes a real Indian experience," he intoned.

That was back in the mid-1980s, in a Bay Area that—unlike New York or London—lacked the range in price and regional variety to be considered an overseas Indian culinary capital. Since then, we have been blessed with an encouraging Indian restaurant boom, emanating

mostly in the South Bay and Berkeley and to a lesser extent in San Francisco.

One of its prime, if unlikely, focal points is the Santa Clara County intersection where El Camino Real meets Halford Avenue. Shopping centers sprawl over all four corners, in a bounty of boutiques, hair salons, and hardware stores. It's only when you get close up that you notice Sanskrit signs in the windows. Welcome to the commercial heart of the Indian Silicon Valley.

Don't let the lack of a more picturesque ethnic setting put you off; it doesn't bother the locals a bit. Ask one of them, Veena Birla, to pinpoint the secret of her own family's success in these precincts, and the answer is an unqualified endorsement of South Bay–style merchandising. "One-stop shopping," she says, with undisguised reverence. "People only want to park their car once when they go out. *Acha!* This is the genius of the American shopping center."

In the Birla interpretation of that genius, you can commission a sari, peruse the latest Hindi videotapes, and pick up a sack of *basmati* rice, all in Birla-owned establishments within sight of a single parking space. But what really draws crowds to the southwest corner of El Camino and Halford is **Sanraj India Cuisine**, the restaurant that Veena and her husband, Hira, oversee in their share of a Santa Clara shopping center.

American though the setting might be, the Birla kitchen is a bona fide outpost of Veena and Hira's native Punjab. Their chefs turn out *parathas* (flaky whole-wheat bread) and seven other classic northern Indian breads, including the popular teardrop-shaped wheat bread called *nan*. They cook the latter in a genuine *tandoor,* the traditional clay oven also used to roast succulent

People and Their Neighborhoods

Where they live: There are no Indian residential neighborhoods. Mostly engineering or medical professionals, Indian-Americans can be found in many middle-class suburbs, especially in Santa Clara and Alameda counties.

Where they gather: The two primary Indian commercial districts are University Avenue in Berkeley and around the intersection of Halford Avenue and El Camino Real in Santa Clara. The best way to locate Indian foodstuffs—and follow the community's rapid development here—is to pick up copies of the free *India Currents* monthly magazine in restaurants and shops.

Estimated Bay Area population: 50,000.

portions of spiced chicken and lamb. Simmering in nearby pots are a northern Indian rice *biriani* flavored with saffron and nuts, and a southern Indian *gosht vindaloo* that mixes lamb with potatoes in a searing curry of garlic, chili, and vinegar.

The Birla enterprises, which also include a *chaat* or "snack" shop, might be enough to satisfy every need of a Western Indiaphile. But that's not necessarily the case for the Silicon Valley's thousands of Indian residents. Many are professionals, with the disposable income to insist on choices. The result is a wave of Indian businesses—led by restaurants—that has made the El Camino-Halford crossroads a Bay Area curry capital.

Sujatha's, where those reveries on

Indian authenticity overcame us, occupies a cheery storefront in the northeast quadrant of the intersection. Behind the counter stands Reddy Mocherla, genial proprietor of an eatery that satisfied even our fussy Indian friend's definition of the genuine. For starters, it offers no fewer than three separate *thalis*.

On the day of our conversation, he had selected the Sujatha special, which consisted of *chole bhatura* (chick-peas prepared in a spicy sauce and served with an enormous round of puffy deep-fried wheat dough), plus *dahi vada* (lentil-flour spheres floating in yogurt), potato-stuffed *samosa*, and *jalebi* (pastry twirls infused with honey). At less than $5 it was a steal. The same price fetched the vegetarian *thali*,

delivering a flaky *paratha* in place of the *bhatura*, rice, a *dhal* (lentil) curry, the peas-and-white-cheese mixture known as *mattar paneer*, and a cooling pool of yogurt flavored with black mustard seeds. One dollar more bought the nonvegetarian *thali* that added a chicken or lamb curry.

It was more than the presence of *thalis* that reminded us of Mocherla's native Hyderabad, near the geographical center of India. Sujatha's counter itself was a technicolor spectacular in the uninhibited Indian manner, loaded with *chaats* and sweets. There were pyramids of cashews and *vatana* (spiced dry peas) alongside glorious pieces of *burfi* and spheres of *ras malai*. The first of these terms refers to milk-

Tandoori: India's Famed Clay-Oven Cooking

The chief culinary claim to fame of India's north is the *tandoor*: a jar-shaped clay cooking vessel, heated to very high temperatures, that the Mogul kitchen borrowed from Persia. Though the word *tandoori* tends to suggest chicken to most people, it wasn't until the mid-19th century that it was employed for meat; before then, only bread was prepared in a *tandoor*. Until the late 1940s, moreover, its use was limited to India's upper borderlands, now the Pakistani Northwest Frontier Province.

Today it seems as though nearly every Indian restaurant in the Bay Area feels obliged to include *tandoori* dishes on its menu. Hereabouts, they're done best by the chef who presides over the tandoor at the aptly named Indian Oven. The rack of lamb we had one

evening at this extraordinary San Francisco establishment had been marinated in a mixture of yogurt and spices. Seared on the outside by the white-hot tandoor, it remained succulently pink in the center, just the way it should be. The portion was generous, and the flavor was memorable.

One of Indian Oven's distinctions—other than its being run by a collective of chefs trained at a professional culinary institute in Poona—is its willingness to experiment. In effect, it is to Bay Area Indian food what places like the Zuni Café are to its Mediterranean traditions: a meeting ground for the tested and the imaginative. Case in point: Indian Oven's quail—something you'll never find in India but a dish you'll certainly remember.

based confections; the second is a kind of sweetened cheese, served in a cream flavored with rose essence.

"Business is very good," Mocherla allowed, passing us a portion of the *ras malai*, which he considers his kitchen's masterpiece. "Many of the Indian engineers and scientists who work in this area consider us a second home."

As it happens, Mocherla has since contributed his part to yet another burgeoning second home for Bay Area Indians—aimed at academics rather than electronics workers. If the southern stretches of El Camino are outside the geographical range of your hankering for a *thali*, try heading for Berkeley instead. There, along University Avenue, an East Bay Little India is fast developing, with at least half a dozen restaurants and snack shops at last count. One of them—bigger in both menu and space than its Santa Clara cousin—is Sujatha's number two.

Indian Restaurants: The Top Choices

• **Bombay Cuisine** This restaurant, which shares its building with an Indian spice market, features the cuisine of Gujurat, the state between Bombay and Pakistan from which thousands of the Bay Area's Indian residents have emigrated. The Gujuratis have their own table, and it ranks with the subcontinent's finest. Certainly no one would quarrel with that premise after a dish of Bombay Cuisine's *patra*, half-inch-thick rounds of deep-fried taro leaves sprinkled with sesame seeds and coriander and served with a sharp turmeric chutney. The *khaman dhokla*, wonderfully light steamed squares of seasoned, puréed chick-peas, is further proof. A main course of *baigan bhartha*, eggplant curry with peas, is another top choice here, confirming the reputation Gujuratis have as India's premier vegetarian chefs. 2006 Ninth St, Berkeley (415) 843-9601. Lunch and dinner Tues–Sun. Major credit cards. Moderate.

• **The Ganges** Pure vegetarian cuisine—no eggs or gelatin—cooked by Gujurati-born Malvi Doshi, who regularly serves a number of dishes encountered in no other Indian restaurant in the Bay Area. At the warm, intimate Ganges, Doshi prepares different curries and other vegetable dishes each day and offers them on a quartet of preset dinners. She's truly a genius. We reached that verdict at our first meal there, halfway into an enormous banquet that opened with the crisp lentil wafers called *pappadams* and closed with *kulfi*, a rich ice cream laced with saffron, cardamom, almonds, and pistachios. In between came two chutneys and remarkably light *pakoras* (savory fritters) of broccoli, cauliflower, and potato; a *dhal* soup sharp with the flavor of clove; a curry of potatoes and cabbage with black mustard seeds; *kofta* curry, "meatless" meatballs of spiced black-eyed peas; saffron rice; *chapatis*; and a truly memorable creation of baked banana stuffed with coconut, fresh coriander, chili, and lemon. From beginning to end, every dish was prepared from scratch in Malvi's modest kitchen. 775 Frederick St, SF (415) 661-7290. Dinner Mon–Sat. MC, V. Moderate.

• **Indian Oven** Housed in an airy

Victorian storefront in the lower Haight, Indian Oven is an offbeat but elegant place that may well offer the most creative twists on Indian cuisine you'll ever experience. The basic dishes are derived from the classics of Bengal and Madras, Kashmir and Kerala, Hyderabad and Gujurat, but every one of them reflects the personal imagination of the collective of chefs who work here. From the tandoor, there's *hussaini* lamb kabob, a trio of ground lamb "sausages" stuffed with dried fruits and pistachios. Crave curry? Try the turmeric-and-cumin-infused chicken *massala* or the Kerala-style prawns in chili-laced coconut milk. The comfortable dining room, done in white linen, English china, and contemporary art, is anchored on one side by the tandoor and on the other by an ebony baby grand. 237 Fillmore St, SF (415) 626-1628. Dinner daily. MC, V. Moderate.

- **Maharani (San Francisco)**
- **Maharani Sweets and Snacks (Berkeley)** Rajiv Gurjal was born in Malawi and schooled in London and has been a principal in the Bay Area in such eminent establishments as North India and India Garden. Nowadays, this polished and witty entrepreneur is a partner in two more local restaurants, both of which offer superlative dining experiences. On the Berkeley side of the bay, there's the first Maharani, featured in our sidebar on the Indian *mathai*, a snack-and-sweet shop. The *mathai* specialties are what you should concentrate on there. The San Francisco branch, by contrast, is a full-fledged dinner house. The decor is lovely; there's even a back

Mathai: Sweet Objects of Indian Affections

A *mathai* is a classic genre of sweet-and-snack shop that exists all over the subcontinent but in few places outside India. For years, its aficionados could only wax nostalgic about the spectacular sweetmeats, puddings, and elaborate "dry snacks" that are part of every expatriate Indian's fondest memories of the old country. They'd trade tales of famous *mathais* like the Nanking in Delhi, where lines form each afternoon when the capital's wheeler-dealers gather for high tea.

One glance at the delicacies turned out at the growing number of *mathais* that have finally begun to appear here in recent years and you'll understand why Mrs. Field's cookies are scant consolation for a homesick Maharashtran or Punjabi. One bite at Berkeley's **Maharani Sweets and Snacks** and you'll be equipped to trade nostalgic tales of your own.

On any given day, the *mathai-wallah* there assembles an array of up to 16 separate sweets, representing every region from the northern Punjab and Bengal to the deep tropical south. Tastewise, they run the gamut from straightforward honey-sweet to complex flavorful explosions of cinnamon, cardamom, and pistachio.

Aesthetically, they alternate between representational illusion and outrageous abstraction. A favorite from the first category is *gulab jamun*, deep burgundy spheres of dried whole-milk and soft cream cheese that look for all the world like irridescent plums. The second

room with Mogul-style booths in which the diners recline on pillows to the strains of sitar music. As for the food, it's exceptional—the tandoori chicken couldn't be juicier, and the *dal mahkni* is outstanding. 1122 Post St, SF (415) 775-1988. Lunch Tues–Fri, brunch Sat–Sun, dinner Tues–Sun. Major credit cards. Moderate. 1025 University Ave, Berkeley (415) 848-8844. Lunch and dinner daily. Major credit cards. Inexpensive.

• **New Delhi** For years, Ranjan Dey has been the proprietor of one of Hong Kong's favorite Indian restaurants, the New Delhi. Today, this veteran from Britain's last Asian imperial outpost is trying his hand in San Francisco. He picked quite a place to begin: The New Delhi is ensconced in what was once the grand ballroom of the fabled Ramona

includes specialties that could have inspired postmodernist geometric sculpture; the Maharani's taffylike *burfis*, for instance, resemble polychromatic studies of the rectangle and trapezoid. They come in five varieties—plain, chocolate, coconut, almond, and chick-pea—and many are studded with nuts and spices, or shine under layers of thin, edible silver leaf. The use of precious metals in foods originated under the 16th-century Mogul emperors, who were convinced that they imparted strength to their warriors.

Like the sweets, Indian dry snacks are sold by the pound. In effect, Indian dry snacks are the forerunners of California trail mix—highly nutritious and marvelously seasoned compositions of nuts, puffed rice, lentils, chick-peas, and slender dry noodles called *seve*. (In India, a good mix is literally regarded as money in the bank; we

were once given a chili-spiced dry lentil and peanut snack in change when we purchased stamps at a small post office near Mysore.)

Perhaps no food is more indigenous to Bombay than *bhelpuri*. It's a blend of food styles: a seasoned combination of *seve*, puffed rice, and other items from the dry-snack shelf, tossed with boiled potato, mint, and tamarind chutneys, onions, and yogurt *raita*. The resulting mélange of flavors and textures is indescribably delicious.

True Bombay types always order *bhelpuri* with a side of *gol gappa*, tiny rounds of thin, fried-bread pockets that are filled at the table with potatoes, chick-peas, and a pungent tamarind-and-cumin sauce. They take practice to eat properly; each must be popped whole into the mouth or the liquid is prone to pour down the diner's chin.

Hotel on Ellis Street. Dey has done a marvelous restoration job. As in Hong Kong, he is out to win gourmet hearts with a grand buffet dinner every Monday night, featuring at least 15 items. One dish to look for here, among the relatively conventional curries, is *palak kofta kashmiri*, a truly memorable vegetarian preparation in which a mound of braised spinach is "stuffed" with dried fruits and served in a rich curry sauce. 160 Ellis St, SF (415) 397-8470. Lunch and dinner daily. MC, V. Moderate.

• **Pasand Madras Cuisine** Southern Indian food was practically unknown here before the arrival of the first Pasand in Berkeley. Today, three branches, from San Rafael to Santa Clara, are bringing such Madrasi staples as *masala dosa*—a large lentil-flour "pancake" stuffed with potatoes and chilies—to an appeciative Bay Area public. The meat curries, while not native to the south, are also produced with care. The San Francisco branch, incidentally, is a noted jazz bar. 2286 Shattuck Ave, Berkeley (415) 549-2559; 802 B St, San Rafael (415) 456-6009; 1875 Union St, SF (415) 922-4498; 3701 El Camino Real, Santa Clara (408) 241-5151. Lunch and dinner daily. Major credit cards. Inexpensive.

• **Sanraj India Cuisine** Hira and Veena Birla, who hail from the Punjab, have opened a restaurant that, among other things, features the breads for which the Punjab is famous. The menu lists eight varieties, ranging from simple *chapatis* and leavened *nan* to deep-fried *pooris*, *paratha* stuffed with spiced potatoes and peas, and *Kabuli* or *keema nan*, respectively stuffed with nuts and raisins or minced lamb. There is even an "assorted basket" that includes three different breads. 3650 El

Indian Food Glossary

There is no standard transliteration system for Hindi in use in Indian restaurants. We have selected the most common spellings.

Achar: Pickles.

Aloo: Potatoes.

Biriani: Rice mixed with meat or fish.

Brinjal: Eggplant.

Chaat: "Snack," including *aloo chaat*, boiled potatoes seasoned with chilies, coriander, and other spices; *appam*, rice-flour pancake from southern India; *bhajias*, vegetable fritters; *bhelpuri*, deep-fried small bread rounds stuffed with vegetables; *dhokla*, lentil-and-rice-flour cake, steamed and then fried;

gol gappa, wheat rounds served with legumes and potatoes; *pakoras*, northern Indian name for *bhajias*; *pappadam*, crisp "chips" of fried flour; *samosas*, deep-fried stuffed triangles; *vada*, chick-pea-flour dumplings served in yogurt.

Dahi: Yogurt.

Dhal: Legumes, usually lentils, simmered with spices.

Do piaza: Onions; a dish of meat or poultry cooked with onions.

Gosht: Meat; *bhuna gosht*, spicy fried meat.

Kabob: Skewer-grilled meats, poultry, or fish; *boti kabob*, meat kabob basted with butter; *hussaini kabob*, meat kabob often simmered in a sauce after grilling; *seek kabob*,

Camino Real, Santa Clara (408) 247-4360. Lunch and dinner daily. Major credit cards. Moderate.

• **Sujatha's** A Little India has been growing along University Avenue in Berkeley since 1985 or so, when a crop of promising subcontinental kitchens began to appear. With the 1989 arrival of Sudhakar "Reddy" Mocherla and his Sujatha's, the casting is complete. If you have any doubts, just follow the crowd of Maharashtran, Punjabi, and Madrasi students and professors to this spot, where Mocherla curries favor with those who favor curry. A fuller description of his *thalis*, or set meals, appears in the introduction to this chapter. But it's Sujatha's array of sweets and dry savory snacks that brings tears to Indian eyes. Mocherla offers half a dozen varieties of *burfi*, milk-based confections that come in several colors of the rainbow. He has rows of *halwa*,

jamun, and *chum chum*, the tasty cheese drums Bengalis love. There are also piles of spiced dried lentils, noodles, and nuts, plus the wildly hued "hot mix," a fiery blend of the lot. Sujatha's, 48 Shattuck Square, Berkeley (415) 549-1814; 1584 Halford Ave, Santa Clara (408) 984-5280. Lunch and dinner daily. MC, V. Inexpensive.

---

ground-meat kabob; *tikka kabob*, cubed-meat kabob cooked in a tandoor.

Korma: Meat or poultry braised in yogurt or cream.

Lassi: Sweet or salted yogurt drink.

Masala dosa: Lentil and rice-flour "pancake" stuffed with spiced potatoes.

Massala: Meat or poultry braised with medley of spices.

Mattar: Peas.

Murgh: Chicken.

Palak: Spinach.

Paneer: Cheese.

Raita: Cucumber-and-yogurt condiment.

Roghan josh: Lamb *korma* (see above).

Roti: Breads, including *bhatura*, deep-fried wheat bread; *chapati*, whole-wheat griddle bread; *idli*, rice-flour bread or cake; *nan*, tandoor-baked flat wheat bread; *paratha*, flaky, buttered, griddle-cooked whole-wheat bread; *poori*, deep-fried puffed whole-wheat bread.

Saag: Green vegetable, usually spinach.

Shirnee: "Sweets," including *burfi*, flavored condensed-milk "cakes"; *gulab jamun*, dairy-rich balls served in a very sweet syrup; *halwa*, confection made from grains or vegetables, often carrot; *jalebi*, deep-fried pastry "pretzels" coated with syrup; *kulfi*, ice cream; *ras malai*, cheese balls in cream or thick milk.

Tandoor: Clay oven used to cook marinated meats, poultry, seafood, and breads.

Iran: Gifts from the First Gourmets

Persian cuisine is a hard sell in America. The reasons are obvious. But the logic makes no sense. Whatever political turns the image of Persia—renamed Iran in 1935—has taken in the past decade, it is a nation whose influence on civilization stretches back to the dawn of recorded history. Nowhere is that legacy more evident than at the table. From the Straits of Gilbraltar to the Straits of Malacca, across the Mediterranean to the Spice Islands of Southeast Asia, "Persian" is an eloquent cultural idiom.

Hereabouts, we look to Mahmoud Khossoussi for a modern articulation of that idiom. As he points out, the great Persian poet Omar Khayyam wrote parts of *Rubaiyat*, his famous musings on wine, women, and song, in a *maykadeh*, more or less a cross between a tavern and a restaurant. So, not surprisingly, that's the name Khossoussi and his partner, Pirouz Tehrani, decided to give their own place on Green Street in North Beach. "Mo," as his friends call him, presides over the kitchen of **Maykadeh**, our favorite Middle Eastern restaurant west of the Levant.

It's one of many Iranian-owned establishments that have appeared in the Bay Area since the 1979 revolution stranded tens of thousands of Iranian students and professionals in California—more than a quarter million in Los Angeles alone—where they have often taken up new roles as entrepreneurs. The distinctive qualities of their cuisine are evident immediately in the starter known as *sabzee*, which is the mandatory first bite of any authentic Persian meal. Literally, it means a plate of "fresh herbs"; invariably, it also includes wedges of goat's-milk cheese and onions. The herbs at Maykadeh are basil and mint, and they are eaten along with the warm pita bread that arrives at the same time.

If this description seems familiar even to diners who have never entered an Iranian restaurant, that's because it is; *sabzee* is the model for the first course served traditionally in virtually the entire Muslim

Fine Persian rugs traditionally served as the Iranian dinner table, with plates set on a white cloth atop a leather mat covering the carpet.

Chelo: Rice Fit for a Sultan

San Franciscans are accustomed to thinking of Chinatown as the home of the nation's most serious rice consumers. But there are those in the gourmet world who say that no one, not even the Chinese, outclasses Iranians in this department.

In the first place, they don't steam just any old rice. Iranian *chelo*—a delicate mound of which accompanies every dish at fine Iranian restaurants—is made from the rice strain known as *basmati*. Grown only in certain limited stretches of the Middle East and the northern Indian subcontinent (though California and Texas farmers are trying to expand its range), *basmati* is the Jane Fonda of rices. Its grains are the most slender, the longest, and the firmest in existence.

What's more, it has a character all its own. After harvest, Iranian and Pakistani farmers spread *basmati* rice above a fire in a closed earthen room for three days. That smoky flavor comes out when it's steamed, especially if you toss the rice with saffron and butter, as Iranians do. When it's served, the diner often mixes a raw egg yolk into the hot *chelo* and then sprinkles it with with *sumak*—the powdery spice made from the red berries of a plant that is a distant relative of our own (inedible) Western sumac and has been used as a general seasoning in the Fertile Crescent since the days of the Babylonians.

Iranian chefs also prepare a crisp form of *chelo* called *chelo ta dig*. They combine boiled rice with egg and cook it in a thin sheet until it is a golden brown. The crusty sheet is broken into pieces and served with kabobs and stews.

world—and also in the lands where it once held sway, from Greece to the western provinces of China. At the very heart of this world six centuries ago were Khossoussi's ancestors, the polished Persian sophisticates who transformed successive waves of nomadic warriors—Arabs, Mongols, Ottoman Turks—into one of history's most highly developed cultures. Persian Farsi became the language of Islamic poetry. Persian experts supervised silk manufactures in Genghis Khan's China. Persian artists set medieval Cairo's aesthetic fashions.

More to the point, for hundreds of years Persian culinary genius fueled the kitchens of the eastern Mediterranean Basin, Arabia, the Indian subcontinent, and landfalls as far east as Sumatra. Scarcely a dish on the menus of Athens, Istanbul, or Tangier does not owe some inspiration to Persia.

For us, one dish—offered at Maykadeh and most other Bay Area Iranian restaurants—neatly sums up the complexity and sophistication of the original Persian table. The dish is called *ghorme sabzee*, "epicure's combination." It might help to begin by pointing out that,

according to Khossoussi, the word *ghorme* was, indeed, borrowed from Farsi by the French. The first gourmets, in other words, were the Persians, whose agricultural accomplishments—and culinary finesse—date back 8000 years.

This dish confirms the pedigree. It begins with lamb shanks, which are braised with onions, scallions, leeks, garlic chives, parsley, red beans, and a rare herb imported from the Middle East that has no English language equivalent. At a critical moment in the preparation, Khossoussi adds something called *adveeye*, which he describes as "a mixture of six separate roots—the actual contents are a carefully guarded secret for every chef, you understand—plus cinnamon, dried limes, and *sumak*, a seasoning made from dried red berries." The results, which mingle sharp, pleasantly sour spices with a rich sauce base, are nothing short of sensational.

Ghorme sabzee is one of many *khoreshts*, roughly "stews," that punctuate the Persian menu. Their spinoffs, it should be noted, are clearly present in Moroccan *tagines* and the original Punjabi curries. But the most influential legacy of Persia's table lies under a cloud of smoke in another corner of Mahmoud Khossoussi's kitchen. This is where Mo cooks his kabobs—the Farsi word for anything grilled over coals. He has made one concession to local taste: the coals are mesquite. The chicken, lamb, and beef kabobs themselves, however, are readied strictly according to custom. Marinated in spices, homemade yogurt, and lime, they make a good case for the assertion that the Persians are the world's best grillmen.

There's no doubt about their influence on this score. Variations on the theme of grilled, skewered meat have been passed on as kabobs to Turkey, Afghanistan, India, and the Arab world, and reappear only thinly disguised as Greece's *souvlakia*, Russia's *shashlik*, and Asia's *satays*. "It's a product of commerce," Mo says. "We Persians were trading with countries as far away as China 1500 years ago." Indeed, there were Persian settlements in Chang An, today's Xian, the fabled capital of the Tang dynasty. And there are still Persian-style kabob houses—*maykadehs*—in Xian's bazaar today.

Iranian Restaurants: The Top Choices

• **Kasra** On Clement Street, amid dozens of Chinese kitchens turning out *jiao zi* and *bao zi*, stands Parviz Mehrazar Shirazi's contribution to the Middle Eastern scene. Named for the traditional dining hall of a Persian castle, the Kasra restaurant serves up an extraordinary *mirza ghasemi*. A specialty of northern Iran, it combines chopped and broiled eggplant, tomato, spices, and loads of garlic in an appetizer certain to seduce any disciple of the noble bulb. There's a long, friendly bar to wait at if a table isn't open yet. 349 Clement St, SF (415) 752-1101. Lunch and dinner daily. MC, V. Moderate.

• **Khayyam's Chelo Kabab** *Fesenjon*, a specialty at Khayyam's, is a chicken dish that makes memorable use of two products of the northern Iranian garden: walnuts and pome-

granates. They are blended into an astonishingly rich and sweetly pungent sauce, ideally suited to a jug of wine, a loaf of bread, and thou. Launch your meal with *cucoo*, a vegetable-and-egg "omelet," or *kofteh*, a sphere of ground meat, beans, and rice seasoned with dill. As the name suggests, this is also a house that prides itself on its grilling expertise. The chefs turn their kabobs right in the window. 1373 Solano Ave, Albany (415) 526-7200. Lunch and dinner Tues–Sun. MC, V. Moderate.

• **Maykadeh** What can you say about a restaurant that uses filet mignon in its version of hamburger (Iranian *kofta kabab*) and sprinkles genuine Iranian saffron (retail price: $3000 per pound) on top of its rice? "Eat there!" Maykadeh, the establishment featured in the introduction to this chapter, boasts a superlative kitchen, refined atmosphere, and polished management. Select from a wide array of grilled kabobs—the *joojeh*, or marinated chicken, is expecially good— or from the rich, braised dishes known as *khoreshts*. The grilled lamb brain is phenomenal. 470 Green St, SF (415) 362-8286. Lunch and dinner Tues–Sun. MC, V. Moderate.

The Fertile Crescent: Cuisine from the Cradle of Civilization

Today, sadly, the area that once nurtured Mesopotamia and Babylonia is not known chiefly for its civilizing climate. But remnants of the cuisines of ancient cultures, and modern Middle Eastern ones as well, have reached restaurants half a world away in the Bay Area.

ally he joined the Jeremiah Tower team at the Balboa Café, where his talents as a cook were revealed.

The point to his latest identity—as the owner/chef of the superb **Yaya** restaurant south of Market—is that the elements of the Middle Eastern table can be adapted quite successfully to the tastes of nouvelle San

Iraqi Meets Nouvelle

Yahya Salih was born and raised in Baghdad, Iraq, which he left in 1976 to attend university in the United States. Like many a bright young lad torn between books and bills, he wound up washing dishes; eventu-

Francisco (a point made just as successfully by Fazol Poursohi at Faz Restaurant and Bar).

Salih makes no claim that his is an Iraqi establishment, traditional or otherwise; it's undeniably Mediterranean/Californian. But nearly every dish reflects something of his birthplace. You can't miss it in the opener that three of us lingered happily over on a late spring evening: Iraqi-style flat bread dipped in a dish of dark, full-bodied olive oil laced with thyme leaves and sesame seeds. Salih regards this rather elaborate, distinctly Middle Eastern combination as a must; he doesn't even charge for it.

Elsewhere on the menu, the evidence of the Proche-Orient is more subtle. Steamed oysters would remind no one of Iraq—except for the light dressing of yogurt and mint. Coho salmon do not swim in the Tigris or Euphrates, but grilled and served under an aioli seasoned with tamarind, they are convincing reminders of the spice trade that made ancient Persia—which included Baghdad—wealthy. So, too, is lamb with green peppercorns, a spice carried home from India in Arab caravans.

Bourek, cheese baked in pastry leaves and nestled on spinach, owes its crispy, paper-thin dough wrapper to the kitchens of the Byzantine empire and its vegetable base to Persia's early gardens. Some scholars maintain that the pastry leaves in question, known to the Greeks as *filo*, are yet another Persian invention; certainly one of the most popular *filo* preparations, *baklava*, is part of Persia's large repertoire of sweets—although, according to food writer Tess Mallos, it is also claimed by the Turks and Syrians.

• **Yaya**, 397 1/2 Eighth St, SF (415) 255-0909. Lunch Mon–Fri, dinner Mon–Sat. Major credit cards. Moderate.

Egyptian Fare at the Cairo Caf

Attif Hassan's career opened at the ripe old age of six when his father died. Grandfather Abraham, intent on providing a secure future for his progeny, bought little Hassan a restaurant in Cairo. Now he has a second in Marin County—and the singular distinction of running what may be the Bay Area's only Egyptian dinner house.

The **Cairo Café** in Mill Valley's

Ancient Egyptians transformed the staff of life: the hard, chewy breads of older cultures became lighter loaves, and the Egyptians discovered how to make dough rise.

Strawberry Village is a long, long way from the pyramids of Giza and Hassan's Liberty restaurant back on the Nile. Just beyond a freeway off-ramp, the tiny dining room is flanked by a Safeway and a busy laundromat.

But its menu is sure to make any Egyptian nostalgic. Hassan offers two versions of *ful midammis*, long-simmered fava beans that compose the national dish of his homeland. In cities and villages alike, vendors tend bubbling pots of these legumes, ready to sell them to passersby for breakfast, lunch, or just a snack. Hassan prepares the *ful* with onions, dill, and garlic, in the style of Cairo; and with *tahini* (sesame-seed paste), olive oil, and chopped fresh tomatoes, just as an Alexandrian would serve them.

Cairo Café's assortment of *mazza* (appetizers) is a quartet of specialties, each claimed by Egypt as well as several of its neighbors. The platter includes *felafel*, mashed chick-peas mixed with half a dozen spices, formed into balls, and then deep-fried; a mound of lemony, cumin-scented *hummus* (puréed chick-peas); and *baba ghanoug*, creamy, smoky eggplant blended with olive oil, sesame, garlic, and cumin.

Almost all Middle Easterners like to eat vegetables filled with savory mixtures, and Hassan obliges with stuffed grape leaves, cabbage leaves, bell peppers, and potatoes. An order of the latter brings a pair of tomato-sauce–topped spuds bulging with a mixture of ground beef, rice, parsley, and onions. The same tomato sauce covers baked catfish, a dish that alludes to the freshwater Nile carp and mullet that have nourished Cairenes for thousands of years.

Contemporary Cairo abounds in nightclubs, most located along the road to Giza, featuring internationally famous belly dancers. They cater to foreign businessmen and to Persian Gulf potentates in search of what's banned in Riyadh and Oman. Hassan is not to be outdone by the old country. On Friday and Saturday nights, diners share the café's close quarters with a hip-swinging belly dancer who juggles a pair of silver swords with impressive, if somewhat nerve-racking, finesse.

• **Cairo Café**, 104 Strawberry Village (Seminary Drive off-ramp), Mill Valley (415) 389-1101. Lunch and dinner Tues–Sun. MC, V. Moderate.

Palestine: Savories from the Levant

Palestinians are the premier shopkeepers, professionals—and emigrants—of the the Arab world. Their overseas ranks include the operators of nearly 500 Arab-owned small groceries in the Bay Area plus a number of fine deli restaurants that often provide the best—and least expensive—Middle Eastern delicacies around.

One such establishment is the **Cleopatra** in San Francisco's Sunset District, where you'll fine such Fertile Crescent classics as *foole*, *muttabal*, and *fatteh*. The first is a simmered bean dish that is the national repast of Egypt and a mainstay of the entire Levant, although no two cooks agree on its classic preparation. At the Cleopatra, its ingredients are whole and mashed favas, chick-peas, parsley, garlic, and a pool of robust olive oil. *Muttabal* will remind diners of *baba ghannouj*, the vegetarian specialty served

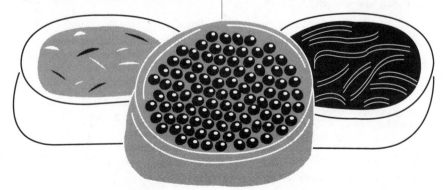

from Athens to Iraq; it is a rich mix of eggplant, sesame, and lemon.

But what Cleopatra really excels at is *fatteh*, a kind of Egyptian savory bread pudding that might have been the real reason Marc Antony tarried too long on the queen's barge. It combines *hummus* (crushed chick-peas, sesame paste, lemon, and garlic) with shreds of freshly baked pita, spiced ground lamb, and toasted pine nuts.

The family that runs Cleopatra has its origins in Jerusalem's Old City but mastered *fatteh* in Egypt. The tragedies of Middle Eastern war and politics sent family members, like so many Palestinians, across the Jordan and the lower Nile before they arrived in California. The menu also includes such all-American fare as a grilled cheese sandwich and steak and eggs, further proof that these victims of diaspora remain forever adaptable.

Palestinian Restaurants: The Top Choices

• **Cleopatra** In addition to the specialties described in the intro-duction to Palestinian food above, this modest Sunset District estab-lishment serves kabobs, *souvlakia*, and a large selection of Middle East-ern desserts. It also does a brisk take-out and catering business, with a whole stuffed roast lamb their specialty. 1755 Noriega St, SF (415)

753-5005. Lunch daily, dinner Mon–Sat. No credit cards. Inexpensive.

• **Just Like Home** If you enjoy the likes of *hummus*, *kibbeh* (balls of ground lamb and bulgur), and *tabbouleh*, you'll be right at home at Just Like Home. The kitchen prepares daily specials, including a number of *tagines*, or "stews," and a delicious dish that will spark the interest of every adventurous eater—spleen stuffed with onions, garlic, and spinach. Just Like Home is also a well-known producer of Middle Eastern baked goods and prepared foods, with products sold through-out the region. 1924 Irving St, SF (415) 681-3337. Lunch and dinner daily. No credit cards. Inexpensive.

• **Sunrise Deli and Café** Simply walk into this friendly place and feast your eyes on the front coun-ters, crammed with Levantine exot-ica. There's freshly made *felafel*, ready to be tucked into pita bread, and rounds of *lahmajoon*, the Arme-nian cousin to Italian pizza. The choice is difficult, but the beauti-fully garnished *shawarma* plate is always a good bet: a large portion of rotisserie-grilled marinated beef and lamb arrives surrounded with creamy *hummus* and warm pita. 2115 Irving St, SF (415) 664-8210. Lunch and dinner daily. No credit cards. Inexpensive.

Afghanistan: Echoes of a Nomadic World

T he bullies of history have not treated Afghanistan kindly. It was overrun by Alexander the Great on his way to India and robbed blind by Genghis Khan's Mongol hordes on their march to the Middle East. In more recent years, Afghans have been battling Russians and other Afghans, with many fleeing the country.

According to Mahmood Karzai, there are about 6000 Afghans now living in the Bay Area, mostly in Concord, Fremont, Hayward, and San Jose. Karzai and his wife, Wazhma, are the proprietors of the elegantly appointed, astonishingly inexpensive **Helmand** Restaurant, one of at least three Afghan dinner houses that opened in the Bay Area in the late 1980s. Named for the great Afghan river that winds northeast from the Iranian border, the Helmand offers dishes that reflect the extraordinary culinary mix that incorporates the cuisines of Central Asia, the Indian subcontinent, the Middle East, and sometimes beyond.

Indeed, one of this landlocked nation's—and Helmand's—best dishes may well have been left behind by the Mongols. A plate of *aushak*, boiled leek-filled wheat triangles topped with both a yogurt-mint sauce and a beef sauce, unmistakably recalls the dumplings of the Far East. Other echoes of the nomadic world resound in dishes like *chowpan seekh*, a grilled rack of lamb on paper-thin flat bread (a cousin of the *nane lavash* bread of Iran) that is an upscale takeoff on the Afghan *chowpan*, or shepherd's, campfire meal. One change that diners here will probably welcome is Helmand's considerable reduction of the oil and fat content present in

truly authentic Afghan dishes. A real *chowpan*, for example, values nothing more highly at the table than the fat from a sheep's tail.

The culinary links are further evident in such Afghan menu listings as *sabzy* (spinach) and *challow* (steamed rice). The former turns up in Iran as *sabzee*, although there it refers to a plate of fresh herbs, and in India as *sabzi*, where it is a dish of mixed vegetables. *Challow*, of course, has a direct cousin in Iran's famed rice dish called *chelo*. Thus, the links encompass language as well as kitchen traditions.

Today's émigrés are not the first Afghan colony in the Bay Area. Years ago, San Francisco boasted the New World's sole settlement of Pakhtuni Afghans, 200 strong, who lived as late as the 1950s in the Western Addition around Fulton and Webster. They worked mainly as peanut and ice cream vendors, and were said to be descendents of camel drivers brought to the Nevada deserts in a failed attempt to move silver out of the Mother Lode aboard dromedaries.

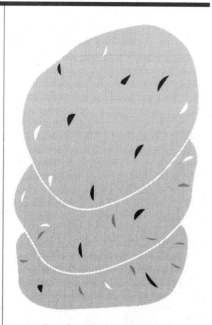

Afghan Restaurants: The Top Choices

• **Helmand** With the opening of Helmand in late 1989, Mahmood and Wazhma Karzai brought a real touch of class to San Francisco's Broadway strip. They also made it possible to sample an unusual cuisine seldom represented in these parts. Besides the kitchen glories discussed in this chapter's introduction, a couple of additional items are worth mentioning: *kaddo borawni*, baked pumpkin atop a garlic-flavored yogurt sauce, and *bowlawni*, leek-and-potato-filled pastries served with yogurt and mint, are a pair of first-rate appetizers. 430 Broadway St, SF (415) 362-0641. Lunch Mon–Fri, dinner Mon–Sat. Major credit cards. Moderate.

• **Kabul Afghan Cuisine** The cuisine of the South Bay Afghan community has an estimable representative in Najib Naimi. His Kabul Afghan Cuisine offers Afghanistan's classic dishes, including a trio of nicely charbroiled kabobs—the traditional beef and lamb, plus a nontraditional chicken. (Back in Khyber Pass country, the locals occasionally grill goat and camel as well.) The best way to eat these succulent chunks of meat is with pieces of *lawash*, the thin but hearty Afghan bread that Naimi supplies with every meal. 833 West El Camino Real, Sunnyvale (408) 245-4350. Lunch Mon–Fri, dinner daily. MC, V. Moderate.

Ethiopia: Complex Plates of Africa

A frica has not made a conscious impression on the world's palate. The operative word is "conscious": The customs of the West African kitchen were certainly transported, with generations of slaves, to the Americas, where they played their subtle part in the development of a New World melting pot that extends from the Mississippi basin through Brazil.

But what of old Africa? In the United States, the question was moot until recently, because there were

zations, complete with generations of master chefs and demanding diners. The proof lies in the traditions of Ethiopia, which offer as much refinement and time-honored complexity as many European cuisines (and a good deal more than some). For reasons that embrace both classic immigrant ambition and geopolitical tragedy, you can test that thesis today in the Bay Area.

The opportunity dates back to the establishment in the 1980s of a string of modest, comfortable Ethiopian

few indigenous Africans here, much less African cooks, to answer it. It was easy to take a culinary view that echoed the sentiments implied in the term "dark continent." By that logic, the light of gastronomy faded out somewhere in the Mediterranean, except for a few providential flashes of European influence.

The truth, of course, is that Africa cradled several brilliant ancient civili-

restaurants along the East Bay's Telegraph Avenue corridor—Sheba, the Café Eritrea d'Afrique, Asmara, and the Red Sea in Oakland, the Blue Nile in Berkeley. Eventually, they were joined by Fana in downtown Oakland and two slightly upscale San Francisco cousins, Nyala in the Civic Center and Rasselas in Pacific Heights. Others have appeared in the Haight and as far south as San Jose.

The people of Ethiopia were among the earliest cultivators of grains; some botanists believe that strains of wheat, barley, and sorghum were grown on the Abyssinian Plateau long before the time of Christ. The Ethiopian staple, however, is *teff*, a milletlike plant that exists only in the foothills of the Choke Mountains, where the Blue Nile begins its long journey to the Mediterranean. This grain is used to make *injera*, a unique fermented bread that is the focal point of the classic Ethiopian meal.

Not surprisingly, *teff* is hard to come by in America. But the diligent experimentation of "Mama" Kefaye, chief cook and presiding genius of Rasselas, has produced what a veteran Africa hand tells us is a good facsimile of the *injera* he recalls from Addis Ababa. The result is a soft, almost spongy round that looks rather like a large bubbled crêpe and vaguely resembles strong sourdough in taste. As diners soon learn, *injera* also serves as silverware and dinner plate.

"When you wanted to try the best in traditional African cooking," San Francisco teacher and former Peace Corps official Bob Siegel says, "Ethiopia was where you went. In most other places, dinner was a simple matter of steamed grain and some kind of sauce, or British or Portuguese colonial holdovers. There was nothing to compete with *doro wat* or *kitfo*."

Doro wat, which Ethiopians regard as their national dish, is a highly seasoned chicken stew. The word *wat*, in general, refers to a long-braised meat, fish, or vegetable, prepared with *berberé*, a potent mélange of chilies, ginger, nutmeg, cloves, and other spices. A milder alternative is the genre of stews known as *alecha*, which refrain from the use of *berberé*. Both are flavored with *niter kebbeh*, a spiced, clarified butter.

Dr. Samuel Johnson's popular romance *Rasselas*, the wholly invented tale of an Ethiopian prince, endowed Mama Kefaye's ancestors with the mannerisms and tastes of Georgian London. Imagine the shock of the doctor's contemporary, the Scot adventurer James Bruce, when he arrived in Addis in 1769 and found its real princes banqueting on raw beef rather than Yorkshire pudding. The dish that shocked Bruce was *kitfo*, an Ethiopian version of steak tartare bound with the omnipresent *niter kibbeh*, *berberé*, and extra chilies and accompanied by a kind of cottage cheese.

The menu at most Ethiopian restaurants is rounded out by extraordinary vegetable dishes, based primarily on lentils, chickpeas, and greens and drawing heavily upon the spice shelf. It is these dishes that inspired the vegetarian cuisine of Jamaica's Rastafarians, who view themselves as heirs to the culture of ancient Addis.

Whatever you order, the etiquette is the same: tear off a section of the *injera* "plate," wrap it around a portion of an entrée, and eat. In Ethiopia, honored guests are personally served by their hosts, in which case these edible bundles are known as *gurshas*, which translates loosely as "mouthfuls."

Some of the *gurshas* might well be called *boccacini*, since certain items on local Ethiopian menus are recognizably Italian—*lasagna al forno* and pasta with prawn sauce are often featured. Indeed, nearly every Bay Area Ethiopian restaurant offers *espresso*, *cappuccino* and *caffe latte*, culinary vestiges of Rome's imperialist past in Africa.

Many of the Bay Area's Ethiopian-born residents are from Eritrea, which was an Italian colony from 1890 to1941, when the British invaded. Eritrea's problems didn't end with the defeat of *il duce*. The coastal Eritreans never fully accepted their 1962 incorporation into greater Ethiopia, and for years a terrible civil war has raged in the region. The war seriously compounded the effects of the drought and famine of the 1980s, accelerating the flight of refugees to staggering proportions in the last few years.

According to Mulugenta Gerefa, executive director of the Ethiopian Refugee Resettlement Project in San Francisco, about 6000 Ethiopian citizens, mostly from Eritrea and the neighboring province of Tigre, are now in Northern California.

Ethiopian Restaurants: The Top Choices

• **Café Eritrea d'Afrique** Oakland's Café Eritrea d'Afrique, which accurately bills itself "a cozy place to be," is an all-purpose social club, information center, and coffeehouse for Ethiopian newcomers. It's one of the most pleasant, least costly places to eat in the East Bay. And as brothers Haile and Aerfaine Beyne, its owners, pointed out to us, its fine kitchen reflects yet another element in the cosmopolitan nature of Ethiopian cuisine. Instead of *wat* and *injera*, the Café Eritrea specialized in *couscous*, *shehan phool*, and *fatta*, respectively steamed semolina, seasoned fava beans, and an intensely garlic-flavored bread salad. They all come from the Arab north, home of Africa's second grand culinary tradition. 4069 Telegraph Ave, Berkeley (415) 547-4520. Lunch and dinner daily. No credit cards. Inexpensive.

• **Nyala** Just a few steps from the Civic Center, municipal bureaucrats and opera lovers alike know they can enjoy first-rate meals at the restaurant that first brought Ethiopian food to San Francisco. Like many establishments in Ethiopia itself, Nyala offers both African and Italian specialties. Among the highlights of its menu's offerings are an ample Ethiopian vegetarian feast with three separate braised "curries" and pasta with prawns in the style of the Italian colonial city of Asmara. 39 Grove St, SF (415) 861-0788. Lunch and dinner daily. Major credit cards. Moderate.

• **Rasselas** In a sideroom off one of the Bay Area's top jazz bars, extraordinary food from Africa's most extraordinary table is served to an enthusiastic clientele seven days a week. For more on this fine restaurant, see the introduction to this chapter. 2801 California St, SF (415) 567-5010. Lunch and dinner daily. Major credit cards. Moderate.

• **Red Sea** This charming restaurant is located right across the street from San Jose City Hall. Order its five-dish combination dinner and you will receive *injera* topped with sculpted mounds of pure exotica: *yebeg wat*, lamb chunks braised with onion; plus an *alecha* of chopped sirloin in a blend of spices; legumes with turmeric; puréed peas with tomatoes and chilies; and cabbage mixed with potatoes and carrots. If you like a lot of fire, add a dollop of *berberé*, the explosive red-pepper condiment that is the catsup of Ethiopia. Cap off the experience with a cup of spice-scented coffee and then marvel at the modest check. 684 North First St, San Jose (408) 993-1990. Lunch Mon–Fri, dinner Mon–Sat. MC, V. Moderate.

EUROPE

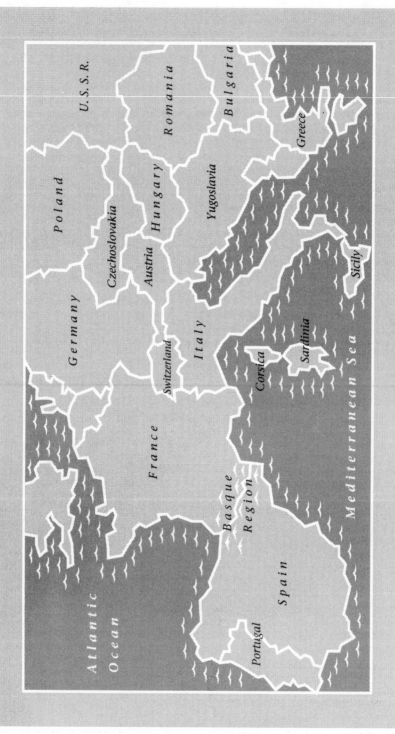

Italy: Immigrant's Feast

A century ago, San Francisco was almost, but not quite, the secret of Santa Flavia. It was begrudgingly shared with five other Italian villages and with certain fortunate neighborhoods in Genoa, Lucca, and Palermo.

The secret was this: A golden city lay 10,000 miles to the west, at the other end of the earth—a city more Italian in its promise than Italy itself. Its undulating rises and valleys were more sensuous than the Tuscan hills. The vineyards of its countryside were miraculously generous. Its coast outdid the spectacular Ligurian cliffs, and the bounty of its offshore shoals was the stuff of Sicil-ian fantasy. In that secret was born our lasting romance with Italian culture—and Italian food.

Word of San Francisco was carried into Genoa's harbor by returning sailors in the 1850s. It reached Lucca a few years into the '60s, skipped past Rome and Naples, reappeared in the mountains of Calabria a decade later, then lept the Messina Strait.

From each of the nine villages and neighborhoods where it rested, the secret drew people west. And without anyone, in America or in Italy, understanding quite how it had happened, San Francisco was forever changed. It had become

People and Their Neighborhoods

Where they live: Santa Clara County is home to roughly one in four Bay Area Italian-Americans, with another half of the population divided among San Francisco, San Mateo, and Alameda counties.

Where they gather: The epicenter of local Italian urban life is San Francisco's North Beach district. An echo of the region's rural Mediterranean past still lingers in the small Sonoma County town of Occidental, in the form of venerable restaurant-hotels that were built to serve Italian railroad workers.

Estimated Bay Area population: 185,000

more than an Italian dream. San Francisco was an Italian city.

Never mind that the Italian-born population here peaked at 27,000 in 1935, or that the Cantonese of North Beach now outnumber the district's combined total of Sicilians, Calabrians, Luccans, and Genoese roughly 50 to 1. Numbers have nothing to do with why San Francisco was Italian in 1935 and is still Italian today.

Sheer physical resemblance is part of it. On the wall of our office hangs a photograph of Terrasini, the Sicilian village from which the Vivianos made their way to America. Viewed from the Tyrrenhian shore, medieval Italian towns like Santa Flavia and Terrasini are jumbles of pastel cubes strewn along ochre ridges: a foreshadowing of Telegraph Hill and North Beach.

San Francisco, too, is largely a landscape of pastel cubes climbing ridges of ochre—visually, a city in the Italian manner.

In cultural terms—and at the table—it is the sum of dramatically conflicting parts, a reconciliation of historical Italian opposites. Other American cities had their Little Italys; but each was really a Little Naples or a Little Catania. Only in San Francisco was the chaotic, fragmented mosaic of Italian regionalism made whole.

San Francisco called to the people of Lucca: a breed of traveling salesmen so firmly attached to their peculiar profession that they seemed incapable of settling down. The Luccans and their relatives from the nearby village of Porcari held a global monopoly on the manufacture and sale of religious statuary. In San Francisco, they plied a different global trade: they are our best known merchants in olive oil and sausages.

San Francisco called to the Sicilians of Santa Flavia, Palermo, and Trabia: fishermen who loved and hated the sea. They loved it as their sustinence. They hated it because Sicilian history is a 3000-year tale of successive maritime invasions—from Phoenicia, Greece, Rome, Germany, Normandy, Spain, France, even, in 1943, from America. In San Francisco, they remained fishermen nonetheless, and are yet the mainstays of the wharf's pasta houses and crab stalls.

San Francisco called to the Calabrians of Verbicaro. Almost all farmers in the old country, rooted for a millenium in the unforgiving granite of the southern Apennines, they were the least likely voyagers and yet proved to be among the most resourceful. From a trickle in the 1880s, emigration from Verbicaro to San Francisco grew to a tidal wave in the '90s. In San Francisco, dispossessed Calabrian farmers began their careers as shoeshine boys and transformed themselves into lawyers and industrialists.

San Francisco called to the Ligurians of Genoa, Lorsica, and Sestri Levante. They are an adventurous people, the Ligurians, a people who have never resigned themselves to the supporting role—"Venice's lesser rival"—that popular history unfairly accords them. It was the Genoese who first gave the siren call of San Francisco its Mediterranean voice, settling here in the 1860s as produce vendors and introducing the marriage of Italian sensibilities and food that still makes the Bay Area one of America's favorite places to eat.

Much of that popularity flows from the fact that Northern California offers such a wealth of opportunities to discover genuine Italian cooking—to explore at the table the same complexity that marked the Bay Area's early Italian immigration.

In the simplest gastronomic terms, Italy is divided into north and south; one measure of a better Bay Area menu is that it carefully distinguishes the two. The division roughly follows what was once an ethnic border, the ancient demarcation between the Italy of the Etruscans, the predecessors to Caesar's Rome, and the Italy that was long ago an overseas territory of the Greeks. On a map, picture it as a line drawn across the Boot from a point halfway between Rome and Naples to the Adriatic coast halfway between Pescara and Ancona.

North of the line, cooks are far more likely to use butter, rice, and fresh egg pastas and to give veal, game, and other meats the central role in a meal. South of the line is the realm of olive oil and dried pastas, where the diet typically includes vegetables, fish, and some pork, and there is a blending of imported, sometimes exotic ingredients—figs, dates, almonds, pistachios, pine nuts, coriander, cumin—that reflect the 3000 years of foreign invasions.

Superb Italian dinner houses of both traditions are scattered all over the Bay Area, and our selections are not confined to North Beach. There are many other urban pockets where Italians settled in large numbers and established restaurants: San Francisco's Excelsior, Mission, and Marina districts; a stretch of Oakland's Telegraph Avenue near 50th Street; Jackson Street near 12th in San Jose.

Rural pockets were settled, too, by newcomers from outside the major immigrant Italian homes. Chief among them were the Ticinese of the Italian-speaking cantons of southern Switzerland, who founded the agricultural colony that is today remembered in the Italian-Swiss vineyards of Asti in Sonoma County.

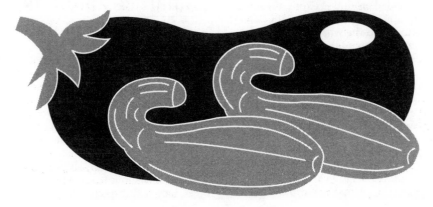

Other Italian-speakers—dairy farmers and poultry raisers in Sonoma and Marin—hailed from the mountains of Lombardy, north of Milan.

Genoese and Sicilians pioneered the fruit and canning industries of the Santa Clara Valley. To the north, in addition to the Ticinese, vintners from the Piedmont and elsewhere planted the barbera, zinfandel, pinot noir, and cabernet grapes that would eventually make the Napa and Sonoma area one·of the world's great wine producers.

Together with their cousins in the fishing fleets and urban *salumerie*, Italian farmers—unknown almost everywhere else in the United States—made it possible for the Bay Area to be Italian in ways that other cities could never equal.

Notwithstanding the breadth of "Italianness" in the Bay Area, it is clearly North Beach that holds chief title to our Italian legacy, anchored by the imposing towers of the Church of Saints Peter and Paul and enveloped in the irresistible fragrance of roasting coffee.

As a strictly topographic entity, North Beach is a gully defined by the west slope of Telegraph Hill and the north slope of Russian Hill. But as a repository of the century-old San Francisco Italian romance, it stretches much farther—from the site of the Genoese-dominated produce district that once sprawled around the foot of Pacific, on up the length of Columbus Avenue to the wharves where Sicilian fishermen launched their feluccas in search of sardines.

Memories are the *pane e burro* of the North Beach restaurant trade. Every weekend they fuel the practical sedans that roll off the freeway, ferrying Bay Area suburbanites—often children of the Beach's children—into the twilight of San Francisco's Italian past. San Franciscans and tourists alone aren't enough to stave off the night; without the

neighbors from Concord, San Mateo, and Cupertino, a lot of the old Beach would probably shut down.

Mostly, the suburban Bay Area patronizes establishments it has known for a generation or more: North Beach Restaurant and Fior d'Italia, Dante Benedetti's New Pisa and the U.S. Restaurant, the family-style kitchens of Green Valley, Capp's, and the Gold Spike.

In short, the commuters are missing the biggest new culinary wave to hit the Beach since Vincenzo Ravenna and Domenico Ghirardelli opened a pasta factory on Pacific Street in 1868. From Battery St to the wharf, a *risorgimento* is blooming.

The evidence has been building for several years now, spawning a dozen or so new restaurants. Northern and southern alike, what they all say is that Italian food is alive—and better than ever—in the West's most famous Little Italy.

Italian Restaurants: The Top Choices

• **Buca Giovanni** In his own quiet way, Tuscan-born Giovanni Leoni led San Francisco out of the tomato-sauce lake of standard Italian-American restaurants. From 1963 to 1981, he was the genius of Vanessi's restaurant on Broadway, where he introduced the dishes of his native Serchio Valley, a Tuscan garden basket not far from Lucca. Leoni's birthplace is known all over Italy for its wild mushrooms, olives, beans, wheat, corn, grapes, cheeses, and roast young lamb and rabbit blanketed with fresh herbs. Now Leoni has made Buca Giovanni the most genuine regional Italian restaurant in North Beach, if not in all the Bay Area. He is the master of a superb cellar trattoria, intimate and congenial rather than trendy. *Coniglio* aficionados return for Leoni's extraordinary rabbit dishes, which on some nights number as many as half a dozen different preparations. Or try his venison-stuffed *tortelloni*; lamb roast stuffed with mortadella, cheese, and herbs; and white beans with fresh sage. All the pastas are made on the premises. Leoni, who changes his menu frequently, is constantly pushing the boundaries of San Francisco taste toward the distant limits of Italian regional possibilities. 800 Greenwich St, SF (415) 776-7766. Dinner Mon–Sat. MC, V. Moderate.

• **Capp's Corner** In the old days, North Beach was known for its family-style restaurants, places where you could get a five-course dinner and some sturdy red wine and still afford a movie. Today, many of the old spots are gone and others have been eclipsed by a change in public appetite. But the venerable Capp's Corner continues to deliver five-courses that honor San Francisco's great Italian dining tradition. Soup, salad, pasta, and dessert accompany such main-course choices as roast beef, chicken cacciatore, and roast lamb. Lunch specials include *osso buco*, tripe with polenta, and clam risotto. The friendly, always-busy bar is an authentic slice of San Francisco neighborhood life. 1600 Powell St, SF (415) 989-2589. Lunch Mon–Fri. Dinner daily. MC, V. Moderate.

• **Ristorante Castellucci** José and Marta Castellucci, owners of this bright, tile-lined restaurant, are Italians from Argentina. Their menu combines an ambitious list of home-made, strictly Italian pastas with the expertly grilled meats that are as Argentine as the tango. Actually, we like to begin a Castellucci meal with neither, opting instead for a delicious platter of polenta, bathed in Gorgonzola sauce and garnished with spoonfuls of tomato sauce. Feather-light gnocchi comes in a light pesto sauce, or try the superb

> # Wine came to Italy even before the written word. Prehistoric tribes in the region made the drink "magically" from wild grapes thousands of years before the Romans.

frittura mista of sardines, calamari, and prawns. Then on to the Pampas for the Castelluccis' wonderful *churrasco à la chimichurri*, a substantial grilled veal steak that has been marinated in garlic, a bit of chili, parsley, olive oil, and vinegar. More memorable yet are the grilled house-made sausages served on a bed of garlicky spinach. 561 Columbus Ave, SF (415) 362-7727. Lunch and dinner Mon–Sat. Major credit cards. Moderate.

• **Enoteca Mastro** Marc Anthony

and Diane Mastro started out with a homey Albany *enoteca* (wine store), carrying *vini* from the Boot only. Soon after, they decided to match their interest in Italian vintages with their love for Italian food. The result is a delightfully casual trattoria whose tables share quarters with cases of wine. The menu, which changes daily, lists just five first courses, two or three pastas, and two main courses. The offerings aren't exactly *piatti dei paisani*, but they do favor the hearty over the fussy. If it's a *crostini* night, order up a plate; the trio of toast toppings includes chicken liver, mushrooms, and creamy blue cheese. The fettuccine with olive oil, garlic, basil, pine nuts, and Parmigiano-Reggiano is a first-class interpretation of the cuisine of Marc Anthony's ancestral homeland. As for wine, select any bottle from the store, pay the retail price, and its yours at the table for a modest corkage. 933 San Pablo Ave, Albany (415) 524-4822. Dinner Tues–Sat. MC, V. Moderate.

• **Gira Polli** The story of Gira Polli opens in the mid-'80s, when Michele and Norine Ferrante spotted the world's most spectacular rotisserie. The place was Palermo, Michele's hometown, and the rotisserie could roast 128 chickens simultaneously over a great fire of aromatic wood. The Ferrantes couldn't resist that oven, so they brought one home to San Francisco and started Gira Polli. They prepare the plump birds in true Sicilian fashion (rubbed with garlic and herbs and basted with olive oil) and each serving comes with roasted potatoes and bread rolls. Start the meal with tomatoes and fresh mozzarella; the cheese is made in the Ferrantes' own factory in the East Bay. 659 Union St, SF (415) 434-4472. Lunch and dinner Tues–Sun. MC, V. Inexpensive.

• **Grazie** Sicilian chefs often don't do justice to one of the great legacies of their cuisine: *pasta alla carrettiera*. Grazie boldly advertises three separate versions of this so-called cart-driver's pasta: with oil and garlic, garlic and anchovies, or tomatoes, garlic, and basil. The sauces are superb, rich with olive oil and generous with crisp golden garlic. Precede this southern Italian staple with an order of the also strictly Sicilian *caponata*. Take a seat at the counter so you can watch the chefs in action. 515 Columbus Ave, SF (415) 982-7400. Dinner daily. Major credit cards. Moderate.

• **Il Fornaio** A creation of restaurant entrepreneurial genius Larry Mindel, cofounder of Ciao and Prego. The look is classic Milanese and everything about the place says upscale. Everything, that is, except the astonishingly moderate prices. We are sold on the chard-and-spinach ravioli in a rich walnut sauce, potato gnocchi with a chicken-and-rabbit-flecked tomato sauce, and oak-roasted duck and flank steak. If you can handle it, the *valentino vestito di nuovo* is mind-boggling: a triple-layered terrine of Italian white chocolate, Swiss milk chocolate, and Belgian dark chocolate. The sweetest corners of Europe wrapped up in a single dessert. Levi's Plaza, 1265 Battery St, SF (415) 986-0100. Lunch and dinner daily. Major credit cards. Moderate.

• **La Pergola** Chef Giancarlo Bortolotti, son of the shores of Lago di Garda in Lombardy, has injected new life into this venerable Marina District establishment. The stylish but not stuffy dining room attracts native Italians who come to satisfy a craving for sautéed red and yellow peppers with garlic and anchovies, squash-filled *mezzaluna* in butter and sage, duck-and-rabbit-stuffed *tortelloni* in tomato sauce, and breast of duck in a grappa and juniper sauce. The menu, which changes with the season, also showcases southern Lombardy's renowned Arborio rice

in a "risotto of the day": sometimes it's a classic *pescatora*, with rock shrimp, clams, and scallops; other times it's a trendier dish that pairs the grain with smoked salmon. 2060 Chestnut St, SF (415) 563-4500. Dinner daily. Major credit cards. Moderate.

• **La Traviata** In the late '80s this beloved Mission District restaurant was destroyed by fire. Lost in the blaze, along with everything else, were the dozens of autographed photos of famous opera stars that lined the walls. La Traviata reopened in 1989, in the same location, and charming owner-maître d' Zef Shllaku is once again greeting guests in a dining room filled with the sounds and portraits of opera. His friends, the world's leading divas and *primo tenori*, have graciously restored his photo collection. The kitchen is also back in fine form, preparing velvety sweetbreads with a side of tortellini in cream sauce

and a full list of veal dishes. The gnocchi and the linguine with clams are also recommended. 2854 Mission St, SF (415) 282-0500. Dinner Tues–Sun. MC, V. Moderate.

• **Mamma Tina's** Here's the place to try the cuisine of a region seldom represented in America's Italian restaurants. Apulia-born chef-owner Rino Laneve and his wife, Tina, a Chinese woman raised in Germany, serve the most famous pasta of his southern Italian birthplace (and one of our favorites), *orecchiette alla pugliese*, "little ears" with rapini, garlic, and anchovies. The kitchen also perfectly understands two other southern classics, spaghetti with olive oil, garlic, and chili, and capellini with tomatoes and basil. Launch your meal here with a plate of imported prosciutto and mozzarella or garlicky roasted peppers. The cozy dining room oozes charm, with its monogrammed dinnerware, mosaic-tiled wall, and glowing fireplace. 1315 Grant Ave, SF (415) 391-4129. Dinner Tues–Sun. Major credit cards. Moderate.

• **Mescolanza** Opened in 1988 by Jeff Piccinini, scion of three generations of San Francisco Italian restaurateurs, and his wife, Toni, this very small, very friendly, and very professional trattoria introduced the glories of pasta and *pizzette* to a neighborhood better known for chow mein. Jeff's specialties would be wonderful even if they didn't fetch prices far below the city's *nuova cucina* norm. Each night, there are more than a dozen choices in the pasta category, including a generous *pansotti alla matriciana* (giant homemade ravioli with a fresh tomato and prosciutto sauce), and a selection of gnocchi, linguine, fettuccine, and green tortellini. The *pizzette*, which are baked on a terracotta slab, are surprisingly delicate, yet ample enough for a main course. Precede them with radicchio and imported Gorgonzola, dressed with an herb vinaigrette, and you'll think you're in the Piccininis' ancestral Lucca. 2221 Clement St, SF (415) 668-2221. Dinner Mon–Sat. MC, V. Moderate.

• **Paolo's** In the heart of downtown San Jose, this local institution has met the gastonomic challenges of the 1990s brilliantly under the Allen sisters, daughters of Sicilian-born founder Jack Allen. A longtime meet-

cards. Expensive.

•**Square One** Chef Joyce Goldstein's Square One is known for its highly innovative pan-Mediterranean menu. But once a week, Goldstein goes traditional and prepares the specialties of a single Italian region, often available nowhere else in America. The schedule is a godsend for lovers of Italian cuisine who are unwilling to settle

ing ground for South Bay notables, Paolo's revises its menu regularly, always offering new dishes to tempt the loyal clientele. You, too, will be tempted by wild-boar sausage, stuffed breast of rabbit, roast squab in wine sauce, pasta with prosciutto and mascarpone cheese, and fried polenta topped with *porcini*. Paolo's also presents an astonishing rendition of a southern Italian *tagliarini*, thin noodles tossed with exactly the right amount of virgin olive oil, black olives, whole crushed garlic, pine nuts, fresh basil, and imported Parmesan. And don't ignore the *dolci*: choose from among such wonderful possibilities as assorted *formaggi* accompanied by homemade fig bread and espresso-flavored *gelato*. 520 East Santa Clara St, San Jose (408) 294-2558. Lunch and dinner Mon–Sat. Major credit

for southern tomatoes or northern pesto. The specialties depend upon the region being featured, which could be anywhere from the Piedmont to the Veneto. Midway into the 1980s, author-chef Joyce Goldstein proclaimed this weekly ritual: Every Wednesday evening her kitchen—which stands almost precisely where Italian truck farmers from Half Moon Bay haggled over the price of artichokes at the turn of the century—would feature a different regional Italian cuisine. Since then, Goldstein's renowned Square One restaurant has completed a culinary journey from the tip of Sicily to the Brenner Pass, and has begun the circuit all over again. (See our Mediterranean chapter for more on the varied cuisine at Square One.) 190 Pacific Ave, SF (415) 788-1110. Regional Italian dinner on Wednesday evenings only. Major credit cards. Expensive.

• **Ristorante Venezia** Just blocks from the UC Berkeley campus, this mural-lined dining room is served by a kitchen that brooks no compromises on authenticity. Pastas are cooked to the Italian bite and taste, with sauces relying on intensity of flavor rather than volume. A good example is the outstanding *spaghetti alla puttanesca*, "pasta as cooked by a hooker," a dish that regularly suffers in Italian restaurant kitchens in America. Whether or not *puttanesca* did originate in the red-light district, Venezia's version certainly has the earthiness of street life, imparted by a sauce of chili peppers, fresh tomatoes, sharp black olives, and garlic. The mixed grill of duck breast, liver, and sausage and the *cassata alla siciliana* are also good bets. Go to Venezia on a Tuesday night and hear live opera while you dine. 1902 University Ave, Berkeley (415) 644-3093. Dinner Tues–Sun. MC, V. Moderate.

• **Thelma's Culinaria Italiana** Thelma's may not sound Italian, but at Thelma's Culinaria Italiana on Willow Street, that's a matter of romantic happenstance. "My father was French and my mother Italian," says the proprietor. "Unfortunately for me, his first girlfriend was a Scandinavian named Thelma, and my father absolutely loved the name. So I was stuck with it." Thelma runs a one-woman trattoria in which she often triples as chef, waitress, and maître d'. Meals are served by reservation only, made 24 hours in advance, *grazie*. The menu is whatever inspires Thelma Seine that day. That could be chicken and veal cannelloni with a cream sauce flecked with leeks, or *osso buco* with a side of fettuccine in butter, Parmesan, and parsley. The ambience is country European—flowers, sturdy chairs, bright oil paintings—packed into a room that accommodates 25 diners. 895 Willow St, San Jose (408) 993-1607. Lunch Tues–Fri, dinner Tues–Sat. No credit cards. Moderate.

• **U. S. Restaurant** The definitive San Francisco Italian-American restaurant, nearly half a century young, and as honest and homey as a meal at Nonna's. You can start your day here with a bona fide North Beach Italian breakfast: two eggs, three slabs of spicy Sicilian sausage, a pile of crisp, golden fried potatoes, and a stack of sourdough bread. Later in the day sit down to genuine old-country fare: *coteghino* sausage with beans, garlicky beef pot roast, and tripe with polenta. The U.S. draws a jovial crowd of regulars—cops on the beat alongside devotees from neighboring Chinatown—and warmly welcomed newcomers alike. 431 Columbus Ave, SF (415) 362-6251. Breakfast, lunch, and dinner Tues–Sat. No credit cards. Inexpensive.

Italian Cafés

In Italy, the authentic coffee bar is closely related to the service station. There are no chairs or tables, just a counter with a hissing *caffettiera* on top. The client pulls up at the bar, a short and powerful shot of fuel is drawn from the machine and injected into the tank, and that's that. None of the chitchat, reading, and espresso nursing many of us tend to associate with the Italian café.

Still, an authentically Italian sense of *dolce far niente* is indeed imparted by the kind of fantasy café we'd like the Italians to have invented. North Beach fills that bill as well as any place in the United States, with an array of Italian-owned establishments where you can *far niente* to your heart's content.

In the Bay Area, where coffee bars must number into three figures, there's no point in listing them all.

But here are the best in our most Italian district, each serving sound espresso and many a good bit more.

• **Bohemian Cigar Store** The oldest coffee bar in North Beach, presided over by the children of Mario Crismani, a former Trieste policeman who bought this circa 1930s card club and smoke shop in 1971. Famous for its meatball sandwiches and ricotta cheesecake. 566 Columbus Ave (415) 362-5036.

• **Café Europa** In the mid-1980s, the *signore* Groppi and Tufo retired from the bread business—for years, they were the next best thing to the *pane* at North Beach's Italian-French and Cuneo bakeries—and almost immediately took over the then-Hungarian-managed Europa. Espresso spoken perfectly here, along with rich pastries, polenta, and stuffed pastas. 362 Columbus Ave (415) 986-8177.

• **Caffè Gaetano** Former auto mechanic Gaetano Schiavone used to work his uncle's *caffè* in Napoli. Ask him for a slice of his famous sausage-zucchini frittata. 348 Columbus Ave (415) 397-0435.

• **Caffè Greco** Okay, the owner is Lebanese, but Hanna Suleiman is so devoted to things Italian that we didn't have the heart to skip his immensely popular Columbus Avenue meeting place. He even imports roasted coffee from Italy. 423 Columbus Ave (415) 397-6261.

• **Café Italia** The pool table and soccer memorabilia mark this as the most authentically Italian-patronized of all coffeehouses in San Francisco. A true neighborhood joint in the best sense. 708 Vallejo St (415)

Cioppino: Seafood Mystery

Ask any San Franciscan to identify the city's number one Italian seafood specialty, and the answer is almost sure to be "cioppino." But ask where to eat it, and everyone looks blank. "We have it once in a while," a maître d' at a fancy downtown joint told us when we called for advice. "But I really don't know where you can get it on a regular basis—or where it won't be cooked beyond recognition."

Some experts say this maritime stew was created by the Sicilians who made the crab industry tick here for decades; the legend is that they threw unsold crab and rock cod chunks into a pot at the end of the day, calling out "chip in" to their colleagues. Others pinpoint the recipe's invention to Giuseppe Buzzaro, a Genoese who came to San Francisco during the gold rush, and claim that the name is derived from the Genoese dialect word, *ciuppin*, for seafood stew; still others believe it is an elaboration on the famed *cacciucco* of Tuscany.

Whatever its origin, cioppino has been cherished by generations of San Francisco Italians—yet it appears to be losing its once central role in the local diet.

Fortunately, it holds on in the very place in which San Francisco restaurant dining was born in the year gold was discovered at Sutter's Mill. Surrounded by three-piece suits, and hovered over by a bevy of charming waiters in impeccably white aprons, you can enjoy delicious cioppino in the heart of the Financial District at the **Tadich Grill** (240 California St, 415/391-2372). Its proprietors may be Yugoslavs—the Buich family—but every Bay Area Italophile owes them a debt of gratitude.

362-9315.

•**Caffè Malvina** Franco Bruno, a native of Trapani on Sicily's west coast, arrived in San Francisco in the mid-'50s, took a job selling espresso machines, and has never looked back. One of the best-liked men in North Beach, ensconced in a sunny room with a classic view of Washington Square. Memorable pizzas, salads, and sandwiches. 1600 Stockton St (415) 391-1290.

•**Caffè Puccini** The owner, Lino Simonetti, is a scion of the great composer's summer home, Torre del Lago. Opera-poster decor, an aria-programmed jukebox, and generously packed *focaccetta* sandwiches. 411 Columbus Ave (415) 989-7033.

• **Caffè Roma** Sergio Azzollini is a North Beach booster whose costly renovation of this 1920s bakery— complete with lovely frescoes— played a key role in the late 1970s *risorgimento* of the neighborhood. His brother-in-law, a native of Bari, prepares pastas in the style of Apulia. Caffé Roma's coffee roasting operation is just down the block. 414 Columbus Ave (415) 391-8584.

• **Caffè Tosca** Not really a coffee-house, but so firmly imbedded in the heart of North Beach since 1919 that it can't be omitted. A jukebox that plays Verdi, Puccini, and Bellini highlights an atmospheric bar where the house drink is cappuccino spiked with brandy. 242 Columbus Ave (415) 391-1244.

• **Caffè Trieste** Celebrated for its Saturdays, when opera singers and musicians serenade the crowd. The Giotta family, Trieste's owners for more than a generation, were coffee purveyors to the beats and still offer fine espresso and house-roasted blends. 601 Vallejo St (415) 392-6739.

• **Pasticceria Dianda** An old favorite in a new location. At the turn of the century, Dianda's Italian American Pastry Company opened for business in the Mission, to serve the Italians who migrated there from

North Beach. Now the Dianda family has opened a café right in the center of North Beach. *Panforte* has never tasted better. Green and Columbus Ave (415) 989-7745.

• **Gino's Gelateria** One corner of Columbus at Filbert belongs to Washington Square. The other three are held, respectively, by Gino's Cafferata restaurant, Gino's garage, and Gino's Gelateria— proprietor, Gino Biradelli. The superb gelato is made on the spot; chase it with an *espresso romano*. 701 Columbus Ave (415) 981-4664.

•**Savoy Tivoli** One of the few places in San Francisco where an espresso can be sipped al fresco. More beat than Boot, this is said to be the site at which Allen Ginsberg first howled out "Howl." 1434 Grant Ave (415) 362-7023.

Pizza

Hard though it may be to believe, there was no pizza in San Francisco before 1935, when legend has it that Eduardo Cantalupo turned out the first local pie in a wood-burning oven at his Lupo's restaurant. By the 1950s, pizza was everywhere; but in its evolved U.S. identity, it bore little resemblance to the namesake item that Eduardo ate in his native Napoli, pizza's 18th-century birthplace. (Vincenzo Buonassisi, a leading Italian-food authority, notes that a version of pizza actually dates back to the Romans; what the late 1700s added was tomato.)

Instead of the personal-sized serving—covered with a modest dash of sauce and minimal amounts of cheese and other toppings—that Neapolitans knew, US pizza was baked in stainless-steel ovens and had taken on Eisenhower-era American dimensions. It was as big, mass-produced, and loaded with options as a '57 Olds.

And so it remained until the past decade, when the traditionalist and nouvelle crazes swept everything edible before them. The traditionalists wanted pizza—or the folded-over model called calzone—just as Eduardo's cousins still eat them in Naples today: a thin, crisp crust no larger than a dinner plate, a homemade fresh tomato sauce, a sprinkling of herbs, good mozzarella, and perhaps anchovies or sausage. Whenever possible, it would be baked, as in its ancestral Campania, in a wood-fired brick oven. The nouvelle types wanted essentially the same thing, except for the addition of such upscale condiments as escargot, smoked salmon, and onion confit.

Not everyone welcomed these trends, which insulted longtime American-pizza lovers and more or less doubled the cost of the meal. A Neapolitan-born expert, the redoubtable Guido Polverino of San Jose's celebrated Guido's Pizzeria, even argues that the true Naples pie is impossible here: "The climate in the Bay Area is different from the Campania," he notes. "The dough behaves differently, and the sauce can't taste the same with the local water, air, and ingredients."

Nonetheless, wood-fired ovens and personal pizzas have been proliferating from one end of the Bay Area to the other. At the same time, the American-style pizza—and its subset, the thick Chicago-style deep-dish pie, sometimes known as Sicilian pizza—has hardly thrown in the towel. Lately, its production has been embraced by pizza-baking immigrants from the Italian community of Brazil. (Some of them man the kitchens of the Brazilian-owned De Paula's, Little Rio, Diamond Pizza, and North Beach Pizza in San Francisco, and Nino's in Berkeley.)

All of which is to say that every sort of pizza still has its Bay Area advocates and that ethnic authenticity in this matter lies in the mind of the diner. Lupo's, incidentally, is still around, using a wood-burning oven in its venerable Kearny Street trattoria; its name today is Tommaso, in honor of the late Tommy Chin, the Chinese San Franciscan who was the Cantalupo family's head chef for many years.

All three pizza forms are widely available in the Bay Area, and most folks have their own well-established parlor affiliations. A select list of our favorite pizza options in each category follows.

American Pizzas

• **Guido's Pizzeria and Restaurant**
Guido Polverino has been San Jose's best-known pizza vendor for more than a quarter of a century. His is a red-and-white-checkered tablecloth

kind of place, with pies—three-quarter-inch-thick crusts blanketed with whole-milk mozzarella and punctuated with spicy sausage—that respect both American pizza customs and a traditional Italian spirit. Guido, by the way, is also the undisputed king of South Bay Italian-America soccer; his team, Italia USA, is one of brightest stars of the Peninsula Soccer League. 1372 South Bascom Ave, San Jose (415) 293-6969. Lunch and dinner daily. MC, V.

• **Tommaso Famous Pizzeria** The birthplace of San Francisco pizza, where pies have been baked in the landmark wood-burning oven for more than half a century. The crust is what every first-rate American-style pizza deserves—thin, crisp, and ever-so-lightly charred. Choose from almost a score of toppings or opt for one of the kitchen's preset combos. 1042 Kearny St, SF (415) 398-9696. Dinner Tues–Sun.

Neapolitan Pizzas

• **Prego Ristorante** Those who haunt Union Street frequent the upscale Prego, where individual crisp-crusted pizzas and their cousins, the calzone clan, arrive fresh from the wood-burning brick oven. The cast of pies numbers nine, and the topping ingredients include sausage, pepperoni, prosciutto, smoked mozzarella, eggplant, artichokes, and even shrimp. 2000 Union St, SF (415) 563-3305. Lunch and dinner daily.

• **Spuntino Italian Express** Verdi lovers who know that arias sound sweetest from the Opera House balcony also know to head across the street for authentic Italian pies. Spuntino's classic pizza Margherita, topped with mozzarella, tomato, and basil, is perfect before *La Traviata*. *Quattro stagioni*—"four seasons"—is for those who want a quartet of distinct tastes in one pie hearty

enough to sustain them through the *Ring.* 524 Van Ness Ave, SF (415) 861-7772. Lunch and dinner daily.

Nouvelle Pizzas

• **Pauline's Pizza Pie** Many local pizza historians credit this place with baking San Francisco's first pesto-topped pie. A favorite for years with Mission District locals, Pauline's is a small, friendly spot with a repertoire of more than two dozen toppings. You might find andouille sausage featured one evening and eggplant and goat cheese on another. Everything, fortunately, tastes good on Pauline's thin, crisp crust. 260 Valencia St, SF (415) 552-2050. Dinner Wed–Sat.

• **Ruby's Gourmet Pizza** For those into cornmeal crusts, Ruby's turns out the very best in the Bay Area. The chewy yet crunchy base is a palette for a cupboardful of trendy (and delicious) ingredients, from Gorgonzola, duck sausage, and smoked chicken to leeks and sun-dried tomatoes. The board changes daily, with three special and three regular pies. Don't have time to sit down? Ruby's will sell you the pies half-baked to slip into your home oven. 489 Third St, SF (415) 541-0795. Lunch Mon–Sat, dinner Mon–Sun.

Italian Delis and Bakeries

On the theory that packaged food is to food what the sunlamp is to sunshine, we've spent a lot of time hunting for gaps in the cellophane fog that clouds the modern American table. We are happy to report that one of the largest such gaps in the country is still centered roughly over Washington Square in San Francisco's North Beach.

Within three short blocks, Bay

Area residents can choose from a staggering array of traditional Italian sausages, breads, prepared vegetables, pastries, and other delights—all made in the shopkeepers' backrooms. It's one of our city's grandest eccentricities: Oblivious to the power of mass production, the heroic *fabbricante* of North Beach fight on against an industrial monster that has gobbled up neighborhood bakers and sausage makers across the United States.

Begin at the **Liguria Bakery** (1700 Stockton St, 421-3786), kitty-corner from the square's northeastern angle. Don't be surprised if you hear *mercis* exchanged on the premises; co-owner August Azzalini was born to Venetian immigrants in France, and one of the store's habitués is a retired Swiss boxer who had his nose definitively broken in a Paris 10-rounder. The Liguria's ovens, however, are dedicated to a Genoese classic—the fabulous *focaccia* of Azzalini partners George and Mike Soracco. It is a raised dough, mixed and kneaded to ancient specifications, then topped either with olive oil and salt, olive oil and scallions, raisins, or tomato sauce, and baked in rectangular sheets. Some people describe *focaccia* as "pizza bread," which in Liguria's case, is a little like referring to caviar as fish eggs.

Scallion *focaccia*, especially, is made to be stuffed. "What with?" can be a difficult question for the indecisive, however. In North Beach, the possibilities are endless. Let us opt, therefore, for the nearly impossible: cured meats that simply aren't supposed to exist in neighborhood versions anymore.

"Sure we hang our own prosciutto," Vic Candia declared when we tried our luck at the venerable **Iacopi** butcher shop (Grant Ave at Union St, 421-0757), founded in 1896. Bruno Iacopi, son of the founder, passed on last year, but nephew Leo Rossi, his wife, Darlene, and Vic still press and cure raw ham in the time-honored way, aging it on the premises. Sliced paper-thin by Vic, who was born and raised in these streets, it's everything prosciutto ought to be—rosy, translucent, and just salty enough. Balance it with a slice of Darlene's basil-and-sun-dried-tomato cheese *torta*.

For years, we've been devoted

clients of the **Molinari Delicatessen** (373 Columbus Ave, 421-2337). One of the reasons is their *zampino*, which is a native of Modena, where it's usually called *zampone*. Lots of lunch meat history there: Modena was already celebrated for its porkers in Pliny's time (circa 90 B.C.), and an early Renaissance poet called the town "the fecund mother of sausages." *Zampone* is by all accounts her favorite son. Originally, it was a cured, stuffed pig's foreleg; today in Modena, as on Columbus Avenue, the actual leg has given way to a pork-skin casing.

Molinari's is surely among the classiest, most irresistible *salumerie* this side of the Italian Alps. That's where young Joe Mastrelli's grandfather, the Molinari patriarch, hailed from and where he learned how to make *bresaola*. Joe describes this specialty as "air-dried" beef; seasoned to perfection by the Mastrellis, it is not to be confused with the jerky carried in hikers' backpacks. The best way to eat it is with a little olive oil drizzled on top.

Focaccia is hardly the sole frame for these masterpieces. The **Italian-French Bakery** (1501 Grant Ave, 421-3796), founded in 1880, offers some superb alternatives: a heavy round loaf of Sicilian bread that resembles the French peasant's *pain de campagne*, and *gingelana*, which is slightly sweet, covered with sesame seeds, and baked in a ring.

Dessert can be secured in an establishment that gives new meaning to the American melting pot. Not only is the **Victoria** pastry shop (1362 Stockton St, 781-2015) perched on the edge of Chinatown, it is owned jointly by a Genoese, a Tuscan, and a Sicilian. Veteran Vinnie Solloni—*she's* from near Ravenna—waits patiently while we pace before her display cases trying to make a selection. With almond torte, cannoli, anise cookies, pine-nut macaroons, and *pasti-*

ciotti (a ricotta-stuffed shortbread) to consider, it's never easy.

Afterward, to Luciano Repetto's **Graffeo** coffee company (733 Columbus Ave, 986-2420) for some of the corniest jokes in the world. The coffee, of course, can't be consumed there, but Mario's **Bohemian Cigar Store** (566 Columbus, 362-0536) is only a few steps away, brewing potent espresso from Luciano's dark roast.

More of the Best Delis and Bakeries

• **Danilo Bakery** Some of the best baked goods in North Beach are found on the shelves of this small shop, where the taste and ambience is pure small-town Italian. It will be hard to choose from among the crisp breadsticks, sweet lattice-crowned pie filled with Swiss chard and topped with pine nuts, *focaccia*, *panettone*, and sturdy *pane* baked in the shape of a hand. 516 Green St, SF (415) 989-1806.

• **Dianda's Italian American Pastry Co.** The Dianda family, which hails from Lucca, took over this turn-of-the century *pasticceria* in the early '60s. Located in the heart of San Francisco's largest Latino neighborhood, Dianda offers scores of extraordinary sweets, including anise-flavored *biscotti* and coconut macaroons, *zuppa inglese*, and *torta di mandorla*. The cordial staff handles requests in English, Italian, and Spanish. 2883 Mission St, SF (415) 647-5469.

• **Florence Italian Deli and Ravioli Factory** As with so many Italian delis in San Francisco, Florence is also in the business of making raviolis. Stop here for polenta and *ceci* beans in bulk, and take advantage of what seems to be a continuous sale on imported olive oil. 1412 Stockton St, SF (415) 421-6170.

> Never underestimate the power of pasta. Italy's other favorite passion, Sophia Loren, once said, "Everything you see I owe to spaghetti."

• **Genova Delicatessen and Ravioli Factory** A tightly packed little shop carrying fresh pasta, a wide assortment of canned and packaged Italian ingredients, cured meats and cheeses, homemade frittata, and almost everything else you need for a true Italian feast. They can even outfit you with a pasta machine. 4937 Telegraph Ave, Oakland (415) 652-7401.

• **Il Fornaio Bakery** This lovely sun-splashed bakery offers wonderful regional breads rarely seen outside of Italy, plus pizza, pastries, and cookies. You'll also be tempted by their ricotta-stuffed raviolis and assortment of flavored whole egg pastas. 2298 Union St, SF

(415) 563-3400.

• **Lucca Delicatessen** Located in the Marina, one of San Francisco's oldest Italian neighborhoods, Lucca turns out handmade raviolis, roast chickens redolent with herbs, and a host of salads and other cold dishes, including delicious pickled pigs' feet. Unlike many of its competitors, this shop is open on Sundays. 2120 Chestnut St, SF (415) 921-7873.

• **Lucca Ravioli Company** No relation to the previous entry; the name is the same only because so many Luccans went into the delicatessen business. Currently run by the amiable Michael Feno, this wonderful Mission District institution has been in operation since the 1920s, when Italian was commonly heard in the neighborhood. All of the staples are here, from dried pasta and olive oil to anchovies and imported *prosciutto crudo*. The raviolis come in two flavors, cheese and meat. This place has among the best deli prices in the Bay Area. 1100 Valencia St, SF (415) 647-5581.

• **Panelli Brothers Delicatessen** There's always a line at lunchtime for Panelli's sandwiches, generously stuffed with salami, mortadella, *coppa*, or whatever you like. Salt cod is displayed in wooden crates, and dried pasta in countless shapes lines the shelves. 1419 Stockton St, SF (415) 421-2541.

• **Viviande Porta Via** Once you're inside this bountiful *salumeria*, you can gaze right into the kitchen. That's where the action is, where everything from *caponata* and *insalta di calamari* to *crostini* and *amaretti* are made. Proprietor Carlo Middione watches over the preparation of fresh pork sausages, stuffed veal breast, *pizza rustica*, and much more. There is also a carefully chosen selection of cheeses and cured meats. A small dining area accommodates a regular lunchtime crowd. 2125 Fillmore St, SF (415) 346-4430.

Basque: Classics from the Shepherd's Table

We know exactly what you'll think when we say the **Basque Cultural Center**—on Railroad Avenue in South San Francisco!—is one of the most authentic French restaurants in the Bay Area. You'll

3000 fellow Bay Area Basques to manage a bona fide French Basque provincial dining room in their center. The result is a warm, jovial establishment that looks, sounds—and cooks—just like its counterparts in Marticorena's native

imagine folding chairs and card tables, a cavernous hall, and heaping amounts of overstewed beef. You'll think we don't know the difference between *carré d'agneau persillé* and tuna casserole.

Wrong, *nos amis*. We know the difference. More important, so does Louis Marticorena, a true son of *les Pyrénées* and formerly the head chef at La Bourgogne. Marticorena could have retired after San Francisco's most famous French restaurant closed in the mid-1980s. Instead, he accepted a mandate from his

Bayonne countryside.

Bayonne, the gastronomic center of the Basque region, owes much of its culinary reputation to its superb charcuterie. Marticorena's lunch menu recognizes the legacy with a pair of grilled *boudin noir* atop a rich tomato purée; a stack of classically skinny, perfectly crisp french fries stands alongside. The sausages themselves come from those celebrated San Francisco charcutiers Marcel et Henri. Equally satisfying is a plate of broiled lamb chops, done medium-rare as requested.

The Cultural Center is the chief landmark of a Basque world in the Bay Area that was once focused around a string of boardinghouses and restaurants on and around Broadway in North Beach. It was born with the arrival of shepherds from the French-Spanish border regions, who drove flocks in the San Joaquin Valley and in Nevada. The Basques first came during the gold rush; later they settled throughout the western states, where they became the premier herders. In 1951, when a lack of shepherds threatened the health of the West's sizable sheep-ranching industry, Congress enacted legislation that allowed Basques to enter the United States with permanent-resident status.

Today, that memory lives on in a few establishments in the Bay Area, notably Des Alpes Restaurant and the Basque Hotel. At these and other Basque haunts scattered across central California, the dining is usually family-style, with huge tureens of soup arriving at the table, followed by salad, two entrées, and dessert. The Cultural Center is an exception in that it employs an à la carte menu.

Basque Restaurants: The Top Choices

• **Basque Cultural Center** Evenings at the Basque Cultural Center (see chapter introduction) feature a prix-fixe menu that changes daily, along with à la carte selections. But the best time to come to the center is Sunday afternoon at one o'clock sharp. That's when Basque families sit down to a five-course meal for, at this writing, just $14 per person, including tax, tip, and all the wine you can drink. You'll leave convinced that San Bruno Mountain is a peak in the Pyrénées. 599 Railroad Ave, South San Francisco (415) 583-8091. Lunch Tues-Fri and Sun, dinner Tues–Sun. MC, V. Moderate.

• **Basque Hotel** Standing on picturesque Romolo Place on the steep southern slope of Telegraph Hill, this hotel could be the scene of a peasant feast in southern France, circa 1850. The dinner guests are seated at long communal tables, which are soon groaning under platters of such things as roast lamb, duck confit, lamb chops, and the celebrated Basque classic braised chicken with rice, each part of a five-course meal. The choices depend on the night of your visit, and the prices, for European food, are sensationally low. 15 Romolo Place, SF (415) 788-9404. Dinner Tues–Sun. No credit cards. Moderate.

• **Des Alpes Restaurant** From the moment you walk into the *intime* bar that fronts Des Alpes to your first stab at the thin and perfectly crisp *pommes frites*, you'll know you're in the presence of restaurateurs who realize that "French" means more than creamy sauces. For years, this was a retreat for folks who didn't believe in retreat—the anti-Fascist vets of the Spanish Civil War's Basque legion. Among the best main courses (check with the staff to learn what two dishes are being served that night) are leg of lamb, calf's sweetbreads, panfried sand dabs, and a casserole of clams with rice. 732 Broadway St, SF (415) 391-4249. Dinner Tues–Sun. MC, V. Moderate.

Mediterranean: Tastes from Shores that Mirror Our Own

The problem of defining ethnicity shadows every kitchen in which nationality is chosen rather than inherited, or in which the menu reflects something other than an orthodox ethnic identity. Italian is Italian. Period. But in a Bay Area where scores of Italian kitchens have Chinese or Mexican staffs and where distinctly Anglo chefs have won fame cooking Chinese meals, ethnicity is a complicated matter.

Immigration, among other things, can wreak havoc with ethnic identity, introducing new ideas as well as genes to produce something different but still quite "authentic." Sicily, the homeland of millions of Italian-Americans, is the textbook case. As a matter of cultural habit and genetic composition, its ethnicity was one thing a millenium ago, when the root influences were Greek and Roman, and quite another thing after the Arabs, Normans, and Spaniards swept through.

About all that remains fixed in this world of variables is geography. Ethnicity is what you want it to be and what the local conditions will permit. It is a commonplace that Northern California is broadly "Mediterranean" in its look and feel. And so too, increasingly, are its European menus. They take it for granted that dinner life in this most Mediterranean corner of North America should bear some distinct relation to the presence of olive groves and vineyards, citrus orchards and artichoke fields, the sun and the sea.

Together, the land and the Pacific exposure of these shores make for a kind of dialectic that gives fresher meaning to the overused term East-West. The two longitudinal hemispheres have for several years now been engaged in a good-natured tussle at the table for our ethnic soul. Its eventual result, we'd like to believe, will be a novel Northern California synthesis—a new identity in its own right, one part pan-Asian and one part pan-Mediterranean.

It's our destiny, in a way, by the singular virtue of a Bay Area population that includes 1.2 million Asians, settled into a geography that mirrors the charms of Valencia, the Levant, and Palermo. No other place on earth can lay a natural claim to it.

The ever-popular Lalime's in Berkeley stands nicely for the Mediterranean in this dialectic. But it's scarcely the sole example; Lalime's is part of the larger Bay Area pan-Mediterranean world so delightfully bordered by the likes of Joyce Goldstein's Square One and Judy Rodgers' Zuni, to name just two examples.

A stellar first course at Lalime's generously draws upon staples of the Mediterranean kitchen. A scoop of the gutsy French olive paste called *tapenade*, and Italian *bruschetta* (toast) to spread it on, are joined by a fragrant baked onion, a whole head of roasted garlic, and rosemary-and-lemon-marinated French, Greek, and Italian olives. A pile of calamari, seared on an iron plate and bathed in lemon and parsley, conjures up the image of an al fresco meal in Sicily.

One might just as easily imagine sitting down to Lalime's excellent juniper-berry–seasoned pork chop on a bed of creamy cannellini beans somewhere in the countryside between Provence and Tuscany.

Monkfish roasted in a cumin-laced crust and served in a hearty Catalán sauce, thick with orange chunks, seems to embrace not only Spain, but the whole Mediterranean basin.

In the true spirit of Bay Area–style ethnicity, this kitchen is operated by an Armenian from Lebanon, Haig Krikorian, and his French-Canadian wife, Cynthia Lalime.

Mediterranean Restaurants: The Top Choices

• **Bay Wolf** In recent years, Bay Wolf has inaugurated an ambitious approach to Mediterranean cooking. Instead of combining a little of this and a little of that on the same menu, the restaurant features the foods and wines of a distinct region—Tuscany, North Africa, Provence—for a week or two, and then moves on to a new area. One Tuscan menu, for example, included penne with favas, peas, asparagus, and bacon; sautéed sea bass with olives, leeks, and sun-dried tomatoes; and roast lamb with eggplant-Parmesan gratin and a red wine–thyme sauce. Generic Mediterranean dishes appeared, too, such as a country-style terrine of duck drizzled with mustard, and goat-cheese salad. 3853 Piedmont Ave, Oakland (415) 655-6004. Lunch Mon–Fri, dinner daily. MC, V. Moderate.

• **Lalime's** In 1989, Lalime's moved from its original small storefront location on Albany's Solano Avenue to a bright, light-filled, two-story space on Gilman Street in Berkeley. It continues to produce wonderful plates that reflect a pan-Mediterranean culinary sensibility. Some examples of the Lalime's chefs' substantial repertoire are described in our introduction to this chapter. The menu changes monthly and Monday nights are reserved for prix-fixe dinners that usually feature the food of a single southern European region. 1329 Gilman St, Berkeley (415) 527-9838. Dinner Mon–Sat. MC, V. Moderate.

• **Square One** Joyce Goldstein, whose Italian gastronomic credentials are covered in our chapter on Italy, oversees a kitchen with solid culinary moorings that span the Mediterranean basin. That means that one night Moroccan-style *couscous* is on the menu, and on another night, the *cùscusu* of Sicily's Trapani shows up. The upshot is that every night at Square One promises an innovative menu to tempt the Mediterranean soul. 190 Pacific Ave, SF (415) 788-1110. Lunch Mon–Fri, dinner daily. Major credit cards. Expensive.

• **Zuni Café** What started in the early 1980s as a tiny café with sandwiches and espresso has evolved into one of California's most distinguished restaurants. Much of the credit for Zuni's success goes to head chef Judy Rodgers, whose instinct for great Italian and southern French menus has given her kitchen a large coterie of followers. Pizzas are cooked in a wood-burning brick oven, in the style of Naples, and a fresh seafood bar delivers a *plateau de mer*, à la French seaside bistro. Pastas may be tossed with julienned roast duck or a walnut sauce; polenta comes ribboned with creamy mascarpone. The look of the place is trendy, but the food is wonderfully down to earth. 1658 Market St, SF (415) 552-2540. Lunch and dinner daily. Major credit cards. Expensive.

Spain: Tapas, Paellas, and Sweet Serenades

T he boys in the band were play-
ing "Cielito Lindo." At the
long, long dark wooden bar,
a gentleman of 60 or so carefully cultivated years took an elegant
stab at his *pulpo à la Gallega*. He
sipped his *rioja* and looked up at us.
The saxophone sang an arpeggio.

Maybe it's due to an overwrought
imagination, but we could have
sworn he was Fernando Rey. **El Oso** is
that kind of restaurant—it is the
Spain that overwhelmed Ernest
Hemingway and sired Placido
Domingo. Two parts undistilled
romance and one part dignified
civility.

Ataulfo Perez Briz was born in
Santander, on the moody Bay of
Biscay. Later, he did stints as a
restaurateur in Mexico and as the
proprietor of San Francisco's popular La Terraza mariachi club, before
opening El Oso in 1988. During his
career, he claims to have served the
regal likes of King Juan Carlos and
Queen Sofia. At his restaurant, in
other words, tapas are an honest
gesture to tradition rather than a
bow to fashion. The real thing, even
without Juan Carlos in attendance.

You can take your tapas at the
bar or, ignoring old-country custom,
in the dining room, which has the
dimensions of the great Castillian
plain. The *tortilla de patatas* (potato
omelet), *callos à la madrilena* (tripe
and sausage in a tomato-and-
pepper sauce), and "Fernando's"
Galician octopus, infused with
garlic, are especially good choices.
The portions are less authentic;
they're double the size of their counterparts in Santander.

Tapas began making the scene here
in a big way in the 1980s, not just at
El Oso, but also at the longtime
Richmond District favorite Alejandro's Sociedad Gastronomica,
which features the dishes of Peru
and Mexico, along with those of
La Madre España. (Now just about
everyone seems to offer tapas, whatever their ethnicity.)

There's nothing new about a
Spanish presence in the Bay Area.
Spaniards discovered the place for
Europe, after all, and Spaniards were
among the most fervent of the gold-
panning forty-niners. In later years
many Spaniards worked in the Bay
Area's sugar refineries and ports and
farmed in Alameda and Santa Clara
counties. North Beach, with its Our
Lady of Guadalupe church, was the
heart of the community, and it was
there, at 827 Broadway, that the

region's most important Spanish social club and cultural center, Union Española de California, was established in 1923. Today, the union, with nearly 300 members, has built a large, handsome headquarters out on Alemany near Geneva, where there are endless stores of Iberian charm and a restaurant, Patio Español, that welcomes all comers.

Spanish Restaurants: The Top Choices

• **Alejandro's** *Sí, amigos,* it's true that Alejandro Espinosa is a Peruvian and that his menu lists a number of Peruvian dishes—*papas à la huancaina* and seviche—and some Mexican classics. But regulars are justifiably wild for his selection of Spanish tapas (even though some of the items are more likely to be found in Lima than in Madrid). Among our favorite small plates here are *tortilla española,* a potato-onion omelet; pig's ears marinated in olive oil and lemon; *chorizo salteado,* sausage cooked in olive oil; and *pejerrey regozdo,* deep-fried smelts. With more than a dozen choices, you can easily make a meal from the tapas menu. If, however, you decide to venture into the dinner entrées, the *zarzuela,* a seafood stew laced with sherry, is strictly Spanish and *muy bueno.* 1840 Clement St, SF (415) 668-1184. Dinner daily. Major credit cards. Moderate.

• **El Oso** As this chapter's introduction points out, El Oso's kitchen staff understands tapas. But do try to leave room for some of their other Iberian culinary accomplishments. From Spain's north comes *lomo de cerdo adobado,* charcoal-grilled pork loin with a sauce of puréed red sweet peppers. Valencia contributes a pair of paellas. Each main course comes with a delicious bowl of *sopa de pescado*—and a new song from the band. 1153 Valencia St, SF (415) 550-0601. Lunch and dinner daily. Major credit cards. Moderate.

• **Patio Español** For 50 years, North Beach was home to the Union Española de California. In 1983, its members—the sons and daughters of Spain—purchased land in San Francisco's Excelsior District and shortly after broke ground for a new cultural center. Today, in addition to its role as a meeting place for the Spanish community, the center is home to the excellent Patio Español restaurant, where the public is invited to dine on what is surely one of the best paellas in the state: scooped from its traditional metal pan at tableside, the large portion of saffron-seasoned rice comes studded with prawns, clams, mussels, pork, and chicken. But this classic Valencia feast is not your only choice here. The menu is a gold mine of Spanish regional specialties, from quail baked with raisins, pine nuts, and sherry to Castillian-style pork braised in saffron to lamb with sherry and peppercorns, in the manner of Asturias. If you find yourself waiting in the small side bar for a table, order a couple of tapas. The *calamares fritos,* the *tortilla española,* and the full-flavored *jamón de serrano* are dishes to make a Sevillan homesick. 2850 Alemany Blvd, SF (415) 587-5117. Lunch and dinner Wed–Mon. Major credit cards. Moderate.

Portugal: Legacies of a Seafarer's Cuisine

C hef Lionel Sousa and wife Aira are from Graciosa, a tiny island of the Azorean archipelago, set almost dead center in the Atlantic Ocean 900 miles west of Lisbon. That makes them doubly appropriate for a survey of Portuguese food in the Bay Area. The Azores are the ancestral home of most of the region's 90,000 Portuguese-Americans, most of whom live in Santa Clara and southern Alameda counties. And the islands were also Portugal's first stepping stones to an empire that would eventually stretch from today's Indonesia to Brazil—an empire that was responsible for bringing the chili pepper to India and *bacalhau a Gomes de Sa* to Macao.

What sent the Portuguese into the mysterious Atlantic in the early 15th century was the search for spices, the crucial preservatives of food in a nonrefrigerated age. Until the discovery of the Azores opened a potential sea route to the plantations of Southeast Asia, Venice had monopolized the lucrative spice trade through its overland connections with central Asian merchants.

What sent us to San Jose's Alum Rock Avenue Little Portugal and the **Sousa Restaurant,** on the other hand, had less to do with Oriental spices than it did with a nearly insatiable hankering for the dishes that Portugal perfected during its monumental oceanic adventure. Portuguese food, above all, is a seafarer's cuisine, relying heavily on the preservative properties of salting, vinegar marinades, and sturdy seasoning. Its main courses were developed to suit shipboard galleys that might not encounter fresh vegetables or meat for months on end; for the Portuguese, these intensely flavored dishes soon became a matter of preference rather than necessity.

Bacalhau is the most famous of them. Technically, it is nothing more than filleted codfish, salted and sun dried, an item that sounds prosaic until you've tried one of the 365 delicious preparations that the Portuguese claim to have created for it. "A different recipe for every day of the year," says our chum Rui, the Sousa's amiable waiter. "We call it *o fiel amigo*, 'the faithful friend.' " At Sousa's, the faithful friend is served in the style devised by a notable Porto restaurateur, one Gomes de Sa, who devised a casserole in which the *bacalhau* was alternated with slices of potato and onion and liberally doused with olive oil.

A cautionary note on *bacalhau*: it's not for the salt wary, a fact that hasn't stopped the faithful friend from becoming a standby on the menus of Greece, Italy, Spain, southern France, and Jamaica. The same caution applies to many Portguese dishes, which tend to reflect the salting and spicing that their nautical origins required. Two examples are *carne à alentejana*, a specialty of the Portuguese south in which fresh clams are mixed with pork, garlic, tomatoes, and peppers; and *alcatra*, a beef pot roast that is a classic of the Azores. Both will have you calling for repeated glasses of *vinho verde*, the refreshing "green wine" of Portugal.

So too will *polvo* stew, a braised octopus cooked with wine and garlic, which, like salt, served originally as preservatives. In Portuguese, wine and garlic translate as *vinho e alhos*, a phrase that India adopted as *vindaloo* shortly after Vasco da Gama completed his epic voyage to Goa in 1499. For the record, the chili pepper made its earliest appearance in an Indian curry 112 years later, exported from the Americas by the Portuguese, along with potatoes, cashews, and chocolate.

Portuguese Restaurants: The Top Choices

• **Margaret's Place** Margaret's cozy place in Santa Clara boasts a chef from the Algarve who knows the dishes of mainland Portugal as well as those from Margaret's native Pico. (That's the volcanic Azorean island pictured on her dining room wall.) On the island menu, there's *alcatra*, large chunks of beef simmered in wine and herbs. A bit pricier are *polvo*, octopus stewed in red wine, and rabbit sautéed in lemon butter, white wine, and spices. From the Algarve, the chef offers the true masterpiece of Portuguese cooking, *bacalhau*, salt cod fried with potatoes and tomatoes. 57 Washington St, Santa Clara (408) 248-2575. Lunch and dinner daily. MC, V. Moderate.

• **Patusco's** This is an old-fashioned family restaurant tucked away in an Alameda bowling alley. Don't be put off by the all-American ambience and the half-Italian menu. Proprietor Fernando Patusco, a native son of the 12th-century Portuguese fortified town of Guarda, near the Spanish border, hasn't forgotten his roots. One of his favorite memories inspired the restaurant's Portuguese rice, an outsized platter of rice tossed with clams, squid, fish, pork, and onions and seasoned with a bit of chili pepper. His very tasty *mariscada*—squid, clams, shrimp, tuna, salmon, mussels, and broccoli in a highly seasoned broth—brings to mind a hearty bouillabaisse. 300 Park St, Alameda (415) 523-2525. Lunch and dinner daily. MC, V. Moderate.

• **Silva Family Restaurant** As much a social club as a restaurant, this warm establishment in San Jose's Little Portugal makes guests feel like they, too, are members of the Silva family. One of the appetizers here is *amêijoas à Bulhão Pato*, clams steamed with lots of garlic and coriander (and named for a poet!). Daily specials include some hard-to-find Portuguese classics, such as fried rabbit and the bean-and-meat stew known as *dobrada*. For dessert, turn around and look east: the Silva family dining room shares quarters with the Silva family ice-cream shop. 1525 Alum Rock Ave, San Jose (408) 729-4011. No credit cards. Moderate.

• **Sousa's** The staff of the Bay Area's Portuguese consulate is said to frequent Sousa's, the most upscale of the South Bay's Portuguese restaurants. The dining room is appointed with the beautiful tiles that are a Portuguese hallmark. For more on its menu and staff, see the introduction to this chapter. 1614 East Santa Clara St, San Jose (408) 926-9075. Lunch and dinner daily. MC, V. Moderate.

Russia: Smoked Sable and Siberian Dumplings

L ong before there was glasnost—"maybe 40 years, who remembers?" a babushka tells us—there was the **Cinderella Bakery and Restaurant.**

A line stretched out the Balboa Street door when we arrived at noon on a Saturday. Half a dozen people were patiently waiting for one of the nine tables that fill a small room adjacent to the shop where baked goods are sold. A low murmuring in Russian rose from the dining area. Near the window, a man of gray-bearded, Tolstoyan dignity gazed into his teacup, and at the far wall, two turbaned women who might have walked Nevsky Prospekt with Diaghilev whispered in deep, conspiratorial tones over *kotletki* and borscht.

We linger over this portrait because Cinderella is nearly the last of a breed we once took for

granted, and a certain atmosphere has much to do with its charm. After World War II, San Francisco was an important center of Eastern European exile culture. Well into the 1960s, the Richmond District was especially rich in its nuances, and little bakery-restaurants like Cinderella, Acropolis, Miniature, and Park Presidio Bakery lent a note of old Moscow cafédom to the westside scene.

In fact, as the soy-sauce bottles on Cinderella's tables illustrate, the note was doubly distant. San Francisco's Russians came largely from Shanghai and from Harbin, Manchuria, remnants of a community that had fled Europe once and fled Asia later. The soy sauce, however, is just a Chinese accent, to be drizzled cautiously onto piroshki. The language of Cinderella's kitchen is as warmly Russian as the bear hug and the samovar.

It's imperative to order *pelmeni* here. The vast wheat-growing plains of Siberia, Byelorussia, and the Ukraine engendered the world's most pronounced affection for the dumpling, and *pelmeni* are its favorite objects. At Cinderella they are walnut-sized, delicate morsels, stuffed to the bursting with seasoned minced beef. A couple dozen come to the order, immersed in a light chicken broth.

The problem is that a bowl of *pelmeni* leaves scant appetite for the menu's other attractions: lamb with kasha (buckwheat groats), the cheese-filled dumplings called *vareniki*; stuffed peppers and cabbage; cutlets of chicken, fish, or beef; and a quartet of hearty soups—spinach, barley, or *rassolnik*, if you aren't in the mood for borscht.

Sirniki, mysteriously listed under "sandwiches," are a Russophile's reverie. Second to wheat in the food pantheon of the steppes is dairy, and dairy is what this dish is all about. Essentially it is a plate of cottage-cheese fritters, shaped into oval patties before frying, then served with as much sour cream as you care to ladle on.

Incidentally, the breads— both whole wheat and white—are fresh from the oven and irresistible.

What brought us back to Cinderella in the first place should be fairly obvious: After eight years of listening to Washington's ravings on the evil empire, we Americans have suddenly declared the Eastern Bloc acceptable—even fashionable. Glasnost is where it's at (and hopefully, will still be when you read this).

Moreover, the Bay Area is also where it's at, quite literally, for thousands of Eastern Europeans who arrived more recently than the Asian expatriates on Balboa Street. An estimated 1200 Soviets per year are now settling in San Francisco alone. Where are they eating?

One answer is the **Irving International Foods Café-Deli**—not an inspiring moniker, but the emporium is so heavily laden with delicacies that it will instantly remind the old Russian hand of the celebrated Moscow Gastronome No. 1. (Merchandising names just aren't a Soviet strong point.) At MG No. 1, the idea is takeout, drawn from the capital city's biggest spread of sausages, cheeses, caviar, and smoked fish. Efim Sinyak, the Kiev-born owner of Irving IFCD, has taken things a step further, adding a mezzanine café section for those who want to eat on the spot.

Our own habit is to make a selection of cured meats and fish, always including smoked sable, which is arguably better than lox (at half the cost), if not as good as smoked eel (alas, at nearly twice the cost). The sausages come from the true epicenter of contemporary Soviet exiledom, Brooklyn's Brighton Beach, aka Little Odessa, which speaks for itself about authenticity.

But you may prefer to choose from the prepared dishes that Sinyak's staff cooks up each day. Not long ago we sat down there to a feast of cabbage rolls stuffed with rice, meat, and plenty of fresh dill; a first-rate chicken *kotletki*, which, for the uninitiated, is ground and seasoned chicken that has been breaded and fried; and boned carp stuffed with a wonderfully spicy filling.

There's much more, including huge sheets of homemade Napoleon pastries to tempt those with a sweet tooth. The Napoleons, by the way, harken back to an earlier Russian opening to the West in the 19th century, when French influence on the upper classes was so enormous that some Czarist courtiers stopped speaking (and eating) Russian altogether.

Russian Restaurants: The Top Choices

• **Acropolis Bakery and Restaurant** Perhaps the most mixed of San Francisco's culinary mixed metaphors is the Richmond District's Acropolis— Athens in name, Moscow in cuisine, and Taipei staffed and owned. Although its cuisine has been steadfastly Russian for half a century, the Acropolis was run by Greeks until 1985, when Taiwanese immigrant Kitty Quon took over, after mastering the recipes for everything from *pelmeni* to *sirniki* and borscht. Kitty held onto Maya, the Russian pastry chef, so there's no question about authentic input. In fact, the sole concession to the ethnicity of the new ownership is the addition of Chinese potstickers to the menu. Kitty swears they're a response to the demands of Russian customers, émigrés who came to California from the venerable European settlement at Harbin, in potsticker-crazy north China. 5217 Geary Blvd, SF (415) 751-9661. Lunch and dinner Tues–Sun. MC, V. Inexpensive.

• **Cinderella Bakery and Restaurant** Nostalgia hangs heavy in the dining room of this Balboa Street establishment, which is described at length in our introduction to this chapter. It's no wonder Cinderella has hung on while so many other old-time Russian restaurants here have vanished. The food is prepared with the utmost care, which an entirely new generation of Russian immigrants is learning to appreciate. 436 Balboa St, SF (415) 751-9690. Lunch and early dinner Tues–Sat. No credit cards. Inexpensive.

• **Irving International Foods Café-Deli** At first glance, the International is just a place to secure the delicious sausages and smoked fish that Slavs so love. But upstairs on a mezzanine, there are half a dozen tables where you can sit down to a plateful of the delicacies that fill the counter below, or sample some of the hot Russian specialties that are prepared each day. The actual menu pretty much depends on the chef's mood, but regular entrées include stuffed cabbage rolls, chicken cutlets, and braised beef. 1920 Irving St, SF (415) 753-0401. Lunch and early dinner daily. No credit cards. Inexpensive.

• **Petrouchka** For a taste of pre-Bolshevik evening decadence, try Petrouchka, over on College Avenue in Berkeley. The name comes from a popular Russian children's fairy tale of a doll that comes to life, dies, and is reborn—a Pinocchio of the Urals. (Stravinsky, charmed by the doll's resilient spirit, composed the now-classic *Petrouchka* for the Ballets Russes. It premiered in Paris in 1913, with Nijinsky on stage.) A dozen years ago, that same spirit prompted three Berkeley women to open the quietly elegant Petrouchka. They gathered the recipes of their Russian grandmothers, hung the walls with prints by Chagall and Kandinsky, and introduced the culinary traditions of their ancestral homeland to the East Bay. The restaurant has different owners now, but those traditions (and all the recipes) live on. 2930 College Ave, Berkeley (415) 848-7860. Lunch and dinner daily. MC, V. Moderate.

Eastern Europe:
Not for the Faint of Appetite

The hearty cuisines of Eastern Europe are woefully underrepresented in the San Fransisco Bay Area's wonderful ethnic restaurant mix. Our dining-out options can't begin to compete with those of Polish Hamtramck in Detroit, Little Budapest in Cleveland, or Chicago's Croation South Side. But what we lack in numbers, we make up for in effort and quality.

Hungarian Rhapsodies

On all matters Hungarian, we defer immediately to the charming George Csicsery, Oakland writer and filmmaker, descendant of Magyar warriors and grandson of a Budapest parliamentarian. It was with George that we ventured to the unlikely reaches of Newark in search of Hungarian rhapsodies.

We found them, both musical and gastronomical, at chef George Kloczl's **Hungarian Huszar** restaurant, where a strolling violinist and concertina player accompanied our goulash and *lángos*.

Paprikás and goulash are probably the only Hungarian dishes most Americans recognize. Maybe too familiar: we skipped the *paprikás* in deference to George's urgings for more exotic fare. But we did try a goulash, veal braised at length in a paprika-and-tomato sauce. It came with *galuska*, nice little flour-and-egg dumplings, and was far less prosaic than its near-kitsch reputation would suggest.

At the end of a lengthy paean to the beauties of Lake Balaton, where swims the noble *fogas* (Hungary's answer to the pike), George convinced one of us to order *Szegedi halászlé*, named for the city of Szeged where Hungary's finest salami and paprika are made. This famous fish soup was hearty and delicious, despite the substitution of Louisiana catfish for *fogas*, though perhaps too much restraint was observed in the seasoning. As for our Magyar, he appeared to be opting for quantity, in the form of an evening special that was a one-plate guide to Hungarian meats. It boasted smoked sausages, a pork chop, and back bacon, as well as stuffed cabbage and pickled beets.

Notable, too, was a remarkable appetizer: mushroom slices that had been formed into a sphere with a duck liver center then dipped in egg and bread crumbs and deep-fried. It came in a mushroom-dotted wine sauce.

As for the *lángos*, it is a fried bread so reminiscent of central Asian equivalents that it must surely owe its presence in Hungary to invaders from the East who swept through

periodically to test the mettle of the Csicsery clan and its neighbors. Cross the border from Yugoslavia into Hungary south of Balaton, and you pass a wide field marked with a sign that reads "former camp of Attila the Hun," whose troops were as crazy for *lángos* as George is.

• **Hungarian Huszar,** 36601 Newark Blvd, Newark (415) 796-8061. Dinner Tues–Sun. Major credit cards. Moderate.

Perogies Please!

Northern California transplants who grew up in Chicago, Cleveland, or Detroit have long harbored a fondness for *perogies* and kielbasa that the Bay Area failed to satisfy. That was true until Darlene Bearde, née Malazdrewicz, of Winnipeg, Manitoba (where thousands of Slavs emigrated around the turn of the century) had an inspiration.

Darlene has strong personal feelings about two places that claim the *perogie* as their own. She is the daughter of a Polish father and a Ukrainian mother. And she had spent years in the Bay Area regretting the absence of good Slavic food—until she decided to do something about it. The something is **Perogies Please!**, at the Emery Bay Public Market in Emeryville, headquarters of Darlene's budding *perogie* empire. She is the manufacturer, purveyor, and distributor of the answer to ex-Chicagoan's daydreams.

At this point, definitions are required because the word *perogie* can mean very different things to different people. The Russian-Manchurian Cinderella Restaurant in San Francisco's Richmond District, for instance, features four versions of the *perogie*, all of which are prepared in a flaky pastry crust and baked in long pans, something like Greek *spanakopita*. The fillings

are meat, fish, cabbage, and mushroom; in token of her Manchurian birthplace, the Cinderella chef also uses Chinese bean-thread noodles!

All delicious, really, but about as far from what Darlene calls *perogies* as could be imagined. Hers are boiled or fried dumplings, about two inches in diameter, stuffed with four mixtures: potato and onion; potato, bacon, and cheese; cabbage, onion, and dill; or mushroom, onion, and herbs. She serves them with melted butter, onions, and sour cream (and even sells them, packaged, for cooking at home).

Darlene can also turn a *knish* (potato dumpling), flip a *latke* (potato pancake), and stuff a wild Polish *golompki* (cabbage roll). But her genius really shows in having the good sense to order sausages from the Krakoos Sausage Company in the South Bay, which makes no fewer than five kinds of kielbasa. The Ukrainian version is among the finest we have ever set teeth into—and we are people who regard sausages as a genuine art form.

• **Perogies Please!,** Emery Bay Public Market, 5800 Shellmound Ave, Emeryville (415) 547-8400. Lunch and early dinner daily. No credit cards. Inexpensive.

Slavic with a Venetian Accent

In a San Francisco that prides itself on a wide variety of regional culinary options, **Albona** is a handsome little place that carries regionalism to the logical extreme. It features the cuisine of Istria—a former Italian province that was transferred to Yugoslavian sovereignty after World War II and has historically blended Latin and Slavic traditions.

Istria, as owner Bruno Viscovi will tell you, was a valued part of the Roman Empire 2000 years ago and

from the 14th to late 18th centuries served as a prime source of ship-building timbers and hearty sailors for the galleys of the Venetian republic. (Incidentally, it was also the birthplace of Mario Crismani, founder of the popular Mario's Bohemian Cigar Store that over-looks Washington Square.)

The Viscovi family hails from the town of Albona, which Belgrade has renamed Labin. "My menu is based on the things we ate at home when I was a boy," Bruno says. There is no mistaking the relationship between part of that menu and its counter-parts across the border in nearby Trieste and the Veneto. Albona's *gnochetti de semolina* is a kissing cousin of northern Italy's familiar *pastina in brodo*, light egg-and-cheese wheat dumplings in a full-flavored meat broth. The influence of Venice is literal in *polenta e brodeto vene-zian*, a memorable seafood dish featuring grilled cod and rectan-gles of polenta in an extraordinarily rich sauce of fish, squid, tomato, and balsamic vinegar.

Still, what makes Albona notable is not its resemblance to any univer-sal Italian standard; it's the remin-der that many regional traditions are rooted in cultural marriages. For the Viscovis, this marriage speaks to the influence of Istria's Croatian neighbors and to its 19th-century interval under the flag of the Austro-Hungarian emperor.

You can't miss the melting-pot legacy in the delicious *capuzi garbi*, shredded cabbage that has been braised with prosciutto. *Crafi albo-nesi* look like a cross between Slavic *vareniki* and Italian ravioli, though they come with a brown sauce of sirloin tips that Bruno Viscovi himself refers to as "a kind of goulash—you know, like they serve in Budapest." The *crafi* filling of three cheeses, pine nuts, and raisins puts one in mind of the Turk-ish sultans who unsuccessfully sought to extricate Istria from the Venetian doges in a war that lasted nearly 500 years.

Best of all is the marvelous *arrosto de maial*, roast pork loin, a dish that would have pleased any of Istria's various overlords. The meat itself is cooked to a perfect moist turn. At its center is an assertive stuffing of herbs and sausage, and alongside sits a portion of that delicious *capuzi garbi*. Dessert lovers will be more than satisfied with chocolate-ricotta torte or curacao-scented flan.

• **Albona Ristorante Istriano,** 545 Francisco St, SF (415) 441-1040. Dinner Mon–Sat. MC, V. Moderate.

Germany: Schnitzel Nostalgia

T he German community in the Bay Area is surprisingly large, numbering some 230,000 people. But they are no longer concentrated in certain neighborhoods, and their cultural world here has shrunk to a shadow of its former self.

In the 1950s, San Francisco alone claimed more than one hundred German associations and lodges, among them the Teutonia Football Club and a clutch of *säengerbunde*,

nity—primarily Danes, Finns, and Norwegians—populated Buena Vista Hill and the nearby blocks around Market and Duboce.

With time, they looked to other careers—and other neighborhoods. But one thing hasn't changed: They still all head to Church Street for heaping platters of *Eisbein*, Wiener schnitzel, and sauerbraten at **Speckmann's**.

Out front, on the Church Street side, there's a deli with a full range

"singing societies." They shared Noe Valley and Dolores Heights with thousands of Swedes who had arrived as seamen and settled down. The Germans taught school and brewed the city's beer; the Swedes were construction workers. Another large Scandinavian commu-

of cold meats and sausages. The dining room behind it is a museum of Bavarian atmosphere. The small first-floor dining room, with its color photographs of snowy mountains, Dortmunder beer lanterns, and chairs with heart-shaped backs, recalls a *gasthaus* at the edge of the

Schwarzwald. Dirndl-clad waitresses deliver steins of Gosser draft and platters of sausage to hungry *männer* at the narrow bar. A sign near the kitchen advertises Christmas goose dinner for $15 dollars; the gentleman behind us at dinner is humming Strauss; visions of *stollen* dance in our heads.

The fantasy expands with the arrival of a massive hors d'oeuvre board of pickled herring and beets, roast beef salad, cold cuts, eggs with caviar, pickles, and a basket of hearty pumpernickel and dark rye. One of our companions orders a second Gosser in preparation for his *kalbsnieren mit spatzle*, veal kidneys in a pool of mushroom gravy shored up by a pile of wonderfully knobby *spatzle* noodles. Another opts for *kasseler*, a pair of smoked pork loin chops accompanied with mashed potatoes, gravy, and vinegary sauerkraut. *Wunderbar!* But also far too much dinner for this table. The waitress understands when we decline the strudel.

> Pretzels get their name from a word meaning arms or branches. The twisted shape was originally thought to resemble a person's arms in prayer.

German Restaurants: The Top Choices

• **German Cook** A pair of fat, succulent bratwurst flanked by vinegary red cabbage and panfried potatoes. Golden brown Weiner schnitzel and stuffed pork chops. Juicy *hackbraten* (meatloaf) covered in brown gravy and partnered with boiled spuds. Old-fashioned German cooking at old-fashioned prices is what downtown San Francisco's German Cook is all about. Plus, the atmosphere matches the food—a handpainted mural of a middle European landscape, a wall of cozy booths, plenty of jovial banter, and a staff that inspires a sincere *danke*. 612 O'Farrell St, SF (415) 776-9022. Dinner Mon–Sat. No credit cards. Inexpensive.

• **Speckmann's** Once you have visited Speckmann's, you'll understand why we featured it in our introduction to this chapter. Put simply, it not only has good food, but it also has ambience with a capital *A*, right down to its oompah music, German-speaking clientele, and mile-long beer list. The entrées are so large that we wonder how anyone is ever able to sample from the scrumptious dessert tray, a spread that does Germany's great torte tradition proud. 1550 Church St, SF (415) 282-6850. Lunch and dinner daily. MC, V. Moderate.

Greece: A Trio from the Wine Dark Sea

Old-timers in San Francisco's Greek community, many of whom emigrated here from Greek settlements in Turkey and elsewhere, recall, even as late as the 1950s, a small, but thriving Hellenic commercial district south of Market around Third and Folsom. In those days the Greeks lived mostly in the Mission, Richmond, and Potrero Hill districts and enjoyed evenings out in the handful of tavernas that lined lower Eddy Street into the 1970s. Only the tiny Athens Greek restaurant holds on in that neighborhood, in the 100 block of Mason Street. The number of Greek-Americans here has never been large; the 1950 census counted fewer than 9000 Greeks in the whole Bay Area; in 1980 the figure was little more than double that.

Even so, we've never understood why good Greek restaurants are so scarce in the Bay Area. In Detroit, Chicago, and New York, they're ethnic mainstays. It's not so much that these cities have overwhelmingly Greek populations; it's that Greeks in the East seem to gravitate almost automatically to the food business. Here they don't.

Enter Vicki Serveta, who believes that San Francisco can be as Greek as Detroit and Chicago. Back east in Motown and the Windy City, she won a loyal following with her *skordalia* and shish kebab. Emigrating to the Bay Area, she was disappointed to find that Greek food was plain hard to find.

In 1988 she decided to do something about it and opened **Athens By Night**, a lively taverna on Valencia near 15th, not far from a fine little Greek market and one of the Bay Area's oldest Greek churches. Her authentic menu and old-country ambience has built the restaurant a devoted following among folks new to Greek food and those who still recall the warm breezes floating off the Aegean.

Greek Restaurants: The Top Choices

• **Athens by Night** Vicki Serveta wants to give her customers more than Greek food. She wants to give them the experience of being in an old-country taverna, complete with live music and warm conversations. Her Greek fans feel that she has done just that, and they crowd her place on weekends. The dining room looks like a grotto, right down to cascading water and birds in cages. A cold appetizer combination plate comes heaped with all the Greek favorites: *melitzanosalata* (eggplant salad), *taramosalata* (creamed cod roe), *tzatziki* (yogurt and minced cucumber),

and that wonderful *skordalia*, potatoes puréed with garlic and olive oil. You can follow that up with one of the Athenian favorites that is beloved by Greeks around the world: chicken or lamb *kapama*, in which the meats are braised in wine and tomatoes; *keftedes*, spiced meatballs; or *moussaka*. The menu also includes such favorites of the Greek table as the *filo*-and-spinach pie called *spanakopita*, the rice-stuffed grape leaves known as *dolmas*, and a variety of grilled meats. 811 Valencia St, SF (415) 647-3744. Lunch and dinner daily. MC, V. Moderate.

• **Athens Greek** This tiny home-style stop, the last culinary remnant of San Francisco's once-thriving taverna district, is in the capable hands of Yianna Makris. She cheerfully presides over both the stove and the dining area, which is made up of just a counter and three tables. Some regulars swear by her *moussaka*; others champion her braised-lamb dishes. Both camps, however, endorse a glass of retsina as the best way to wash down the meal. 39 Mason St, SF (415) 775-1929. Lunch and dinner Mon–Sat. No credit cards. Inexpensive.

• **Stoyanof's Café** Georgi and Elenka Stoyanof, Greeks from Macedonia, spent 40 years in the restaurant business in Istanbul before opening their attractive San Francisco Sunset District café with son Angel. In other establishments, *filo* usually comes out of a box. At Stoyanof's, Georgi makes the thin, delicate sheets of dough by hand and then wraps them around fillings of spinach or cheese. There are also salads of spinach and feta and of fish mixed with fragrant olive oil, *moussaka*, and shish kebabs. Plus, Georgi's marvelous *filo* reappears in the dessert menu's honey-drenched baklava. 1240 Ninth Ave, SF (415) 664-3664. Lunch Tues–Sun, dinner Tues–Sat. Major credit cards, dinner only. Moderate.

LATIN AMERICA
& THE
CARIBBEAN

Mexico and Central America: The Heritage of the Mayans

The Bay Area's Mexican-Americans sometimes make the case that they're not ethnics—all the rest of us are. On the Spanish side, they've been residents of the Pacific Coast for nearly five centuries; on the Indian side, their tenure reaches back more than 100 centuries, the exact number depending on which anthropolgist is doing the reaching.

In either case, every other nationality is a johnny-come-lately to the Bay Area melting pot. And every "ethnic cuisine" hereabouts is a historical addendum to the table that the forty-niners found on these shores when they jumped ship at the Golden Gate. Well into the late 19th century, Mexicans—or more precisely, their *Californio* cattle-baron relatives—were the old establishment in the region, led by families with names like Berryessa, Vallejo, and Bernal that still march across the Northern California map.

By the end of World War II, there were nothing more than names on a map to recall the 70 enormous *ranchos* that once ruled the entire Bay Area. Their local world had shrunk to a small neighborhood around Our Lady of Guadalupe church in North Beach, a few blocks below Folsom between Fifth and Eighth streets, and a piece of the Mission District along South Van Ness. The 1950 census counted less than 35,000 Spanish-surnamed people in the region.

Today, thanks to a Latino immigration wave whose actual proportions can only be guessed at, Mesoamerican culture has made a dramatic comeback here. The most conservative estimates place the Spanish-surnamed population in 1990 at 900,000, the vast majority of whom are of Mexican and Central American lineage. There's no doubting the culinary impact: after Chinese and Italian, Latin American restaurants are certainly the most numerous dining spots in the Bay Area.

The dominant theme is Mexican, which—thanks to the likes of Taco Bell—has become nearly as familiar to *Norteamericanos* as the pizza. We take the Mexican table for granted, seldom reflecting that it is one of the world's most distinctive and influential cuisines. From corn and chilies to the tomato and chocolate, Montezuma and his Aztec kitchen had plenty to offer the Spanish kitchen, and generations of Mexican cooks did just that: they blended the methods and ingredients of the Old and New Worlds so thoroughly that they produced something entirely distinct from both. (Not always to their healthy advantage; one of Spain's contributions was the idea of frying in lard, having delivered the pig to the Americas.)

If authenticity is the chief criterion of cultural renewal, then the rise of the Bay Area *taqueria* is its most convincing Mexican harbinger. You recognize that, even if you've never been south of the border, the minute you walk into the **Taqueria San Jose** (2830 Mission St). Located near the Mission District epicenter of the fast-expanding Latino community, it's the perfect expression of the simple-but-honest fare that budget-

People and Their Neighborhoods

Where they live: The residential center of the Bay Area's Latin American community is San Francisco's Mission Street corridor, from 14th Street all the way out to the Daly City line. But Hispanic numbers are growing rapidly in the East Bay, along a line that follows East 14th Street from Oakland's Lake Merritt south to Hayward. The east side of San Jose has also long been an important Hispanic settlement, as is Redwood City in San Mateo County.

Where they gather: According to the conservative figures of the US Census Bureau, the number of Spanish-surnamed people in the nine-county Bay Area nearly tripled between 1960 and 1980—when it really began to soar. One result is a thriving commercial life, especially evidenced in a vast proliferation of restaurants run by Salvadorans and Nicaraguans (and augmented more recently by Peruvians and Brazilians). The Mission District of San Francisco, with its heart running south through the *barrio*—24th Street from Mission Street to Potrero Avenue—remains the focal point of Hispanic social life in the region.

Estimated Bay Area numbers: 900,000-1.2 million, including those of Mexican and Central and South American ancestry.

conscious eaters dream of and only the best little restaurants achieve.

Turnover is part of the secret: leading San Francisco *taquerias* reckon

their daily customers in the hundreds. That says, "Only fresh food is served here"—sometimes at a pace that leaves the customer breathless.

What's fresh is a wide array of meats, ranging from the accessible *carne asada* (grilled flank steak), pork or chicken cooked in green sauce, and *al pastor* (marinated strips of pork cooked on a rotisserie), to various preparations of innards, including tongue, brains, and calf's head. You want authentic? You got it.

What's done with them is primarily tacos and burritos, though the former will be a surprise to Taco Bell regulars. The corn tortillas in a genuine *taqueria* like the San Jose are quickly warmed on a grill and remain soft; a pair of them, stacked and loaded down with the meat of your choice plus beans and the hot *salsa* of your tolerance, cost less than $2. The wheat-flour burrito versions, about a buck more, are so hefty they require two hands to tote.

A further sign of authenticity is the row of large ceramic or glass jugs that hold quintessentially Mesoamerican tropical refreshments—tamarind, melon, and the rice-based *horchata*.

We use the term Mesoamerican deliberately, because both the population and restaurant booms reflect the upsurge locally of a culture that stretched from the Bay Area to Panama before the conquistadores arrived. One of the ironies of the current immigration is that it is once again uniting the descendents of that legacy, which is rooted in the grand Mayan Indian past that was as much the glory of today's Guatemala, El Salvador, Honduras, and Nicaragua as it was of Mexico.

Mexico has been the chief preserver of the pre-Columbian tradition, more "Indian" than any of its neighbors except Guatemala. It has also heavily influenced their dining habits. Of the numerous Central American restaurants opening hereabouts in recent years, many include Mexican items on their menus. This has lead to a common misconception that there is no difference between the cuisines of Mexico and her southern neighbors.

Not so. The fiery chilies are missing in Central America, and some of the most common dishes in El Salvador and Nicaragua are quite foreign to Mexico. Banana, plantain, and yuca, the starchy root also known as cassava, play much more prominent roles in Managua and San Salvador. Vinegared onions and tomatoes are used as condiments there, instead of explosive salsa. Even where there are apparent carryovers, the preparation—and often the name—may be very different. *Menudo*, the classic tripe soup of Mexico, has several vegetables added in its Nicaraguan and Salvadoran counterpart, which is called *mondongo*. The Mexican tamale usually involves a coarse-grain cornmeal wrapped in corn husk; to the south, *tamals* are often softer-textured and cooked in plantain leaves. *Carnitas* (roast pork) becomes *frito*.

Another familiar term in unfamiliar guise is the *empanada*. In Central America it is a cheese or meat-filled banana turnover, rather than the wheat pastry that bears that name elsewhere in Latin America. There are also terms no Mexican would recognize. Nicaraguans, for example, are passionately opinionated about *vigoron*, which vies with *gallo pinto* as their national dish. A proper *vigoron* must have just the right proportions of yuca, shredded cabbage, and deep-fried pork rind, doused perfectly with lemon. In Spanish, *vigoron* roughly means "invigorator," a curious moniker for such a hearty concoction.

Central American cooks turn out an exceptional dish called *indio viejo*, a mixture of shredded beef, spices, and corn flour. It translates into "old Indian," no doubt a reference to the ancient importance of corn, which grows 20 feet tall in Nicaragua, where it is harvested by men on horseback. Another masterpiece is *baho*, lean, tender chunks of steamed beef surrounded by yuca and plantain. *Pescado en salsa*, although a great favorite at Bay Area Central American restaurants, is not precisely the same fried fish eaten in Managua. It can't be: Lake Nicaragua, the enormous inland sea less than 50 miles from the capital, has some very peculiar denizens— saltwater fish from the Caribbean, including sharks, that have adapted to a freshwater environment.

The rich diversity of the Central American table is particularly obvious in the refreshments department. For reasons of health as well as pleasure, Nicaraguans and Salvadorans drink beverages based on such diverse ingredients as hominy, cocoa, jicaro seeds, tamarind, barley, corn, and tropical fruits. Not to mention coffee, of course, a principal export.

For Nicaragua, especially, the culinary breadth is no accident of culture; this intensely fertile country is a leading agricultural producer, when it is allowed the peace to produce. At its best, the Central American land yields a well-balanced and varied diet, even if it falls short of *haute cuisine* or Mexican complexity.

But needless to say, these haven't been the best times for Central America. And one result is another example of that peculiar irony of political crisis: a North American restaurant trend fueled by the arrival of refugees.

Mexican and Central American Restaurants: The Top Choices

• **Antojitos Nicas (Nicaraguan)**
Antojitos, right across the street from the Managua Intercontinental Hotel, is arguably the best-known restaurant in Nicaragua. Its name literally means "little whims," refer-

ring to an array of classic snacks beloved of all Nicaraguans. Today that tradition is pursued with gusto in San Francisco's own Antojitos Nicas Restaurant by co-owners Maria Emelina Perez and Isabel Olivares. Their antojitos are far from little— except when the bill comes. A good start is the *empanada de maduro con queso*, a fried turnover of ripe plaintain stuffed with cheese and topped with shredded greens. The house special, *nacatamales*, hand-wrapped in parchment paper and corn husk, are filled with delicious chunks of braised pork, raisins, onions, green pepper, olives, and rice. 3829 Mission St, SF (415) 282-9114. Lunch and dinner daily. No credit cards. Inexpensive.

• **Aqui Me Quedo (Salvadoran/ Nicaraguan/Mexican)** There are few reminders of the original Mesoamerican diet more cogent or exotic than a dish served in this pleasant Mission Street eatery, whose charming name translates as "Relax Here." The centerpiece is *atole*, a "drink" of ground corn and water spiced with clove and served in a coconut shell, that harkens back directly to a Mayan favorite. Around it are long, deep-fried cornflour cylinders, plantain chunks, and a "dumpling" of yuca mixed with egg, all served in a thick, sweet syrup. The idea is to eat one of the sweet bites, then chase it with a gulp of the sharply contrasting *atole*. 2240 Mission St, SF (415) 626-4879. Lunch and dinner daily. No credit cards. Inexpensive.

• **Sakura Del Sol (Salvadoran/ Japanese)** Latin or Asian? That used to be a chronic lunchtime dilemma in the San Francisco melting pot. Then came Victor Contreras with the ideal solution: two chefs in a single restaurant, producing some of the finest Japanese and Salvadoran food in town. The ambience and aesthetic are Japanese, reflecting the influence of eight years that

Victor and chef Oscar Osmin Chavez spent, respectively, in the dining room and kitchen of Japantown's estimable Sapporo-ya and Fukusushi restaurants. Enter chef number two, Anna Maria Huezo. Not content to bring some of Japantown's best tempura to the Mission, Sakura Del Sol has added Anna Maria's famous *carne asada*, *pescado frito*, and *platanos fritos*. 324 South Van Ness Ave, SF (415) 863-8184. Lunch Mon-Fri. No credit cards. Inexpensive.

• **Casa Aguila (Mexican)** We have no doubt about the name of one of the happiest Mexican restaurateurs in the Bay Area these days. It's Luis Angeles Hoffman, whose Casa Aguila, out in the un-Mexican Sunset District, has lines of waiting customers outside its Noreiga Street door even on Tuesday nights. The wait earns a free tamale when you sit down in one of the Aguila's bright, cheery booths. In addition to large portions and middling prices, Aguila offers some regional themes. An example is *puerco de Morelos*, in which the meat is first cooked in seasoned broth, then panfried with garlic, onions, chilies, and tomatoes. 1240 Noriega St, SF (415) 661-5593. Lunch and dinner daily. Major credit cards. Moderate.

• **El Tazumal (Salvadoran/Mexican)** The owner of San Francisco's El Tazumal, Rigo Pacheco, was among the pioneers of Salvadoran cuisine in the Bay Area. In a restaurant with comfortable, nicely appointed surroundings, his chefs turn out a superb version of the dish Pacheco says is a Salvadoran national obsession. It's *carne deshilachada*, a kind of Central American version of the Joe's special, in which eggs, minced beef, tomatoes, onions, and peppers are fried together. For years, the Pacheco kitchen has also been noted for its beef tongue cooked in tomato sauce. El Tazumal is really two restaurants these days—a fast-food *pupuseria* and a dinner house. 3522 20th St, SF (415) 550-0935. Lunch and dinner daily. MC, V. Moderate.

• **El Zocalo (Salvadoran/Mexican)** What compels the attention of El Zocalo's faithful clientele is a superlative rendition of the *pupusa*, El Salvador's national dish. The thick, handmade cornmeal tortilla, patted around a filling of cheese or pork and then cooked on a griddle, is served with an especially good *repollo*, shredded cabbage and carrot in a tart dressing (a mixture peculiarly translated on the menu as "sauerkraut"). One *pupusa* sets you back exactly one buck at El Zocalo. Five cents more fetches a *tamal de gallina*, potatoes and chicken in a surprisingly light cornmeal jacket. For the big ticket item (around $6), you can't beat *pescado frito*, an entire deep-fried white fish served with french fries or rice, beans, and salad. 3230 Mission St, SF (415) 282-2572. Lunch and dinner daily. No credit cards. Inexpensive.

• **La Quinta (Mexican)** A truly modest little Mission joint, La Quinta is described by its loquacious owner, José Tapia, as offering "typical Mexican country-style food." For breakfast, José's crew cooks up mean *huevos rancheros*, eggs smothered in fresh chilies and tomatoes, and serves them with handmade tortillas. Of an evening, you might have enormous portions of *chile verde* (pork in green sauce) and *chiles rellenos* stuffed with cheese. José also turns out the classic Mexican weekend specials, *menudo* (tripe soup) and *birria* (braised goat). The decor reflects his eclectic taste and humor: on the wall hangs a tender image of the Virgin of Guadalupe, a huge poster from *The Magnificent Seven*, and, unaccountably, a photo of the 1931 All-Jewish Baseball Team of Benton Harbor, Michigan. 2425 Mission St, SF (415) 647-9000. Lunch and dinner daily. No credit cards. Inexpensive.

• **La Rondalla (Mexican)** This warm family establishment has been around so long that a couple of generations of Bay Area residents think of it as the place they first tried Mexican food. Many of them find it unnecessary to go anywhere else. Time has done nothing to lower La Rondalla's standards or to change an atmosphere best exemplified by

walls covered with photos of decades of family duck-hunting trips. All the Mexican standards are handled superbly by the kitchen, from enchiladas to *carne asada*. Terrific mariachi music on weekends and late closing hours round out the attractions of one of San Francisco's most beloved restaurants. 901 Valencia St, SF (415) 647-7474. Lunch and dinner daily. No credit cards. Moderate.

• **Las Cazuelas (Nicaraguan)** According to one of our most cherished conceptions of "authenticity," a restaurant should seem more like a relative's home than a stranger's business. Las Cazuelas owner Raul Arauz, formerly of Managua, makes his diners feel part of the family. Each day, under a large color photo of Lake Managua, Don Raul puts the finishing touches on one of his home-made desserts, served free with every meal; it was pumpkin pie the last time we ate there. Try his wonderfully named *pescado frito à la Tipitapa*, made in the style of a fishing town on the southern shore of Lake Managua. It's a fresh black bass, fried and then topped with a vinegary sauce of onions, peppers, and tomatoes. 6123 Mission St, Daly City (415) 239-9302. Lunch and dinner Wed-Mon. No credit cards. Inexpensive.

• **Las Palmeras (Salvadoran/ Mexican)** Las Palmeras is Ernest Punzet's third and most ambitious homage to the cuisine he came to love after making his way from Deutschland to Central America (and later to California). In addition to the familiar Salvadoran classics— steak with onions and tomatoes, *pupusas*, fried plaintains and thick cream—Las Palmeras offers several outstanding house specialties. *Sopa de frijol* makes a wonderful poor-man's cassoulet: its enormous portion of stewed white beans and pork suggests that Herr Punzet hasn't lost the Teutonic taste for hearty fare. Prices are rock-bottom here and at Punzet's other two Mission Street establishments—La Santaneca I and II, respectively near 24th Street and Richland Street. There'll be plenty of money left to indulge in a half liter of Spaten beer. 2721 Mission St, SF (415) 285-7796. Lunch and dinner daily. MC, V. Inexpensive.

• **Las Tinajas (Nicaraguan)** The Chang family, Nicaraguans of Chinese descent who emigrated here from Managua, offer one of the more complete Nicaraguan menus in the Bay Area. For those who are not familiar with this cuisine, Las Tinajas provides ample opportunity to learn quickly, in the form of three separate combination platters that survey the possibilities. One is even a vegetarian plate, built around the rice-and-bean mixture

---

Pupusas:
The Perfect Pat

In Salvadoran restaurants, one name always tops the *antojitos* list. It is the *pupusa*, a stuffed cornmeal round that is the hamburger of its homeland and is fast becoming a Mission District standby. At many of the unpretentious diners heavily patronized by the Latino community, you hear it before you eat it. A rhythmic pat-pat-pat comes from behind the counter, as the pupusa makers slap handfuls of yellow dough into perfect shape, almost magically filling them with cheese, meat, or both. The rounds are quickly grilled, and then delivered with *repollo*, a vinegary shredded cabbage mixture; the customer slices open the *pupusa* and adds *repollo* to taste.

known as *gallo pinto*, fried cheese, and plantains. There are several daily specials, including Tuesday's *baho*, a preparation matching up steamed beef, yuca, and plantains. 2338 Mission St, SF (415) 695-9933. Lunch and dinner daily. American Express. Inexpensive.

• **La Taqueria Menudo y Pupuseria (Salvadoran/Mexican)** A hot juke box. The TV tuned to a soap opera beamed out of Morelos. A mural depicting Jalisco's San Jose de Gracias church. This modest taqueria has exactly the right ambience. It also has every imaginable taco filling, from carne asada and *lengua* (tongue) to *sesos* (brains) and *chili verde*. Or try the hearty Salvadoran banana-leaf-wrapped *nacatamal*, which bulges with pork, chicken, raisins, potatoes, tomatoes, green chilies, and *masa harina*. Wash it down with a glass of cold *tamarindo* juice or one of *horchata*, a blend of rice water, cinnamon, and vanilla. *Menudo*, the tripe soup Mexicans consider the sure panacea for tequila hangovers, comes *pequeño* or *grande*, with chopped onions, chili peppers, and lemon for spiking the broth to taste. 4591 Mission St, SF (415) 333-0604. Lunch and dinner daily. No credit cards. Inexpensive.

• **La Victoria (Mexican)** You enter this longtime popular favorite either from the conventional doorway on Alabama Street or, more picturesquely, by walking through the bakery that fronts 24th Street in the heart of the *barrio* and winding your way through the back rooms into the kitchen. Whatever the route, the destination is a dining room staffed by some of the cheeriest waitresses and cooks you'll ever meet. Chat with them over a platter of *chile verde* or an enormous bowl of *birria*, a fantastic goat stew in the style of the state of Michoacan. Doctor it to your taste with cilantro and lemon, then wrap the delicious chunks of meat in a tortilla. 1205

Cortés found more than gold at Montezuma's table. The Aztec ruler's golden cup held chocolate, a revered elixir that he drank in rituals and before visiting his wives.

Alabama St, SF (415) 550-9309. Lunch and dinner daily. No credit cards. Inexpensive.

• **Los Jarritos (Mexican)** The *amiga* behind the Mission's youngest old favorite is Dolores "Josie" Reyes. For almost three decades this warm Jaliscan and her sister Margarita have been welcoming diners to the New Central Café on South Van Ness. In late 1988, Josie opened Los Jarritos, just a few blocks away. It already has the feel of a neighborhood institution. The restaurant throbs with friendly Mexican banter, punctuated by the steady patting of the tortilla maker. Come Fridays, devotees of Josie's home cooking stream in for the daily special of *posole*; on Saturday and Sunday they stop by for a steaming bowl of *birria*. If you don't know what these dishes are, it's time to learn, and Los Jarritos is our best local school. The restaurant's

name refers to Josie's collection of hundreds of tiny earthenware cups that hang from the ceiling and decorate the walls. "Back home, when someone dies," she explains, "the men console each other with tequila all day long, filling and refilling these jarritos." 90l South Van Ness, SF (415) 648-8383. Lunch, and dinner daily. No credit cards. Inexpensive.

• **Mi Mazatlán (Salvadoran/ Mexican)** On Friday nights at Mercedes Quintana's very modest Mi Mazatlán, an itinerant three-piece mariachi band often stops in, in hopes of exchanging a song for a few bucks, and a handsome, shawl-shrouded woman offers red roses for sale. Señora Quintana specializes in seafood, and one of the best dishes to order here is the unusual *campechana*, small octopus and shrimp in a full-bodied broth flavored with a touch of chili and lime and loaded with chunks of avocado, chopped tomato, and fresh cilantro. The Mi Mazatlán kitchen also turns out first-rate *pupusas*. 2401 Harrison, SF (415) 648-7226. Lunch and dinner Wed-Mon. No credit cards. Inexpensive.

• **New Central Café (Mexican)** Ever since the mid-'50s, the New Central Café of Dolores "Josie" Reyes and her sister Margarita has been a firm stop on the Mission District schedule of San Francisco. And no wonder: not only does Josie serve the finest homemade tortillas this side of her native Guadalajara, but she also turns out a mean plate of *huevos con nopales*. In gringo, that's scrambled eggs with cactus, cilantro, onion, and pepper, accompanied with rice and refried beans. The cactus isn't dangerous—it has been pared down to the tender inner meat—but it is certainly delicious, especially under the New Central's fresh green salsa. If *huevos con nopales* sounds like an unusual breakfast, it's pedestrian compared to another morning selection: *chicharrones* (pork skins) stewed in hot sauce. 301 South Van Ness Ave, SF (415) 431-8587. Lunch and dinner daily. No credit cards. Inexpensive.

• **Nicaragua (Nicaraguan)** Henry Abarca, co-owner of the popular Nicaragua, is indisputably one of the founding fathers of Central American cuisine here. Since the spring of l973, when he opened the restaurant with his mother, Carmen, Abarca has seen several of his employees go on to run fine Nicaraguan and Salvadoran kitchens of their own. Today, the Nicaragua is managed jointly by Henry and his sister, Maria Tercero. Nearly every night they serve a full house in their small dining room, presided over by a portrait of the celebrated Nicaraguan poet Ruben Dario. Try their *yoltamal*, a pleasant surprise to those who associate tamales with a leaden feeling in the pit of the stomach. It is as light and delicate as a soufflé. Like many Nicaraguan and Salvadoran dishes, it comes with *crema*, a delicious Central American version of the French *crème fraîche*. 3015 Mission St, SF (415) 550-9283. Lunch and dinner daily. No credit cards. Inexpensive.

• **Pancho Villa Taqueria (Mexican)** Without a doubt, Pancho Villa serves more meals on a daily basis than any other Latin American restaurant in Northern California. And it serves them to a clientele that gives new meaning to the term "diversity": cops and street-wise hustlers, Koreans and Salvadorans, playwrights and actors from the Eureka Theater, Mexicans from Sonora and Chicanos from East San Jose—everybody seems to love this joint. One reason is the customers themselves, not only because they're their own entertainment, but because their numbers insure constant turnover. Old food is unknown at Pancho Villa. The emphasis is on tacos and burritos, but the fixings—from pork *carnitas* and *chile verde* to *carne al pastor*—are also available on huge dinner plates. 3071 16th St, SF (415) 864-8840. Lunch and dinner daily. No credit cards. Inexpensive.

• **Red Balloon (Nicaraguan)** This tiny storefront on Mission doesn't post a menu, but don't worry that you may be unpleasantly surprised by the check; it's pretty hard to break into double figures—for two! That doesn't mean cheap food, however. Just good, honest meals, at prices the Mission's thousands of Central American immigrants can afford. Try the football-sized *empanada*, which Nicaraguans make out of a plantain-based dough and stuff with chopped pork and rice. 2763 Mission St, SF (415) 285-1749. Lunch and dinner daily. No credit cards. Inexpensive.

• **Taqueria San Jose (Mexican)** Tacos, like any culinary staple, have their aficionados. And what the taco-informed have known for years is that the San Jose provides the best array of fillings in town. Especially good, for those who favor innards as we do, are the boiled tongue and the grilled calf's brains, heaped up on two soft tacos and covered with a fresh salsa of chilies, onions, and tomatoes. A full line of Mexican *refrescos* is available to wash the repast down. There are scores of good taquerias in the Bay Area. But this is our number one choice. 2830 Mission St, SF (415) 558-8549. Lunch and dinner daily. No credit cards. Inexpensive.

• **Tortola (Mexican)** A very contemporary Pacific Heights joint that ex-Zuni Café chef Kathy Riley transformed in the late 1980s. It has the advantage of moving beyond the restraints that modest Mexican restaurants impose on their menus. Yucatán sausage, flavored with chilies, garlic, citrus, and achiote seeds, comes nicely crisp off the grill, in a pool of black beans. Next to it is an extremely successful square of grilled polenta. Wonder what a pair of $10 enchiladas would taste like? They're most respectable— one filled with chicken, topped with a first-rate sauce of pasilla chilies; the other with pork, under a green chili sauce. Alas, the only way you get to try Tortola's estimable tortilla chips is if you order salsa and guacamole. 3640 Sacramento St, SF (415) 929-8181. Lunch and dinner Tues-Sun. MC, V. Moderate.

Caribbean: Creole Rhythms from the Spanish Main

Christopher Columbus, it will be recalled, was looking for black peppercorns in the East Indies when his ships dropped anchor in the West Indies. One of the first things he did there was secure a cargo of chilies, putative peppercorn substitutes that he presented to King Ferdinand and Queen Isabella as an inducement to fund follow-up voyages. Their majesties couldn't quite handle jalapeños, but the money was provided anyhow.

The island where Columbus picked his first pepper was Cuba. That historic moment in 1493 is recalled five centuries later at the **Cuban International Restaurant** with the inclusion of peppers—of the mild, sweet pimiento variety—in virtually every dish. Located somewhat incongruously near the heart of San Jose's Japantown, the Cuban is so familial that it could have been transported whole from your grandmother's bungalow to its second-floor quarters on North Sixth Street. The walls are paneled in knotty pine, the decorations run to framed religious prints and corny sayings, and plastic sheets cover the tablecloths.

If it looks like proprietors Ciro and Edenia Calvo's living room, that's just fine with the restaurant's loyal customers, because what comes to their tables could only be produced by a real Cuban family kitchen. The product is an overseas Iberian cuisine that's just the opposite of Mexico's in its relationship to the old country. In Mexican food, the Native American element thoroughly dominates the Spanish—

corn, chilies, and the chocolate in *mole* are Aztec ingredients. The Cuban table makes use of many New World finds, ranging from black beans and yuca to those sweet pimientos, but there is no mistaking its essential fidelity to España.

The best proof is *lechon asado*, "roast pig," a Spanish favorite now considered a national dish by ex-Spanish colonies as far-flung as the Philippines and Argentina, not to mention the Calvos' ancestral Cuba. It's certainly the indispensable dish to order if you haven't had Cuban food before. In chef Ciro's version, it arrives in juicy chunks with rice, black beans, and yuca, the starchy white tuber that Cuban peasants treat as others treat the potato. Alternatively, the meat can be accompanied with the rice-and-bean mixture picturesquely known as *moro y cristiano*—"Moor and Christian"—plus fried plantains.

The kitchen also prepares half a dozen Puerto Rican and other Caribbean dishes. "We did it for our friends here who come from San Juan and Kingston," Edenia explained when we asked why. "After all, where else could they eat?"

In fact, they do have alternatives. One of the more promising developments on the local dining scene in recent years has been a Caribbean mini-boom. Some of it shares the Calvos' Spanish accent and culinary bent, as in the equally warm and friendly El Nuevo Frutilandia, also purveyors of dishes from both Cuba and Puerto Rico. San Francisco, incidentally, boasts the most venerable Puerto Rican community in the continental United States. In the 1920s, long before the emergence of Spanish East Harlem in New York City, Puerto Rican cane workers from Hawaii were emigrating to the Excelsior District.

Elsewhere, the Caribbean boom has the lively reggae beat of Prince Neville's native Jamaica. Reggae is certainly a subtheme at Neville's Western Addition dining room, where the informed know that the things to order are those Kingston classics, goat curry and salt fish with *callaloo*. The latter, employing cabbage and the salt cod that Cubans call *bacalao*, is a clear link between the English and Spanish West Indies. The curry bespeaks another element in the West Indian table—the contributions of East Indians brought into Jamaica, Trinidad, and several other islands as cane workers.

Jamaican restaurants, although relatively few in number, reflect another longstanding community profile in the Bay Area. West Indians were the first African-Americans to settle here, building a solid business establishment in Oakland as far back as the turn of the century.

Caribbean Restaurants: The Top Choices

• **Cha-Cha-Cha (Pan-Caribbean)**
Run by a Puerto Rican and a Chinese Cuban, this lively Haight-Ashbury magnet attracts an eclectic clientele of local posthipsters, punkers, and downtown investment bankers. One reason is its small plates, in the manner of tapas, that allow the diner to indulge in variety without overeating. The decor is wildly improvisational, and the slant is pan-Caribbean, with stops in Jamaica, Puerto Rico, and Cuba, among other places. The possibilities run from fried calamari with lemon aioli, to Cuban black-bean soup, fish steamed in corn husks, and *arroz primaveras*, rice with capers and pimientos. 1805 Haight St, SF (415) 386-5758. Lunch and dinner daily. No credit cards. Moderate.

• **Cuban International Restaurant (Cuban)** This cozy family establishment in central San Jose (see introduction to this chapter) has been a South Bay favorite for years. In addition to Chef Ciro Calvo's famous roast pork, the highlights include a wonderful *arroz con calamares*, in which rice and squid are cooked in the squid's ink; *tasajo*, strips of dried beef—a favorite of much of Latin America—fried with onions and peppers; and *chilandron de chivo*, a hearty goat stew. 625 North Sixth St, San Jose (408) 288-6783. Lunch and dinner daily. MC, V. Inexpensive.

• **Cuba Restaurant (Cuban)** The ownership of this Mission District standby changed in 1989, but the same chef has been holding forth for two decades. It's a practical, no-frills sort of place—a real neighborhood restaurant where folks hang out at the bar and watch José Canseco, the Bionic Cuban of the Oakland A's, dismember the team's opponents. On weekends, longtime customers know to ask for the *lechon*, which doesn't appear on the menu. It comes with the classic side of *moro y cristiano*, rice mixed with beans. This is also the place to try a Cuban tamale, cornmeal wrapped around a filling of pork, onions, and cilantro.

The menu characterizes it as "tasty"; it's that and more. For a businessperson's escape from downtown, there are daily luncheon specials priced below $5. 2886 16th St, SF (415) 255-2396. Lunch and dinner daily. Major credit cards. Moderate.

• **El Nueva Frutilandia (Cuban/ Puerto Rican)** Co-owners Rosa Rivera and Jo Ann Herr transformed this tiny storefront café into a bright, friendly bistro serving Caribbean home cooking. Among other things, it offers Puerto Rican dumplings, *campesino* favorites that wrap a "dough" of crushed plaintain and yuca around flavorful shreds of pork and olives. They are served with deliciously spiced black beans, rice, and salad. The orbs that resemble oranges on Smokey's counter are *papas rellenas*, whipped potatoes formed into balls around a filling of meat, raisins, and peppers; they are dipped in bread crumbs and deep-fried. The menu also offers a host of the tropical fruit shakes for which the Caribbean is famous. 3077 24th St, SF (415) 648-2958. Lunch and dinner daily. No credit cards. Inexpensive.

• **Geva's (Jamaican)** Set in a pastel-accented house that mirrors the sunny disposition of Jamaican-born Andrea and Opal Baker and their chef-mother, Icilda Vincent, Geva's builds a bridge between the West Indies and the West Coast in more ways than one. What else to say about a menu that offers jerk chicken—a celebrated Jamaican dish in which the bird is cooked in African-influenced "jerk" seasoning, chiefly allspice and chili pepper— as well as a salad of scallops with pesto? Along with the Ethiopian Nyala, Geva's makes for a most exotic stop in the hallowed precincts of Davies Hall. 482-A Hayes St, SF (415) 863-1220. Lunch Tues– Fri, dinner Tues–Sun. MC, V. Moderate.

• **La Belle Creole (Haitian)** Don't just drop in on Gerard Noel. You can only eat at the Bay Area's first Haitian-Creole restaurant if you've made reservations. We have few reservations about what you'll find there, however. Among the possibilities are a delicious roast goat infused with lemon, game birds, and a gumbo that, as Noel points out, has a far longer lineage than anything that upstart New Orleans can offer. His pleasant café is leafy with house plants and full of cheer. 4090 San Pablo Ave, Emeryville (415) 654-6008. Dinner Tues–Sat by reservation only. No credit cards. Moderate.

• **Prince Neville's Original Jamaican Restaurant (Jamaican)** One of the saddest events in the late '80s was the return of Prince Neville, king of Haight Street reggae and master of salt fish, to his Jamaican birthplace. Fortunately for us, the prince found you can't go home again. In 1990, he was back in the Western Addition, presiding over a tiny six-table place on Fulton. The old favorites have also come back to his menu, notably *ackee*, a yellow fruit cooked like a vegetable, with that tasty salt fish. His many curries include one of shark, and his Kingston corn dumplings are better than any pone we've ever had south of the Mason-Dixon line. 1279 Fulton St, SF (415) 567-1294. Dinner Tues– Sat. No credit cards. Moderate.

Brazil: Flying Up from Rio

Before there was a discernible Brazilian presence here—in food or anything else—there were palpable connections between San Francisco and Rio de Janeiro.

Rio's harbor, like our own, is an icon, so self-confident in its heart-rending beauty and identity that it could be mistaken for no other spot on earth. San Francisco and Rio also share a tradition of unabashed sensuality, a freedom of the spirit, that has made them the envy of most of the world (and favorite symbols of decadence to some).

But nothing links the Bay Area and Brazil more powerfully than the unsurpassed complexities of their populations. African, Amerindian, and Arab, Iberian and Italian, Chinese and Japanese: a portrait of Brazil is in many ways the same wonderful mosaic that makes life an irresistible carnival here.

You can sense the connections even in a funky little waterfront diner, **The Java House**, where the bayside setting, food, and clientele conspire to say "San Francisco" with a Brazilian accent. Owner Tulio Silva hails from the state of Minas Gerais, just north of Rio. Silva, a buoyant man in his 30s who joined his sister in the Bay Area in the mid-1980s, introduced a Brazilian menu at the venerable coffee joint on Pier 40 in 1989. "The more I was in San Francisco, the more I noticed how many of my fellow Brazilians were around," he told us one evening, as we watched a couple of Filipino fishermen haul 800 pounds of rock cod from their boat onto the wharf below. "I started running into people I knew," Silva continued, "and before long we would be talking about food."

The view from The Java House is as extravagant as the premises themselves are modest. From one of the Formica-topped window tables, a diner gazes out over the wharves and moored boats toward the first arch of the Bay Bridge. At night, Oakland blinks in the distance.

The time to come, Silva will tell you, is Friday, when he prepares his *feijoada*. (The Java House breaks with custom here, for back home in Brazil Saturday night is traditionally *feijoada* night, in homes and restaurants alike.) Derived from a dish that originated in northeastern Portugal, the Brazilian version of this hearty stew combines black beans, pork, and sausage. It is always accompanied by *farofa* and *couve*, two items that come close to defining the staples of Brazilian cuisine.

Farofa is fried ground manioc, a starchy tuber native to the Amazon Basin that is reputed to pack more calories per acre than any other crop in the world. The rich, golden condiment can be sprinkled on just about everything, or it can be mixed with bits of fruit, olives, or vegetables and served as a side dish. In its uncooked form the flour is called *farinha* and is also used as a condiment. Manioc's more familiar names north of the equator are yuca and cassava; the versatile tuber also surfaces on dessert menus in the guise of tapioca pudding.

Couve is usually, though not always, sautéed shredded kale.

Some chefs prefer to use mustard greens, with liberal amounts of garlic and salt pork. It makes the perfect side dish to Brazil's wide array of rich coconut milk–based dishes—they're almost like curries—that are invariably seasoned with the red palm oil called *dendê*, an African import.

Java House represents the homey side of the California-Brazileiro experience. On the sensual side, the overwhelming choice among San Francisco's newish crop of Brazilian night spots is **Bahia**. In fact, it's really two establishments of the same name: a nightclub on Market at Franklin that pulses with pure Latin rhythms every night of the week and a restaurant just up the block.

The restaurant's tropical atmosphere quickly takes the chill off any foggy Golden Gate night. White walls are covered with huge, bright canavases, the work of painter Alexandra Neto, who with her husband, Valmor, opened Bahia in early 1988. The place hums with Portuguese banter and a soothing samba beat, and the staff look like they just stepped from the pages of South American *Vogue*. To capture the mood completely you can even order a Brazilian white zinfandel (although it delivers more novelty than nuance).

Afterward, wander down to the nightclub, where Africa's greatest cultural contribution to Brazil—a musical flair that knows no bounds—has a packed house gyrating to the erotic call of the *lambada*. Some of Rio and Salvador de Bahia's most famous musicians drop in to jam, unannounced.

You'll note, incidentally, that many Brazilian restaurateurs in the Bay Area have names like Galletti and De Paula. Since 1884, Italians have accounted for almost one-third of all the immigrants settling in Brazil, even outnumbering the Portuguese

arrivals. In the past dozen years or so, a number of them have set themselves up in the pizza business here, launching such wildly successful operations as San Francisco's North Beach Pizza and Nino's in Berkeley.

Brazilian Restaurants: The Top Choices

• **Bahia Brazilian Restaurant** The evidence of Brazil's polyglot population takes a Levantine turn in Bahia's *kebe* appetizer, tasty beef-and-bulgur croquettes introduced to South America by Lebanese immigrants. The croquettes are accompanied with a pleasantly pungent sauce of vinegar, onion, tomato, and parsley that can also be used as a dip for the rich, creamy *coxinha de galinha* (chicken croquettes). The Bahia menu lists all the Brazilian standards—*bobó de camarão* (shrimp in coconut milk), *feijoada*, *muqueca de peixe* (fish with tomatoes)—along with some surprises. *Pernil recheado*, roast pork leg stuffed with carrots, bacon, olives, garlic, and herbs arrives with the requisite *farofa* and *couve*, plus something called *tutu*, which is essentially *frijoles refritos*, Brazilian-style. 41 Franklin St, SF (415) 626-3306. Dinner daily. MC, V. Moderate.

• **Brazilian Fruit Basket** The tropics have relocated to Seventh Street in San Francisco, just steps from the post office and the Hall of Justice, thanks to the Brazilian Fruit Basket. In a cheery little *tasca*, four daughters of Brazil offer a lunchtime menu of what they call "our country's finger food." Among the offerings are beef croquettes, spicy braised chicken, and a wonderful puréed black-bean soup in the style of the Brazilian north. For breakfast there is also *mugunza*, a Brazilian corn cereal. At all times, the bread is homemade, the espresso is strong, and the staff is prepared to whip up one of the fantastic fresh fruit "shakes" so popular in their homeland. You couldn't hope for a more welcome departure from the usual office fare, plus the ladies of the Fruit Basket cater if you can't join them. 107 Seventh St, SF (415) 626-6432. Breakfast and lunch, Mon–Fri. No credit cards. Inexpensive.

• **De Paula's Brazilian Restaurant and Pizzeria** Pedro and Eduardo Galletti are the men behind De Paula's, which they transformed into its present menu format in 1983. It's a place that serves up not only a very good thin-crust pizza, but an equally respectable *xim-xim*

Peruvian Cuisine at Fina Estampa

Back in the gold rush days, San Francisco's connections to Lima were a lot stronger than its ties to the rest of the United States, thanks to a booming maritime trade along the Pacific coast. Peruvian miners were among the most important early settlers at the Golden Gate. Today, a rising tide of immigration from South America is once again familiarizing San Francisco with the rich blend of Incan and Spanish cultures that is Peru. It has also brought us the charming little **Fina Estampa** restaurant, with a menu that includes all the classics an Andean expatriate longs for.

To order like the expats, begin with a seviche of squid, prawns, and white-fish chunks in chili-laced lemon juice, a superb rendition of this Peruvian culinary invention. Pair it with *anticuchos*, skewers of grilled, marinated beef heart—the Andean equivalent of the American hot dog—or with *chicharrón de pollo*, crispy chicken chunks served with lemon sauce and marinated raw onions and tomatoes on the side.

Follow these up with *lomo saltado*, a vinegary sautée of beef strips, onion, potatoes, and tomatoes, or *carnero à la parrilla con yerba buena*, grilled lamb ribs with a sauce of fresh mint, garlic, and oil that puts to shame any other mint sauce we've ever tasted. Rice flecked with corn kernels and golden brown potatoes, the staple of the Peruvian diet, accompany the entrées. Fina Estampa's *parihuela de mariscos*, the bouillabaisse of Peru, is a bowl of tomatoey broth packed with a sea of fish and shellfish. Be sure to try the *ají* (chili) sauce; it's delicious dynamite.

You'll notice that the owners resemble neither Incas nor conquistadores. They're Tamie Takaesu and chef Gus Shinzato, Peruvians of Japanese descent. Other Peruvian restaurateurs now in the Bay Area have Chinese and Italian names, reminders that the Western Hemisphere's ethnic melting pot is not strictly the property of the USA.

• **Fina Estampa,** 2374 Mission St, SF (415) 824-4437. Lunch and dinner Tues–Sun. MC, V. Moderate.

de galinha. In this African-named concoction, chicken and Oriental spices are sautéed with African okra and served with cornmeal polenta. The kitchen also serves a wonderful appetizer of crushed eggplant tossed with a generous measure of garlic, olive oil, and vinegar, a dish that honors a recipe of the Gallettis' Italian grandmother. But the cultural mix is even richer in the deep-fried savory appetizer turnover called a *pastel*, which is accompanied with an addictive chili-laced green sauce. Pedro Galletti explains that in the Brazilian snack shops called *pastelarias* you may find a dozen different kinds of these pastries. "The Portuguese brought the idea to Brazil," says Pedro, "but I'm pretty sure they borrowed it from the Chinese in their colony of Macao." 2114 Fillmore St, SF (415) 346-9888. Lunch and dinner daily. Major credit cards. Moderate.

• **Eunice's Restaurant** In 1985, when Eunice Silva-Taylor first opened her restaurant here, she compromised somewhat between the delights of her native Rio and all-purpose American Creole. Today, she offers far more of Brazil, in a little dinner house resplendent with photos of the Mission's own *carnaval* and her own effervescence. Black women were the culinary decision-makers of Portuguese colonial households. It was they who pioneered the blending of indigenous South American plants, European kitchen idioms, Oriental spices, and their own African ingredients and methods that make the Brazilian table distinctive. Take *bobó de camarão,* for instance. The name is a combination of African and Portuguese words. The shrimp that are its central players are supported by cashew nuts and manioc from Brazil, the coconut milk that binds sauces everywhere in the tropics, and *dendê,* a fragrant oil made from a palm native to Africa. While eating,

try a bottle of Xingu, "the lost black beer of Brazil." According to the journals of Hans Staden, a Dutch explorer who washed up on

Many beliefs surround the humble chicken in Brazil: Lucky in raising chickens, unlucky in love. Disturb a setting hen, lose in business. Suddenly frightened chickens bode good luck or a visit.

Amazonian shores in 1557, Brazilian women used to make the original *xingu* by cooking manioc, chewing it into a paste, adding water, then fermenting it in containers placed underground. 3392 24th St, SF (415) 821-4600. Dinner Tues–Sat. MC, V. Moderate.

• **The Java House** This blatantly friendly waterfront diner, featured in our introduction to this chapter, is the favorite hangout of dozens of Bay Area Brazilians. Come on Fridays, when chef Tulio Silva prepares his famous *feijoada,* and enjoy the lovely view of the Bay Bridge. Pier 40, SF (415) 495-7260. Brazilian food served from 2 to 8 p.m. Tues–Sat. No credit cards. Inexpensive.

Cuisine Index

Location Index

General Index

Editorial
Edited by Amy Rennert
Copy editor: Judith Kahn
Proofreader: Al Riske
Index by Ira Kleinberg

Design
Designed by Laura Lamar
Illustrations: Max Seabaugh
Layout: Caryl Gorski
all of MAX in San Francisco.

Formatting and preliminary layouts:
Rad Proctor and Hal Lewis

Hardware notes
Designed and produced on
Macintosh SE, II and IIcx computers,
with Apple 13" RGB and Radius
two-page display monitors. Proof
printed on Apple LaserWriter Plus
and II NTX printers. Final output
by Digital Pre-Press International on
a Compugraphic 9600 Imagesetter.

Software notes
Illustrations in Adobe Illustrator,
Adobe Systems, Inc.

Typesetting and page layout in
DesignStudio, Letraset, U.S.A.

Type fonts used: Futura, Stone Serif,
designed by Sumnar Stone of
Adobe Systems, Inc., in Mountain
View, and Matrix, designed by
Zuzanna Licko of Emigré Graphics in
Emeryville.

Manufacturing
Printed on recycled paper by Delta
Lithograph Co.

Production director: Sinclair
Crockett